So You're Thinking of Moving to France?

4th Edition – Brexit, Transition, the Aftermath

*A practical guide, hints, tips and suggestions
from someone who did just that*

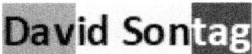

David Sontag

First published June 2019
Second Edition November 2019
Third Edition February 2021
Fourth Edition February 2022
© David Sontag 2019

errors and omissions excepted

All rights reserved
Without limiting the rights under copyright
reserved above, no part of this publication may be
reproduced, stored in or introduced into a retrieval system,
or transmitted, in any form or by any means (electronic,
mechanical, photocopying, recording or otherwise), without the
prior written permission of the copyright owner

Acknowledgements

Front page designed by David Sontag,
courtesy of copyright free images from   http://www.dreamstime.com &
                                                          www.publicdomainimages.net

Brexit Scissors picture courtesy of   http://www.pixabay.com

Regions and Department Maps from
https://www.freeusandworldmaps.com/html/Countries/Europe%20Countries/FrancePrint.html
Phone jack pictures courtesy of   http://www.pixabay.com
School Timetables & Zones from   https://vacances-scolaires.education/
Screenshot of Cadastral plan from   http://www.cadastre.gouv.fr
Screenshot of Chain Link from   http://www.castorama.fr
Screenshot of Etalab/Valuations from   https://app.dvf.etalab.gouv.fr/
Screenshot of France Connect from   http://www.laposte.fr

Lightbulb icon from free clipart on   www.vecteezy.com
Suggestion icon from free clipart on   www.clipartpanda.com
Tip icon from free clipart on   www.clker.com
Warning icon from free clipart on   www.publicdomainvectors.org/

All other images   © David Sontag

Any mistakes are entirely of my own making and I would be happy to correct them in future editions. If you have any comments/questions about the material herein then feel free to contact me on davidsontag@outlook.com

Dedication

To Joanne, for knowing that my dream was your dream and vice-versa, thank you for sharing it with me and embarking on this wonderful journey together.

To little Ava whose arrival gave me the time and opportunity to assemble my previously random collection of thoughts into a coherent document.

To all those friends whose experiences moving and living here have provided invaluable material, sometimes unknowingly, for certain sections of this manuscript.

Also to Josh, Ella and Lady, you would have loved it here.

TABLE OF CONTENTS

Introduction 1
1. Background 5
2. Visits and Visa's 22
3. The Fundamentals 28
4. Finding 'the One' 39
5. Preparation 52
6. The Move 67
7. Settling In 84
8. Traditions 99
9. Everyday Living, an A to Z 104
10. Boys Toys & Other Useful Playthings 200
11. Girls Gadgets 213
12. Amusing Incidents/Only in France 215
Annex A – Questions for Estate Agents 1
Annex B – Everyday Abbreviations 1
Annex C – Useful Addresses 1
Annex D – Public Holidays 1
Annex E – Holiday Absences 1
Annex F – School Terms 1
Annex G – My Meeting with the Local Chasse 1
INDEX

Introduction

Introduction

Why write this guide?

When my wife and I eventually moved to France from Essex back in the summer of 2016 it was the culmination of almost 4 years effort. We knew we had done a lot of research, both in terms of where we wanted to live and the process we would go through to get there. We moved into a newish house – it was only 6 years old at the time – but since then we have encountered numerous pitfalls and potential problems that had to be overcome with both the house & life. None were insurmountable but it has been very much a voyage of discovery since and in some instances we have found out things the hard way as *'Strangers in a Foreign Land'*.

I didn't move here with the intention of writing a book, although I have written over 250 different reviews on Google & TripAdvisor read by some 150,000 people. It's very easy to get complacent with your environment in life so I think it is important for you to challenge yourself every so often and do something that takes you out of your comfort zone to see what you are capable of. (For me two weeks volunteering in the Olympic Stadium during the London 2012 Paralympics watching both competitors and spectators certainly reinforced that notion). Be it to switch careers, to take up a new challenge e.g. to learn how to parachute jump or scuba dive, become proficient in a new language, take up a new technical skill, or overcome a fear of public speaking etc.

In my case writing a book achieved that, although I'd had the previous benefits of writing numerous detailed & lengthy business cases, executive/sponsor's reports and staff guides in my professional life, to do so would be a personal challenge both to write and to publish. But since arriving here in France we have certainly experienced all manner of problems/situations, most of which were unexpected; and these all involved different interactions some of which I expand on in future sections (see brackets) that required speaking at least some French so I think they make me reasonably well qualified to write such a guide, for example and in no particular order:

- Buying cars from both a garage and a private individual (9.15.2);
- Buying various electrical appliances in store (9.82);
- Dealing with wasp infestations in our roof (9.125);
- Understanding/getting familiar with all manner of new tools (9);
- Having to find an emergency dentist 2 days before Christmas;
- Explaining to an Insurance company *'Expert'* what happened after we had an (above ground) swimming pool *'burst'* (9.113.1);
- Getting quotes to replace an unsafe veranda/deck;
- Getting quotes to replace weatherboarding on the house;
- Erecting almost 400yds of fencing to keep our dogs safe;
- Ejecting a three generational family from our garden after they climbed over a fence to steal chestnuts (12.3);
- Ordering 27 tonnes of stones from a quarry for resurfacing and then telling them their invoice was wrong;
- Returning to find our car badly damaged while we had been having a picnic whilst watching horse-racing (12.1);

Introduction

- Suffering storm damage to the house;
- Having to recover data from and subsequently replace a damaged hard-drive on my laptop;
- Being summoned to the Tax Office to answer queries on our tax return;
- Separately attending the local *Finance Publiques* and then returning to the Tax Office to setup an online tax account as my setup code was blocked for some reason and could not be resolved locally.
- Being in my car and breaking down on an unlit elevated urban dual carriageway at night to find my phone didn't work.
- Arguing with local *Chasseurs* about incursions to our garden (7.4);
- Needing to trap Coypu *Ragondin* (9.25)*; and*
- Removing fallen trees from our small lake *Etang* (10.15).

Consequently I thought about writing this book and also because various friends and *'friends of friends'* had asked me about the different aspects of moving here so I just aggregated and expanded all my advice in one place. It is the sort of guide that, had it been available at the time of our move, would have helped us enormously to prepare, settle in and to understand a range of things that are not immediately apparent until they happen to you; and dare I say I would have found it indispensable! The guide is centred around helping someone move to a semi-rural location (on the mainland) like us (although it can't cover every situation in every *département*) rather than being a guide to big city life, but even then I hope there will be certain nuggets that you can take from it and use. It is based on our personal experiences but where relevant it also draws on some (anonymised) friends' experiences with selecting and settling into their French properties before enjoying *'La Belle Vie'*.

As such I hope it is full of useful *'Hints and Tips'*, simple distilled common sense-statements, sometimes of the blindingly obvious (which is easy in hindsight) and practical suggestions and insights that will hopefully smooth your transition into a different culture, a bygone age almost. As it's one that people say is like how the UK used to be 40-50 years ago, with its friendliness, openness, lack of fear and security concerns, and sense of community. Don't move here and continue living to work, the French work to live and live in a far more relaxed manner.

Where applicable, and as you will have noted already, French words/phrases are included *in this format* unless it's in a heading. Although note that if you encounter a French word that is spelt as you would find in English, it <u>will</u> invariably be pronounced differently.

Introduction

What it is and what it's not!

First and foremost this book is about emigrating to France, rather than about buying a second home here (although undoubtedly there will be many elements that overlap). It is based on my personal experience of integrating into French Life and is my understanding of things having lived here. In it I set out some of the problems that we encountered in so doing and in other instances I highlight the sometimes frustrating French bureaucracy you will encounter, but above all it's written with a smile.

It no longer covers chapter and verse of the twists and turns of the Brexit process but focuses instead on the Withdrawal Agreement and Transition as they impact the ability of you to fulfil your dream and move to France.

As to what it's not; it is not a handbook on for example how best to establish one's fiscal residency or how to apply for your Carte Vitale as part of accessing the French Healthcare system once you are here. There are many comprehensive guides out there which explain just that. Equally there are those many publications that talk about making the most of one's retirement etc. etc. I do not intend trying to compete with these guides and so will generally leave anything that requires technical or specialised knowledge well alone. Research those things elsewhere and where relevant find a suitably qualified expert with proper professional indemnity as necessary. Then look in here for the practical implications of doing or using same.

Neither is it a treatise on how to restore or renovate an old house. It is not something I have done and would not care to offer anyone advice about it other than use your common sense, draw up a sensible plan for so doing, don't set impossible deadlines and budget accordingly.

Finally I do not intend making lots of recommendations as to what to buy or where to buy it from, nor endorse specific products, that is not what this book is about. Similarly I will not look to tell you where to go or what to do as there are many tourist type publications out there that are far more detailed and up to date than I could hope to be. Besides, that is outside my scope and you'll find out all that in your own good time when you are good and ready.

Introduction

About the author

I was born and brought up in North London before moving to somewhat greener pastures in mid-Essex in the early eighties. After a brief but unsuccessful flirtation with the military I left school and studied Computing before pursuing a career in that field working as a Computer Programmer and then as a Systems Analyst, subsequently moving into Project and Programme Management and then Consultancy. After I was made redundant for the second time I setup my own Private Service Company and worked on my own account providing Programme, Project Management and Business Change Consultancy to a range of public and blue chip private sector clients for 20 years working with businesses to transform their operations and improve productivity and profitability by rationalising their property portfolios and introducing new ways of working supported by technology enabled change; a need that will doubtless increase post pandemic what with more people working from home. I then opted for early retirement. and spent 18 months assisting a friend with her newly acquired Travel Franchise, introducing rigour into her quoting and booking processes, improving her social media focus and increasing her followers through creation of a publicity video, individual You Tube Channel and a weekly newsletter.

I am married to Joanne, a former gift shop proprietor who had never found a Gift Shop selling exactly what she wanted so opened her own, and spent the next 20 years being the Chief Fairy in her own Curiosity Shop. We have five children between us, and now five grandchildren and live in a small village/commune of around 900 people in the *Corrèze*, one of 3 *départements* that comprise the *Limousin* Region, part of the new administrative area of *Nouvelle Aquitaine* (created on 1st January 2016).

We live here with our two dogs: Alfie an 11-year-old Border Collie, the '*Black One*' who we've had since a pup, undisputed leader of the pack, a sometime neurotic, ultra-protective mummy's boy who will run all day if it means chasing sticks or *rapiettes* (the small Wall Lizards common to Southern France) and the temperamentally different Keno, the '*White One*', (a former street dog who we rescued almost 5 years ago) a 7-year-old Berger Blanc Suisse crossed we think with Labrador/Retriever. Inquisitive, hyper alert, and 6 stone of youthful excitability, exuberance and occasionally misdirected wayward energy, he loves sunbathing, digging holes to try and catch Mice, Moles and Voles, and terrorising hedgehogs, but more about them in a while. So that is us, since moving to France we have embraced the French lifestyle and our *raison d'être* has become:

'Live the life you love and love the life you live'

Background

1. Background

1.1 The Trigger

Why did we want to move to France? To a degree it was *'right place right time'* syndrome. Joanne had spent a number of happy holidays here when she was younger and also when she first had her children. I on the other hand had experienced a couple of enjoyable *'drive through France with the lads'* type holidays but really fell in love with the country when I was lucky enough to work in Paris for eight months during the French Bicentenary which coincided with the Centenary of Opening the Eiffel Tower, and I was assigned to a British Bank in *Place Vendôme*. It was convenient for me, flying out of Stansted (from what is now the Business Terminal but then the only terminal) into Charles de Gaulle Airport on a Monday morning and returning back home on a Friday afternoon.

Shortly after starting there I moved out of the Hotel I was staying in with fellow consultants and rented a furnished apartment in Neuilly, near the business district of *La Défense*. From my balcony on the fourteenth floor overlooking the Seine I could see the Eiffel Tower off to the South East, in front of me the *Arc de Triomphe* beyond which the top of the *Pompidou Centre* was just visible, and off to its left in the hills of Montmartre stood the magnificent white stone edifice of *La Basilique du Sacré-Cœur*. I felt life couldn't get any better. Each day I joined the commuters on the No. 1 Metro line and travelled into *Tuileries* station to go to work. As the months wore on I started staying at weekends particularly during the summer, so captivated was I by the scenery and way of life. I found the city fascinating and my love of France started with that assignment and I have subsequently returned there with Joanne on numerous occasions.

Years later, in 2012, after my stint as a Gamesmaker at the Olympics and Paralympics Joanne and I stayed in an old school friend's farmhouse near Belves in the southern *Dordogne* for a week. We absolutely loved it, in particular the evening market, and it was here that our two earlier worlds collided. When we returned to the UK we found we both missed France terribly and the following month after a particularly arduous commute home one night I said that I wanted us to move here. During the delayed train journey I had figured out we could easily sell up, live mortgage and stress free, with money in the bank, and have a far better quality of life. Luckily Joanne didn't need too much persuading and so our journey began.

You could think us selfish but our various children had left home and although we were both working at the time and therefore our own boss, we knew we could retire early if we wanted to. Above all we figured that it was now *'time for us'* and although we might be 7-800 miles away from the bulk of the family, modern technology meant that we could make a telephone or video-call with ease and because of low cost air-travel the children and their families could come and visit us whenever they wanted to and enjoy true quality time in a relaxing environment.

More importantly we also didn't want to look back at a point in life in say 10 years' time, think of what might have been, wonder *'What If?'* and have regrets that we never grasped the opportunity to move when we could. We very much wanted to live the dream and live in the moment, and as you only get one life we decided to live it?

Background

1.2 The Layout

After this background section I have laid out this guide as follows:
- Chapter 2 covers visiting France and the Visa's you might need;
- Chapter 3 starts with the fundamentals behind moving here;
- Chapter 4 discusses finding *'the One'*;
- In Chapter 5 I talk about how to prepare for your move here;
- Chapter 6 concentrates on the move itself;
- Chapter 7 offers some suggestions to ease the settling in period;
- Chapter 8 highlights some of the traditions you will encounter while living here;
- Chapter 9 moves on to address the practicalities of daily living;
- In Chapter 10 there is a short discussion of the type of tools that may become everyday essentials, depending on your property;
- Chapter 11 looks at those devices that you might wish to use inside or outside the home to simplify life; and
- In Chapter 12 I relate some amusing incidents to give a flavour of our life in France since moving here.

Where I think you would benefit from avoiding the specific traps that we fell into I use this warning symbol.

Where I think there is something not generally known I show it using this symbol.

  Any specific tips or suggestions for you the reader are indicated by these symbols.

1.3 Brexit, Transition and Beyond

1.3.1 Brexit

In previous editions I attempted to summarise the progress (or lack of it at the time) towards Brexit. I see no point in including it here, instead this timeline shows relevant milestones that impacted the overall process.

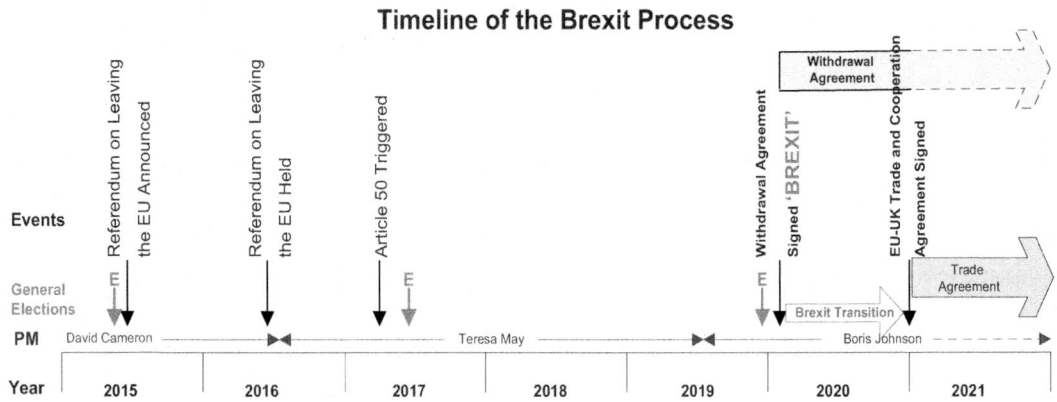

Some might call the result the Accidental outcome of an ill-considered decision, otherwise known as the law of unintended consequences!

Whether you wanted to Leave or Remain, the complete omnishambles of Brexit dominated the news headlines for almost 4 years from the minute David Cameron announced the

Background

Referendum on 20th February 2016 through to the UK finally leaving on 31st January 2020. It absorbed millions of column inches in newspapers, overshadowed News Bulletins and polarised society with seemingly endless political wrangling, prolonged debates and prevarication in Parliament, and it engendered a deeper distrust in the whole political process, parties and politicians, particularly as the one-time central tenet of collective cabinet responsibility fell by the wayside. To a degree it in turn fascinated and infuriated this former 'A' level British Constitution student as it turned past learning on its head with its constant twists and turns, the kind even a Hollywood scriptwriter wouldn't dare make up!

Of course it wasn't just the UK that was impacted, irritated and confused by the whole affair, the best way to summarise this section I think is with the French journalist and TV presenter Bernard Pivot who suggested
adding the word '*brexit*' (no capital) into French. He said it'll mean:
'*a cacophonous, unsolvable debate, a shambolic meeting, a chaotic assembly*'.
Example '*The co-owners meeting ended in brexit.*'

1.3.2 Withdrawal Agreement

The UK finally Brexited the EU on 31st January 2020. In the run up to and integral to that date the UK and EU forged a Withdrawal Agreement (WA) that safeguarded the rights of all expats living in Europe at the time and any that moved here before the end of the ensuing Transition period.

The agreement protected their rights to live, work and study here in perpetuity with many of the same rights that applied when the UK was part of the EU. Under the WA every British citizen living in France at the time had to apply for a new residence status and a new Residence Title - *Titre de Séjour* (formerly known as a *Carte de Séjour*) before 1st July 2020 (then extended to 31st December) or have obtained an official acknowledgement *récépissé* of their application by that point (otherwise they may not be covered by the WA as pre-existing *Carte de Séjour's* would no longer be viewed as valid residency documents). The new *Titre de Séjour* shows that it has been issued under the WA, it is also known as a Withdrawal Agreement Residency Permit (WARP) thus providing one with proof that one's rights are covered by it. As it is also a biometric card one had to visit the *préfecture* to have one's fingerprints taken before it was issued.

As a result of the WA those currently receiving a UK State Pension will continue to receive it, along with any other UK benefits one is eligible for providing that one continues to meet the eligibility criteria, and WA 'Brits' are assured of continuing free healthcare (on the NHS) for any visit they make back to the UK.

However there are two things that the WA doesn't cover which might affect you in that if you subsequently wish to move from France to a different EU country you will now need a Visa whereas previously you didn't. Related to this is how much time you can spend in other EU/Schengen zone countries, in that respect you will fall foul of the 90/180 day rule as it is applicable to all non-EU residents of EU countries as well. Consequently you will no longer be able to spend say 10 weeks in Spain in the winter before moving onto Portugal for 4 weeks before returning to France without the need for a Visa as in total you will exceed the 90 day limit.

Background

1.3.3 Transition

After Brexit an equally tortuous and fraught 11 month *'Transition'* period then followed during which both sides attempted to agree their future relationship and trading terms. During this Transition period, the UK was no longer a Member State of the EU, and no longer participated in its' decision-making processes. A final agreement was cobbled together at the eleventh hour, albeit with unresolved concerns over fishing rights, key labour shortages (fruit pickers, HGV drivers and NHS) and Northern Ireland, and the two parties signed a *'Trade and Cooperation'* Agreement at the end of December that year. The agreement governed the rules applying to future relations and in some instances where there was potential overlap, it superceded the earlier aspects of the Withdrawal Agreement. The Trade Agreement that was reached didn't include agreement on the Services Sector (in which I used to have a vested interest) and in particular Financial Services, that is still to be made.

The UK fully left the EU at the end of the Transition period, midnight on 31st December 2020, and British people have now ceased to be EU citizens, with all the rights that went with that. Consequently France has applied *'third-country citizen'* rules to Britons who immigrate from that date onwards and also to visitors and second-home owners, as the principle of free movement of persons between the EU and the UK no longer applies and EU law no longer applies to the UK.

> **All British citizens legally resident in France at the end of Transition i.e. before 1st January 2021 benefit from the Withdrawal Agreement.**

1.3.4 Coronavirus

Whereas 2019 and the lead up to it was all about Brexit, 2020 was all about Coronavirus and Covid19, even Transition took a back seat. It seemed to conveniently fill the media void from February through the end of the year (until trade discussions finally assumed ascendancy) and introduced a new lexicon of Curfews, Elbow Bumps, Furloughs, Lockdowns, Quarantine Periods, 'R' numbers, Tiers and Travel Corridors amongst other issues. It also introduced the phrases *'Self Isolation'*, *'Social Distancing'* and *'Support Bubbles'* into everyday usage and it made everyone feel like they were extra's in a bad science fiction film and we had all morphed into a dystopian future. France did nothing to dispel that notion in July 2021 by the introduction of a health pass (which prompted 27 consecutive weekends of protest against it) and this month changed it to a vaccine pass but unlike Austria and Germany it hasn't yet gone down the route of announcing compulsory vaccination of its citizens.

1.3.4.1 Initial impact in France

The French response to the Pandemic was possibly the most stringent in Europe. From midday after President Macron announced the initial 2 week lockdown on the evening of Monday 16th March 2020 to go outside without an obligatory piece of paperwork-an exemption travel certificate *Attestation de Déplacement Dérogatoire* – which listed one of 5 reasons for one's journey was risking a 135€ fine. Mask wearing was introduced and exercise in the form of walking, but not cycling, was only permissible within 1km of one's home. Bars, restaurants, schools and non-essential shops were closed. All sport including that behind closed doors was banned until September. The list of reasons was subsequently expanded to 8 when containment was extended by another two weeks. The final extension,

Background

by a month, allowed a further reason - to collect animals from rescue shelters after lobbying by animal protection societies. Some places mainly in Southern France introduced actual curfews whereas for the rest of us it just felt like we were living under one, although

that would become a reality in December. That thought was reinforced by the knowledge that should one venture out one may run into a *Gendarmerie* checkpoint which would ensure you had a valid attestation and were only travelling say to your local supermarket and not one further afield. One possible upside was that it did introduce the wider public both in France and the UK to the pleasures of working at home, and I say this sincerely as working in consultancy it was something I enjoyed on a frequent basis for 30 years or more. As a bonus there was little/minimal traffic on the roads, a complete absence of vapour trails in the sky, and in the fields, forests and woodland, animals thrived.

In particular the national Wild Boar population grew rapidly during that confinement due principally to a lack of hunting, although warmer weather increased their food sources such that female boar were giving birth to more babies (piglets) and the mild winter contributed to increased survival rates. This caused tensions to grow in agricultural communities as it has been estimated that in the last 5 years their population has increased to over 3 million animals. They are most numerous in the *Occitanie* region, especially in the *Gard, Gers* and *Hautes-Pyrénées départements* where the wide-ranging pine forests provide them with food, shelter and the ability to travel around under cover. Also hunting activity was banned during the confinement which helped swell their numbers, as did the reductions in car and train travel which accounts for thousands of them each year.

1.3.4.2   Re-confinement

Thereafter during Summer 2020 there were varying restrictions imposed on meetings, where, how many people etc. Then on the 29th October 2020 France entered a re-confinement period until 1st December, subsequently extended to the 15th, again it was necessary to complete an Attestation, in paper or electronic form, before venturing out. This time, unlike in the initial lockdown it was possible to take your rubbish to the communal tip, after all with nowhere to go many people caught up on all those jobs around the house and garden which created a lot of waste. Also in recognition of the growth of the wild boar population hunters were allowed to continue their activities.

When re-confinement ended it was replaced by a nationwide curfew from 8pm to 6am until the 22nd January 2021, the only exception being Christmas Eve. In mid-January the curfew start-time was reduced to 6pm to counter the effects of '*Apéro Time*' and the end date moved to at least 30th January before being extended indefinitely.

A further (3rd and semi) lockdown was imposed for a month on 1st April, yes really, and the government changed the dates of both department and regional elections, originally due to take place in March they were deferred to mid-June. Curfew start times were extended to 9pm in mid-May and 11pm on 9th June before eventually ending on 20th June (brought forward from the 30th). But amusingly the then Interior Minister (Gérald Darmanin) did ask the Police to show leniency on 15th Jun to allow fans to watch the France v Germany Euro 2020 match particularly if watching outside of their home ☐. That aside, as a semi-confinement rules were less strict than during full confinement, but aimed to limit social

Background

interactions and slow the spread of the virus. You could go out within a radius of 10km from your home without an attestation form and without time restriction, apart from the curfew hours but you needed to carry proof of address if asked for by the police. Although similar to Christmas, exceptions were made for travel over the 4-day Easter holiday when as everyone knows, viruses don't mutate!

1.3.4.3 Conclusion

Amongst the fallout from covid was the imposition of various access and travel rules by different countries to further complicate people's lives. Travel between France and the UK has been no exception, not least the UK introducing a *'Passenger Locator Form'*, completion of which was a bit like a cross between sitting an exam you haven't revised for and reading a Franz Kafka novel. This was compounded by disconnected nonsensical, highly illogical decisions over quarantining and exclusion of business executives, elite sportsmen and politicians from any restrictions.

The longer it has gone on the more one senses that people are fed up with the politicking, blatant profiteering, and yoyoing response of governments to the crisis, albeit supposedly driven by scientific advice, in trying to keep their economies afloat before settling into a darker world of blackmail, bribery and coercion of their populations. Indeed it is difficult to know what the new normal will be?

The Pandemic itself has caused countries to behave in different ways to protect *'National Health'*. They have all introduced measures that previously would have been considered draconian as regards Testing, Travel Restrictions and Quarantine. **Consequently do check on prevailing conditions and requirements before you decide to travel over to France.**

1.3.5 Future Implications, Post Transition

Post Transition you can still move to France, it is just a little more difficult than it was previously as there are different processes to follow, but it doesn't mean you have to give up on your dream as I am sure you can't wait to leave the rat race, embark on your journey and begin to make new memories. That said I have not read any of the 1246 pages of the Trade deal but I have synthesised the extracts appearing in/on the main media outlets and below I examine the main areas of concern and detail some of the more visible changes that are likely to impact you, although I can't account for any of Donald Rumsfeld's *'Unknown unknowns'*. This section should be viewed as a snapshot of the impact at the time of publication as there will of course be teething troubles in the application of new rules and currently trade is far from frictionless as was aspired to, so for simplicity this section will deal with issues alphabetically!

1.3.5.1 Banking

Some French banks are now charging for receipt of transfers from UK banks, irrespective of whether you receive Euros or Sterling. You can avoid this if your UK bank has a French office, or use you an FX dealer.

Britons living in France will no longer have an automatic right to open a basic bank account in the UK as they did when the UK was part of the EU. Certain Building Societies (e.g. West Bromwich) have told EU based customers it will no longer allow them to hold savings accounts.

Background

HSBC have introduced fees for withdrawing cash in France from an HSBC UK account. So don't necessarily close the UK account just don't use it.

1.3.5.2 *Bringing Pets To France*

This is something that is obviously close to our heart, and the biggest change here is that any EU pet passports issued in the UK are now invalid (unlucky Alfie). The reason being that pet passports were not included as part of the formal *'EU/UK future relationship'* negotiations so were not covered by the WA. However the UK has said it will still recognise EU pet passports.

Subsequently the UK was granted Part 2 listed status under the EU's pet travel scheme (EU regulation 577/2013's annexe on pet travel). So from 1st January 2021 the only new requirement has been for those travelling with their cats, dogs (including assistance dogs) or ferrets, whereupon an Animal Health Certificate (AHC) will be needed for any trips to the EU or Northern Ireland. In this case before travelling you must give the vet your pet's vaccination history and then:

- Have your animal microchipped (if it isn't already);
- Vaccinate your animal against rabies *rage* - your pet must be at least 12-weeks old before it can be vaccinated;
- Wait 21 days after this initial vaccination before you travel;
- Visit your vet again to get an AHC for your pet, no more than 10 days before travel to the EU; and
- Treat your dog against tapeworm 1-5 days before arriving.

The AHC then needs to be signed by the vet and it is then valid for:

- 10 days after the date of issue for entry into the EU or Northern Ireland;
- Onward travel within the EU or Northern Ireland for four months after the date of issue; and
- Re-entry to Great Britain for four months after the date of issue.

This has caused problems because the AHC is a complex nine-page form that can take Vets up to an hour to complete and must be renewed every time you take your cats, dogs or ferrets to the EU, and filled out within ten days of travel. Additionally the AHC must be signed by an *'official veterinarian'* (OV). Defra, through their executive agency APHA (The Animal and Plant Health Agency) say on their website that an OV is the term used to describe:

'private practice veterinarians who perform work on behalf of an EU member state. The work performed by OVs is normally of a statutory nature (i.e. is required by law) and is often undertaken at public expense'.

n.b. You should request a dual language certificate in both French and English.

Once you have arrived in France the simplest thing is to ask your new vet about getting an EU passport for your pet. I asked ours when I took Alfie for his Rabies booster last year, they were most accommodating and it just cost the price of a new (EU) Passport, 16€.

1.3.5.3 *Buying And Selling*
a) <u>In the UK</u>

If you are in the UK and buy anything from the EU that costs more than £39 you might get an additional bill for Import VAT. Although you may not necessarily be told when buying if

Background

your purchase costs more than £135 customs duties (that can range from 0% to 25%) may also apply if not already paid by the sender. These additional charges are being requested by courier's on the government's behalf and customers are being asked to pay before they can pick up their package. Delivery companies are having to return the items if customers refuse to pay. For the same reasons, allied to additional haulage costs, European Wine in Supermarkets will now be more expensive.

If you use a Mastercard Credit/Debit card when buying goods from the EU your charges will increase fivefold from the Autumn.

b) In France

Now as a French resident if you buy UK goods (either directly or from the internet) you will find that certain items will be subject to import taxes as well as VAT. Although If you buy articles online there is an exemption for anything up to 150€.

Note That Delivery Companies can now also include administration fees *frais de dossier* due to dealing with customs formalities in bringing in goods from outside the EU.

However purchases of digital software for download e.g: for a Kindle or for your computer are not subject to any Brexit related fees.

1.3.5.4 Car Number Plates

It is no longer possible to fit a number plate that displays the Euro symbol. As of 28th September 2021 drivers have to clearly display a UK sticker on their car/number plate and **not** a GB one, especially if your vehicle has any of the following:

- A 'GB 'identifier with the Union flag (Union Jack); or
- A Euro symbol; or
- A national flag of England, Scotland or Wales; or
- Numbers and letters only – no flag or identifier.

1.3.5.5 Consumer Protection

Note that if one is buying goods from the UK one no longer benefits from EU consumer protection as this will be covered by UK laws, and in the event of a dispute it may well be more difficult to resolve. It is also more complicated to claim back customs duty and VAT on refunds.

1.3.5.6 Customs Related Matters

Between them the EU countries affected by direct sea travel from the UK, i.e. Belgium, Denmark, France, Ireland, and the Netherlands have recruited some 2,000 new customs staff. (See Annex C for details of the customs website and then checkout their section on Personal Imports for a full explanation of what is/isn't allowed). As with many Brexit regulations the following are not new rules, rather it is just the first time that entrants from the UK have been impacted by them. These regulations cover both products of animal origin and most fruit that has either been sent by post, ordered online or sent by individuals. It has been made clear that any Parcels containing banned items will be intercepted and destroyed at the border.

The principal restrictions on food relate to anything that contains meat or dairy. So not only does this cover such items as cheese, ham or sausages but also any products that might contain one of the above as part of their ingredients, similarly anything containing milk chocolate, fudge or fresh custard is not permissible and neither is anything containing

Background

gelatine. Somewhat perversely eggs and honey are allowed if they are intended for human consumption. These are not the subject of a blanket ban, but have limits in place, usually 2kg per traveller. Restricted quantities of fish or fish products are also allowed, so think twice before being tempted to pack the car out.

That said most residents on their return, and most visitors on arrival do tend to pack a few treats into their car/suitcase, be they adult luxuries or former childhood favourites, but beware you may find some of these favourites are now banned in this post Brexit era.

Allowed ✓	Not Allowed X
Bananas	Apples (specifically)
Bread (Not spread with butter)	Biscuits
Coconuts	Bovril (it contains beef stock)
Dates	Cakes
Marmite	Christmas Puddings (with suet)
Pineapples	Flowers *
Tea Bags	Fruit (generally)
Vegan Bovril	Plants *
Vegan Christmas Puddings	Vegetables

* Not without a phytosanitary certificate

1.3.5.7   Driving Licences

Tourists and visitors can continue to drive on their UK licence, and do not need to exchange it nor do they need to obtain an International Driver's Permit.

New permanent arrivals need to apply to exchange their British driving licence within 12m of arrival (from date of validation of one's long stay visa). The *'Applying for a French Driving Licence'* group on Facebook will provide a lot of help with regard to both the process and what documents are required.

The exchange itself is requested through the ANTS website (See Annex C) and you can find more information here
https://www.service-public.fr/particuliers/vosdroits/F1758

When you apply you will receive a document confirming your right to drive (*une Attestation de Dépôt Sécurisée*), which you can use to drive in France until your new licence arrives.

> **tip**: Once you have setup your ANTS account and made your application, log back in from time to time to check on progress. Do **not** rely on receiving an email/message to say there is a hold-up, more information is required or a problem with your application.

n.b. I have been through this process (it took 8½ months ☐) and the requirements for an exchange are very specific. Quite simply if you don't have the correct documents you will find your application is likely to be rejected.

Britons who have a licence from another EU country will not need to exchange theirs, but any non-Britons with a UK licence will need to.

Background

a) <u>Heavy Vehicles or Medium Sized Vehicles/Minibuses</u>

In the UK when you pass your test you are automatically given the right to drive vehicle categories C1, D1, DE, C1E and D1E, whereas in France the Cs and Ds are classed as *'poids lourds'* and are dependent on passing an additional test and a medical. If you are not bothered about driving a small lorry, minibus or towing a heavy trailer then you just need to confirm that you are happy to lose/renounce the entitlement. But if you still want all of the categories that appear on your UK licence, you will ultimately get a letter asking you to supply a medical certificate to allow you to keep your entitlement to drive these categories of vehicle.

If you say *'yes'* and take the medical, then you will have to provide a medical certificate every 5 years until you are 59 and then every 2 years thereafter until the age of 75 and then every year from the age of 76 for HGV (category C), or every year from the age of 60 if you are driving a vehicle for more than 8 people (category D).

Your new French licence will be a full licence unless you had passed your test within the 3 years prior to the exchange in which case it will be a probationary one.

1.3.5.8 *Duty Free*

a) <u>Travelling from France to the UK</u>

Pre-Brexit as a citizen of a member country one could bring in unlimited goods from the EU as there were no limits on personal use. Now, the EU is treated the same as the rest of the world so there are strict limits on what one can bring back duty free. As regards alcohol currently that equates to 4 litres of spirits or 9 litres of sparkling wine, 18 litres of still wine, 16 litres of beer and/or 200 duty-free cigarettes.

Also when returning to the UK from France it will be possible to buy duty-free items (with no TVA nor excise duty) at French airports, on planes, in ports and on ferries.

b) <u>Travelling from the UK to France</u>

Now if you travel from the UK to France you will find that the duty-free shops won't sell you items such as clothing or electronics, but they will still sell you duty-free alcohol and cigarettes within the limits of a litre of spirits (over 22° proof) or 2 litres (below 22° proof) and 200 cigarettes. There are limits on both the value and quantity of other purchases made in the UK and brought back to France after a trip. These are 430€ per person if you travel by air or sea, and 300€ if you travel by car or let the train take the strain. Above these levels French VAT of 20% is payable on the total value of goods (but as you would expect, the duty free element of any alcohol & tobacco purchase is non-taxable). You also need to check the current rules if you intend to bring more than 10,000€ with you in cash. Visitors to France will now be able to buy VAT free goods (on purchases of more than 175€) in certain French shops.

1.3.5.9 *Erasmus Scheme*

Since 1987 the Erasmus scheme allowed free movement and education exchange for students to study languages among a variety of subjects across more than 5,000 registered educational establishments in some 37 countries for between 3 months to a year but access to it stopped as a result of Brexit.

Background

As a replacement the Government introduced the Turing scheme, a global programme whose scope covers 150 countries, but the principal difference is that the former waived tuition fee costs for students whereas these are not covered within Turing.

1.3.5.10 Financial Advice

UK Banks and Financial/Pension Advisors may no longer be able to advise EU residents after Brexit removed the automatic *'passporting'* rights for UK Financial Services in the EU.

1.3.5.11 Health & EHIC

UK residents who are coming to France, including those with second homes, can continue to use any existing UK EHIC (European Health Insurance Card) in their possession whilst it is still valid. These give the holder the right to access state-provided healthcare at a reduced cost or, in many instances, free of charge, during a temporary stay in the EU.

n.b. The EHIC also covers any necessary treatment for pre-existing medical conditions that arise during your visit.

If you don't already have one then you need to apply for a new GHIC (UK Global Health Insurance Card), basically an equivalent (with the same degree of cover) that will be issued in future. **Be aware**, the GHIC is not an alternative to travel insurance. It will not cover you for any private medical healthcare or costs, such as mountain rescue in ski resorts or repatriation to the UK. Make sure you have both a GHIC and a travel insurance policy that includes healthcare in place before you travel.

If you move from the UK to France (now i.e. after the WA) you may be surprised to know that you are no longer entitled to receive free healthcare (on the NHS) if you decide to visit the UK and should therefore purchase travel insurance which includes cover for your healthcare.

1.3.5.12 Internet Domains

As a consequence of Brexit UK companies can no longer use '.EU' domain names for their websites.

1.3.5.13 Mortgages

If you need to supplement any funds you have available to purchase a property by taking out a mortgage within France, 2022 brings some changes that may impact you as the lending criteria for French Banks has been tightened up. The maximum loan period is now set at 25 years and the Loan To Value can't exceed 35%. The amount of deposit required also varies depending in which French region you intend to buy in. Check before committing.

1.3.5.14 Motor Insurance

Since August 2021 it is no longer necessary to obtain an insurance green card to drive one's car in France as all UK vehicle insurance now provides the minimum third-party cover. It is advisable however to talk to your insurance company as to whether they offer any extra cover e.g. for theft and/or damage as not all policies offer the same degree of coverage.

Subsequently if you plan to take any/your French car over to England you need to ensure that your car is covered to drive in the UK by your French insurance company.

Background

1.3.5.15 Now TV
It used to be that UK resident Sky customers could use the Now TV broadband service to watch a limited range of Sky channels while roaming abroad (although) only for 30 days at a time. But as at the end of December 2020 one is no longer entitled to stream one's membership in any EU country but one can still download shows and movies to one's device before one travels, and watch offline outside the UK.

1.3.5.16 Passports
Until 2018 it was possible to renew one's (UK) passport early and extend its life by up to an additional 9 months (however as far as the EU is concerned this additional time does not count), so if you intend to travel into France or the EU from the UK now as a *'third country'* traveller then your passport must:
- Be under 10 years old, i.e. the date of issue has to be less than 10 years ago on the day of travel;
- Have at least six months validity before it expires
(if you renewed it early then any additional months over 10 years will not count towards these 6 months); and
- Contain at least two blank pages.

Post Transition the UK introduced a new blue passport design displaying the words *'BRITISH PASSPORT'* which replaced the previous burgundy passport that referenced the country being a member of the European Union. Anybody who is renews or is applying for a new passport since 2020 will receive one in this new blue design.

Also post Transition, Brits can't just come and go as they used to, they have to abide by the 90 day-rule and as such the passports of British visitors are stamped on entry to and exit from France, allowing border officials to calculate **their 90-day limit in the country**.

However this should not apply to those pre-Brexit British Nationals who were resident in France as they are exempt from having their travel documents stamped when entering or leaving the Schengen area as the 90-day rule does not apply. But there have been numerous cases of such people having their passports incorrectly stamped. Indeed it happened to me as I queued to board a train at Eurotunnel. Customs Officer *douanier* just asked for my passport and subsequently stamped it, not whether I had a *titre de séjour*.

1.3.5.17 Pensions
The WA guarantees that UK state pensioners living in France at the end of 2020 and who have safeguarded their residency rights by obtaining a WARP card will get an annually updated pension. Equally, any future pensioners are covered by the Trade and Cooperation agreement signed at the end of the Transition period which guarantees they are treated the same. However the calculation method for their pension amount changed and is now based purely on their UK NI contributions.

1.3.5.18 Permanently Moving to France
In terms of Emigration I mean moving to France to live *'full-time'* whether or not you still own a property in the UK. It would be advisable to check the current requirements with Customs before embarking on your move. For any/all Customs related queries you can obtain more information in English or French from the French customs helpline on:
From France   08 00 94 40 40 or

Background

From UK   +33 1 72 40 78 50

There is also a useful guide provided by French Customs, written in both French and English (See Annex C) but here is my understanding of current requirements.

a) Declaration of Goods

The UK is no longer a member of the EU, and as such its citizens no longer benefit from facilities offered to EU nationals when crossing the borders of member states. So if you move to France from another EU country, there are no particular customs procedures you need to worry about. However UK nationals and any goods you are transporting are now subject to migration, customs, sanitary and phytosanitary controls which means that certain goods now need to be declared to French customs, and customs duties and VAT needs to be paid on some items.

If you are emigrating to France or you live in France and you are bringing goods to your home, you are in principle exempt from paying taxes on personal goods that you import, providing you have owned them for more than 6 months, although you may need to produce documents proving you have lived in the UK and you are moving to France. That said they can be brought over in one or multiple trips and if you are transporting the goods yourself you need to provide two copies of an inventory of goods and furniture listing their value together with a signed declaration.

n.b. If you plan several trips the initial inventory must include all the things you plan to bring over subsequently.

The exemption applies if you have been living in the UK (or another country outside the EU) for at least 12 months and you have owned the goods you wish to import for at least 6 months before the shipping date (having purchase receipts is useful) and you are bringing the items you want to import within 12 months of relocating. You can find the inventory information on the CERFA website (See section 9.20) where you can download a copy of form 10070 to declare duty-free entry of personal goods from countries outside the EU.

Once again, provided all you are bringing over to France are a load of standard household possessions, and you are clearly moving home, customs officials will likely not insist on a receipt for every item. But if you have something that is extremely valuable then might it be helpful to have some evidence of ownership with you.

b) Exemptions

Some products are excluded from the tax exemption. These include alcohol or tobacco, as well as bicycles and motorbikes, cars and trailers, caravans etc. where it is expected that any/all duties/tax must have been paid in the country of origin, and any professional goods or things that are normally for commercial use such as raw materials.

n.b. Any of these exempt belongings should not be sold within your first year of residence.

c) Household goods you cannot bring to France

Not all your domestic goods can be brought to France and standard customs restrictions apply, particularly to dangerous/illegal items that includes certain breeds of dog! Similarly importing meat and milk-based products is prohibited, except for infant food. If you want to bring your favourite houseplants with you, be aware that there are particular controls on the importation of plants and plant products and you must obtain a phytosanitary

Background

certificate from the Veterinary and Phytosanitary Border Inspection Office (SIVEP) – (See Annex C) who can make exceptions for plants for non-commercial purposes.

d) Removal Companies

If you are bringing a large quantity of/valuable goods to France you will likely be employing a removal company, most of whom will manage the necessary paperwork but do check with them first.

1.3.5.19 Registering Cars

If you intend to bring in your car from the UK and re-register it with French plates the requirements in France have changed and there is now the need to obtain customs clearance, rather than the VAT clearance that was previously carried out See the French customs website for details (See Annex C).

Amongst these changes you will need to order a certificate of conformity from your car manufacturer before you leave as you will need to start to register your car within a month of becoming resident and you will need this certificate.

1.3.5.20 Second Home Sales

As a second home owner one is unlikely to be a French Tax resident so there are some changes if you wish to sell your property. If its' value is less than 150,000€ or you have owned it for more than 22 years then the Capital Gains tax percentage has increased above pre-Brexit levels. If it fails either of the above tests then in addition you have to appoint a tax representative.

1.3.5.21 Sending Parcels to France

As a result of Brexit the UK lost freedom of movement of goods to Europe but, and unrelated to Brexit, since 1 July 2021 following a new EU directive, VAT and Customs Fees are applied to all goods imported from a country outside the EU which has made receiving parcels more expensive. Thus with any parcels that are destined for metropolitan France or its overseas departments the recipients are responsible for paying customs duties, taxes, and customs clearance fees to have the shipment delivered.

a) Preparation

On arrival at the French border all parcels now go through more sorting than previously, customs authorities determine whether you are liable for any customs duties and/or taxes, depending on the nature of the imported goods, their value and their country of origin. They calculate this by reference to the customs declaration and the documents prepared by the sender. Such charges apply to all goods:
- New or used;
- Whatever the value;
- Even if they are for your personal use;
- Even if it is a one-off purchase/Internet order; or
- Whether you are an individual or a professional.

If you intend sending gifts/parcels to France then complete a customs form CN23 starting with your details and those of the intended recipient including their email address if possible, then include a full description of the contents, value, weight and if necessary stating it is a gift. But note that letters are not subject to customs clearance!
n.b. Customs forms for sending parcels to and from the EU are standard across the world.

Background

b) <u>Charges</u>

In addition, extra administration has resulted in higher handling and postage charges for most organisations. Furthermore you can also be charged more for sending goods back to the UK if the recipient rejects additional costs. Overall the possible charges fall into 4 categories:

- Customs Duty;

    Only goods produced outside of the UK or EU are liable. If the goods originate from the UK no duties are payable. Similarly duty is not due for goods sent to France that are provided directly to the buyer when their value does not exceed 150€. Equally no duty is payable on goods to the UK from France provided their value does not exceed £135.

    Goods sent between individuals are exempt from customs duties (and VAT), provided that the value of the goods does not exceed 45€ and that has to be a realistic valuation not a notional figure in an attempt to avoid payment.

    Any customs duties payable should be added to online orders at the time of payment and to parcels at the time of postage. The customs declaration form to be attached to the outside of the package will need to state the country of origin and value in order to benefit from preferential treatment. There may also be import customs duties payable (0-22%) – if goods are not made fully or mostly in the UK as the *'rules on origin'* in the Brexit deal don't exempt goods imported to the UK and then exported to the EU.

- VAT;

    Irrespective of whether a product is zero-rated for customs duties goods arriving in the EU are subject to import VAT and for France that rate is currently 20%. So anything sent from the UK to France/vice versa is not subject to the *'output'* VAT from the country of supply, rather *'import'* VAT is paid in the country of receipt. Before July 2021 this VAT was only applicable to goods valued at over 22€ (apart from alcohol, perfume or tobacco) but this concession no longer applies.

    VAT can also be applied to parcels from the UK containing gifts with a value of 45€ (£39) and over.

- Handling Charges;

    As a result of the complexity of the process and additional administrative costs involved, many UK suppliers no longer deliver to France. If they do and charges are payable, they will need to be paid when the parcel arrives in France in order for it to be delivered. Normally, private delivery companies will directly contact buyers who need to do this.

    If VAT and customs duty have not been paid before a parcel arrives in France, some companies will also hold the parcel in warehouse and charge both *'collection fees'* and *'late fees'* when recipients go to collect them. There are stories of people receiving bills some weeks after parcels containing gifts have been delivered, with the cost being the same or greater than the value of the contents.

- Postage/Delivery Charge

    As a result of these new rules, some couriers have imposed a *'Brexit Surcharge'* and increased delivery costs for sending parcels between France and the UK.

Background

c) Other

Finally, as with many changes in regulation be cautious if you receive emails purporting to come from courier companies or from French Customs asking for additional payments or for VAT payments to be made online as they be phishing scams.

More extensive details of what is and isn't permissible can be found on the customs website (See Annex C).

1.3.5.22 Sending Parcels to the UK

Although you can print standard (*Colissimo* – see section 9.87.3) parcel service labels at home the parcel itself should be taken to a Post Office for sending and **not** put in a postbox. The print process will create four copies (one of these for you the originator) and a 'pro forma' invoice showing the recipient and sender's details and the value. The invoice and the other three copies are then stuck on the outside for the attention of Customs.

Obviously if you use a courier service expect their process to be similar.

1.3.5.23 TV Streaming

Many visitors and indeed 2nd home owners use apps to stream and download different *Sky* services on their laptops, mobiles or tablets whilst they are here. But now if you try and access such services as *Sky Go, Sky Kids, Sky Sports* or *Sky Sports Box Office* you will get an error message as one is no longer entitled to stream Sky outside of the UK as *'cross-border portability of online content'* was not included in the EU-UK deal.

1.3.6 Changes Yet to Come

1.3.6.1 ETIAS

As part of a move to increase European security the EU has created ETIAS (European Travel Information and Authorisation System) which is due for implementation at the end of 2022. It is an electronic travel authorisation similar to the ESTA (US visa - waiver system) and will provide travel authorisation for business, tourism or transit purposes only but **not** for studying.

Thereafter it will become a mandatory entry requirement and visitors travelling to any of the Schengen Area countries that currently don't require a visa will need to apply for an ETIAS online (with no need to visit a consulate or an embassy in person) as they will not be able to cross an external EU border without it. As the ETIAS is not a visa the documentary requirements to obtain one are minimal. One is likely to need only:

- UK passport details: number, expiry and issue date;
- Basic personal information: full name, date of birth, gender;
- Contact details: email address is used for all correspondence; and
- Credit or debit card to pay the ETIAS fees (7€ or £6).

Once approved the authorisation will be valid for 3 years and multiple trips to the Schengen Zone can be made within that time providing the total stay does not exceed 90 days in any 180-day period. Successful applicants will have the visa waiver linked to the electronic chip inside their passport. It will be verified when the passport is scanned on arrival in the Schengen Zone. Visitors will then have their fingerprints and photograph taken and their passport details entered into a database along with their entry and exit dates.

n.b. To stay in France or the Schengen Area for longer than 90 days, a visa or another kind of travel permit is required (See section 2.2).

Background

1.3.6.2   Mobile Phones

The EU banned Roaming charges for Phone Calls and Internet use in 2017, but since Brexit UK providers have not been bound by this rule which affects anyone with a UK mobile. As of January 2022 three of them, vis: EE, Three and Vodafone had announced the reintroduction of such fees for calls, texts and data use in European countries, despite earlier assurances to the contrary. Subtle differences apply for existing, new or upgrading customers and with start dates so best check with your supplier so you can determine the implications for you before moving here but they are likely to offer deals. However this month both O2 and Virgin Mobile announced their customers will not face such charges.

Consumers should be *'protected'* by a new UK rule on unexpected charges – effectively capping mobile data usage (roaming) overseas at £45 a month – unless you have actively opted in to use more – if you rely on your mobile a lot it will pay to double check your potential liability.

However, generally French mobile phones can be used in the UK with no extra charges.

1.3.6.3   Oil Fired Heating

Be aware with regard to heating that any new/replacement oil fired *fioul* heating systems in France are **banned from the beginning of 2022** and this could lead to unbudgeted costs.

N.b. The measure was proposed by a citizens committee looking at ways to '*green*' the French way of life, and the government backed the proposal to bring an end to the use of coal and oil-based heating systems in houses. It also helps towards France's COP26 targets.

1.3.6.4   Votes for Life

Hitherto anybody living abroad for more than 15 years was excluded from voting in UK Parliamentary elections, but buried in the details of the 2021 UK budget was news that the government planned to scrap the rule. An *'Electoral Integrity Bill'* was later included in the Queens Speech and promised to introduce *'Votes for Life'* in the current session of Parliament as it will now eliminate this rule for anyone previously on an electoral register before they left the UK. Those affected will be allowed to vote in the constituencies where they lived before leaving the country, as eligible voters do currently.

At the time of publication the *'UK Elections Bill'* has passed through the Commons and is in the middle of its' second reading in the House of Lords.

Visits and Visa's

2. Visits and Visa's

A fundamental part of coming to France now, whether you intend to live here or not is to ensure that you comply with new rules because as *'Third Country Nationals'* brits no longer have unfettered access to European countries as we did pre-Brexit. From 1 January 2021 UK nationals visiting France are not protected by the WA and can only stay for a total of 90 days in any 180-day period (and that includes second home owners), and you are liable to have your passport stamped on entry. If you move here or want to stay for more than 90 days then you will need a Visa.

But as with any type of travel double-check the requirements before leaving.

2.1　Visits

2.1.1　General Visiting

Any visit to France of less than 3 months by a UK passport holder does not require a visa but you will need health insurance protection (that needs to provide a minimum level of cover of 37,500€ for any medical emergencies, hospitalisation or repatriation in the event of death). Thus you can't just rely on an EHIC/GHIC card, as although they cover emergency care they do not include costs of repatriation if necessary.

n.b. Should one stay beyond the 90-day limit without having obtained a visa then one risks receiving a 198€ fine on departure!

If you intend spending less than 90 days here as a visitor you might still get asked to supply the address where you are staying and provide details of your means and travel insurance when passing through Immigration. If you make multiple visits during the year the European Commission has a useful online calculator to help you work out how many days you have left in your current quota (See Annex C).

All non-EU residents wanting to enter France for a short holiday are legally required to be able to prove where they will be staying. So now if you plan to stay with your family, or at a friend's home, your host is required to obtain an accommodation certificate *attestation d'accueil* from their local *Mairie* (which will cost them 30€) to send to their visitors to show to border/customs officers if necessary. However if you are staying in an Airbnb, B&B, *Gîte* or Hotel don't need one.

n.b. This requirement isn't a result of Brexit but has been in use for non-EU citizens entering the EU for some time, so previously didn't apply.

2.1.2　Entry Documentation

As a non-EU national who wants to visit France Border Agents or Customs Officers can now ask you to show **any** of the following on entry.

- Proof of Accommodation for your stay
  e.g. Airbnb, B&B, Gite or Hotel reservation if you are a tourist; proof of address (utility bill etc.) if you are a second home owner; or *Attestation d'accueil* (See section 2.1.3) if you are planning to stay with family or friends;
- Your return ticket, or proof you have the funds to obtain one;
- An insurance policy that will cover your health costs, medical/hospital treatment and death including the cost of repatriation if required;

Visits and Visa's

- Adequate funds to cover costs during your stay – on a daily basis this equates to 65€ for a hotel booking, 120€ if you aren't staying in a hotel or 32,50€ if staying with family or friends; and/or
- If transiting through France your right to enter your final destination.

As I said earlier, when I returned (Sep 21my passport was stamped but I wasn't asked for any of this documentation.

2.1.3 Proof of Accommodation

If you are visiting family or friends who you plan to stay with when you arrive at the border you may be asked to show an *attestation d'accueil* (Proof of accommodation certificate) CERFA n°10798*04 or details of any pre-booked accommodation and prove you have the financial resources to cover your trip of at least 32,50€ per day, for the duration of your stay. If you don't have either this attestation or any pre-booked accommodation you should be prepared to show proof of funds of at least 120€ per day for the duration of your stay.

Your host can obtain the certificate from their *Mairie* and to do so they will need to provide original versions of the following:
- Their identification (identity card, passport) and for non-French Nationals, a *titre de séjour*;
- Documents proving their status as the owner, tenant or occupier of the accommodation: contract, lease, local tax '*avis*' notice, rental agreement with latest proof of payments etc;
- Recent proof of address: EDF bills, rental payment receipt, utility bills etc;
- Any document justifying their financial status (last three pay slips, last tax assessment) and their commitment to financially support the guest if he/she is in default;
- Any document proving their ability to accommodate the guest in acceptable conditions
(in terms of size of accommodation, no. of rooms, safety, health and comfort etc);
- Details of the duration of the stay and their relationship to the invited party; and
- If the application is for an unaccompanied minor, a statement written on plain paper and signed by the parental guardians of the child should be provided. It should specify the duration and purpose of the child's stay.

Ideally they should check with their *Mairie* has to how much notice they will require to provide it for you as some may want up to 4-weeks' notice. A form will be required for each guest but husbands, wives and children (all with the same surname) and legal partners can be included on the same form. So a family of four will require one form but four non-related friends will each require their own form.

Strangely although the *Attestation d'Accueil* in itself is free they will need to buy a '*timbre fiscal*' with a value of 30€ to obtain it. The *timbre fiscal* can be bought online or in a *Tabac* (See section 9.114).

2.2 Visa's

2.2.1 General

If you intend to move here or visit for more than 3 months then you must obtain a visa. The visa application is made initially online at the France Visas Website (See Annex C) for which

Visits and Visa's

you will need to setup an account. Once the application is completed and processed you will need to book an appointment with the TLS Contact service in London, Edinburgh or Manchester and take in your original documents **and surrender your passport which is subsequently returned with the Visa stamp inside.** Remember, the visa is simply a sticker in your passport, which is why you have to hand in/send off your passport to have the visa stuck into it. The process will take around one month (20 working days) to complete. The final stage is to collect your passport, either in person or having requesting its' delivery by courier. The Visa will only be issued if you can demonstrate that you have both adequate (financial) resources and health insurance cover (with coverage as stated above) for the entire length of your proposed stay and you must be able to show proof of payment.

UK residents have to apply via the French Consulate General in London, residents elsewhere need to apply to the French Consulate in that country. The French consular service has outsourced the initial application step to a number of specialist companies who assess your paperwork. However if questions arise it is the consulate that will contact you.

2.2.2 Types of Visa
Those on visitor visas **must not** do any paid work.

2.2.2.1 *4-6 Month Stays*
To be able to spend four to six months at a time in France one will now need a **visitor's temporary long-stay visa** *visa de long séjour temporaire 'visiteur'* (*VLS-TS visiteur*). (TS = *Titre de Séjour* Residence Permit and while it is valid you don't need to ask for a Residence Permit to remain).

n.b. At the end of 2020 the French Government advised second home owners that if they spent between 4 & 6 months a year here they would have to apply for a *VLS-TS visiteur* as they are considered visitors too.

Note that this visa can't be extended/renewed when you are in France and if you overstay that could result in being refused a visa at a later date and you may well be fined. On expiry you can simply apply for another.

Applicants will be subject to a test of their resources, to ensure they do not become a burden on the French State, to obtain it you will need to show income above the French net minimum wage (See section 2.2.3) for the length of your stay. Cash in the bank is good as no income is guaranteed these days. All the better if you already own a French home as officials may be more lenient if you are close to the threshold limit. You will need to have travel insurance that includes medical repatriation. Family applications are linked (and you will have to list who you are travelling with) but couples will need to apply individually.

2.2.2.2 *Long Stays*
If you want to stay beyond 6 months then you will need to apply for a **long-stay visa** *visa de long séjour (VLS-TS)* (which is equivalent to a residency card) and also show an income above/equivalent to the net French minimum wage. Once issued for stays between 6 & 12 months these visa's allow the holder to come and go during the period (e.g. to allow the holder to return to the UK if required, e.g. to care for an elderly relative).

Visits and Visa's

If you are travelling as and apply as a couple your applications will be linked but be assured your income doesn't have to be double this, probably only a few hundred euros more, but each application is looked at individually.

n.b. Any second home owner's property is taken into account and allows for flexibility to be applied to the amounts required.

If one of you is relying on your spouse's income/pension for example you will need to provide your marriage certificate to prove your relationship. The *'usual'* proofs of income necessary would be the last 3 months of payslips/pension payments or current/savings account statements as savings can be taken into consideration if you can show sums in savings accounts that can supplement any income.

You will also need to demonstrate you will have health insurance cover although if you are retired you will be entitled to join the French Health System after 3 months legal residency.

If one spends more than 6 months a year here (and that would apply to anyone who wanted to move here) they would be considered as French resident which implies Tax Residency (See section 9.115.1).

2.2.2.3   *Business Visa*
There's no doubt that things are now somewhat trickier if you intend to start a business when you move here to France, as you will now need to apply for a **Business Visa**, even if you only intend it to be a part-time activity. **Be aware** that a plain visitor's visa won't allow you to register a business!

a) Purchasing an existing business
You could of course plan to take over an existing business which might simplify things to a degree but a business case will still be required and due diligence is vitally important. If you take this route be aware then that the functioning of the business under its' existing owner as well as your ability to run it in terms of experience or qualifications is taken into consideration as would be your ability to grow the business. This does not just apply to professions such as accountancy or surveying but also to Artisans/Tradesmen who will need relevant qualifications or at least 3 years' experience.
Note that any professional qualifications do not automatically transfer from the UK to France – you will need to prove your qualifications or have at least 3 years' experience as an employee or self-employed.

b) Application Process
You either need to obtain a Business Visa when you emigrate or apply to your local *préfecture* to change the status of your visitor's visa once you are here. Either way you will end up with a *carte de séjour temporaire 'entrepreneur/profession libérale'* at a cost of 225€.

n.b. Whether you apply for the business visa before you move or once you are here the requirements are the same as it's the local *préfecture* where the business will be based who are consulted and it is they who will carry out any business assessment.

Any initial Business Visa that is granted will be based on the viability of your business plan as the French Embassy will want to ensure that once they issue it you will be able to work legally and have sufficient income to cover your cost of living in France. It is only calid for a year, conditional on one applying for it to be validated within 15 days of your arrival in

Visits and Visa's

France, whereupon you must complete all the formalities allowing you to carry out your professional activity. After that first year you have to apply to renew it at which point it will then last for 5 years.

To get one's Business Visa one needs to apply (using CERFA form 13473*01) (See section 9.20 and Annex C) and produce a business plan justifying that your proposed business will be economically viable (See section 2.2.3) and is capable of supporting you/you and your family and this will be applicable whether you intend to start a new business or acquire an existing one. A sizeable amount of documentation will also be necessary, not least the ability to provide precise and thorough information on your proposed project including your business strategy, financial projections for at least 3 years together with the intended legal status of your business (Sole Trader, Limited company etc).

Logically for me this is all a little bit *'Cart before the horse'* as until you arrive and conduct some preliminary market research you have no real idea if there will even be a market for your products or services. Either that or you will have needed to make numerous prior trips as a visitor to do the necessary research. Consequently buying an existing business or continuing to operate an internet business you run in the UK makes it easier to show the economic viability of such an enterprise. Otherwise it would be surely sensible to initially apply for a standard visitor visa until such time as you are clearer about the potential opportunities although see Sections 5 and 5.1 which discuss producing a Business Case.

Your linguistic skills will be taken in to account if you are going to rely on the French market as your proficiency in French will directly impact your likelihood of being able to generate the necessary sales. When you initially apply for the Business Visa if the authorities look favourably upon it, they will issue a receipt which authorises the applicant to obtain their business registration. Thereafter how you decide to operate, as a registered company or micro-entrepreneur etc. is up to you but once your application has been approved you will be allocated a business registration no. *Siret* (See section 9.106) and the Business Visa will be issued. About a month to six weeks later you will be notified that you have been assigned to a relevant social security regime.

c) Other

Small business/micro-enterprises are run by micro-entrepreneurs but the terms are still used inter-changeably with those of auto-enterprise and auto-entrepreneurs even though the two statuses were merged in 2016 and officially the former term replaced the latter.

As a sole-trader in a standard micro-enterprise one has unlimited liability, you are your business as there is no legal distinction between the two like with a limited company, but it is possible to setup a scheme (AERL - See Annex B) to protect against this or one needs to take out Professional Indemnity Insurance. Rest assured however as in 2015 the law changed to at least protect family homes if one was sued.

Note Micro-entrepreneurs are taxed on turnover (you need to record your income and then declare it every 3 months) whereas EURL's are taxed on profits based on formal accounts.

2.2.2.4 *If you have a French Spouse*

In this case you should request the **Marriage Long Stay Visa**, *Visa de Long Séjour (VLS) valant Titre de Séjour (TS) Vie Privée et Familiale* also called *pour époux de Français* which

Visits and Visa's

allows you not only to enter France but remain for more than 3 months and up to a maximum of one year.

2.2.3 Financial Requirements

France has a government-mandated minimum wage, SMIC (See Annex B) and no worker in France, regardless of their status or whether they have an interim, permanent, or temporary contract should be paid less than this minimum pay rate. For calendar 2022 on the basis of the legal working week of 35 hours, the monthly minimum wage will be 1,603.12€ after social charges but before income tax which translates to 10.57€ per hour, making the actual net gross 19237.44€.

Note, that this means an income (**not** Sales) of at least 19237.44€. If your business can't produce this level of income you will need to show how you will supplement it, e.g. from a private pension, savings or from a UK rental. You will need to demonstrate that your proposed venture can provide you with a regular income equivalent to SMIC at the very least although practically the authorities will understand this might not be achievable from the very beginning.

The Fundamentals

3. The Fundamentals

When looking at the fundamentals of moving to France one needn't stray further than Rudyard Kipling's honest serving men vis: Why, What, Where and When. The 'Who' is you, otherwise you probably wouldn't be reading this book, so let's start with the *'Why'*, *'What'* & *'Where'*. Chapter 4 will deal with the *'How'* and the *'When'* will follow.

3.1 Establish your 'Why?'

Generally moving to France and living here is not about *'things'* and it gives one an opportunity to recalibrate your life. The reasons behind our move were quite simple, to enjoy more spacious surroundings, the slower pace and quality of life, not having to worry about setting an alarm each day and to be able to live mortgage and stress free. I said earlier that we felt it was right place right time for us as our various children had all left home and were confidently living their own lives and so we decided that after years of thinking about them and putting them first that it was time we did something just for us.

At the time I was worried I might be bored when we got here so our initial criteria for buying a house included properties that were either large enough to section off or had their own *Gites* I could run.

So as part of your research it is important to establish your 'Why?' e.g:
- Are you simply retiring?
- Do you just want to open a new chapter in your life?
- Do you want a better climate, quality of life, standard of living?
- Do you want land/a small-holding or more space than you have?
- Do you want/need to keep a house back in the UK?
- Do you want to live full-time in what was your Holiday Home?
- Do you want bilingual children or to be bilingual yourself?
- Do you want to buy somewhere to just move in/renovate?
- Do you need somewhere that provides a form of income? etc.

All of these factors will influence both the type of property that you need and its location, use these to drive your search. Simply finding a house, falling in love with it and moving in is a potential recipe for disaster. All dreams need to be underpinned with some kind of foundation else they will quickly turn into a living nightmare. Once you have found your 'why' it will motivate you through the difficult times ahead of actually moving in and help you ignore outside influences or *'noises off'* that can distract and dissuade you.

We saw our house and signed the *Compromis du Vente* (See section 4.9.6) before the *'referendum on the EU'* in June 2016, we then moved in after the outcome had been decided knowing full well that the house we had chosen met our *'Why'*, irrespective of what was supposed to happen politically, and also ticked almost all our other boxes regarding *'What'* and *'Where'*.

Of course then soon after the other advantages of French country living; vis: less busy roads, less people, open spaces, outdoor living, relaxed lifestyle, slower pace and better quality of life and getting much more for our money became added bonuses.

The Fundamentals

> *tip* Don't forget to remove the rose-tinted spectacles from time to time though. Have no illusions, moving to modern day rural France is like stepping back in time to an England of 40-50 years ago with its politeness and emphasis on family values; but some of the more modern aspects of life that we are used to like banking, e-commerce etc. are somewhat dated here at times and it is easy to get frustrated with the slow pace. If you are retired however just take it in your stride, there is always tomorrow.

3.2 Determine your 'What'

So now you have a well-defined idea of your rationale for moving the next basic question is what are you going to do whilst you are here? Reason being is that also has a bearing on the type of property you look for, i.e. will it be solely residential/business/mixed purposes or *'lock up and leave'* as some people move/relocate here but intend to carry on working back in the UK whereas others establish their home as the business or business base?

3.2.1 Establish your budget

I don't understand people who spend at the top end of their budget on their actual purchase and subsequent conversion, why not spend far less (downsize your dream a little) and live more comfortably? If you intend setting up a business then that route forces you to try and start earning as quickly as possible, maybe before its practical to do so.

It won't surprise you to read that here in France as in the UK there is a wide disparity in property prices depending on which part of the country you settle in, consequently although it is stating the obvious the principal contributing factor to your *'What'* will be your budget. Make a long cold assessment of what funding you will have available to make any purchase, be it an advance from a financial institution, the equity or equity release from a UK house sale, an inheritance, lottery win, or even a lump sum taken from your pension pot and set your expectations accordingly. As the old saying goes *'cut your cloth according to your width'*. Do not get seduced by an advert for a barn crying out for renovation, a fairy-tale chateau with pepper pot turrets or a house with extensive grounds or lake without first establishing whether it fits within your price range. In particular if you have grander aspirations like a Chateau remember that it may seem idyllic but look beyond the facade into the actual fabric of the building, in particular the roof and the windows, Chateau maintenance is not cheap and you'll need permission from the state to renovate it as Châteaux are considered historical monuments. The costs are also high as you'll need to employ specialised artisans. Many wealthy families are offloading them for these reasons. You also don't want to buy a *'money pit'*. It would be unwise to select any property and then try and find the money to buy it, especially as any sum borrowed will be subject to fluctuating exchange rates, something over which you have absolutely no control.

3.2.2 What type of property?

Frame your 'what'. By this I mean have it clear in your mind as to whether you want/intend to for example:
- Just move into a property and carry out routine maintenance, i.e. just retire and enjoy your surroundings;
- Renovate a barn/cowshed/property with outbuildings;
- Restore a *Longère etc*; or
- Use it as the base for a business.

The Fundamentals

Irrespective of whether you are not planning to or have no need to work, or simply have the luxury of being able to work from home the majority of the time you need to determine your *'must haves'*/specific wants in which case I suggest that the questions you need to answer about a largely residential property are:
- What type of property?
  Barn, Bungalow, Chalet, Chateau, Cottage, Farmhouse, House, Lodge, *Longère* (all of which will be partly dependent on area);
- What feature (if any) Bread Oven, *Cave*, Inglenook, *Pigeonnier*, Turret?
- What type of construction?

n.b. Stone houses provide a wonderful refuge from the sometimes soaring summer temperatures but if you feel the cold make sure there is an adequate heating system for the whole house as they are notoriously very cold in Winter.

- How many bedrooms?
- How many reception rooms?
- How much land?
- Does it need to have a swimming pool etc?

Remember that one's property priorities are likely to change over time, isolation seems wonderful if you are on holiday but can be overwhelming if you live there full-time, bigger properties appeal or are necessary when one is younger but their upkeep can be challenging with advancing age.

An important point to bear in mind when identifying the type of property that you want is that having UK expectations in France doesn't work in that you may find for example:
- There is only a single toilet for the whole house;
- Fitted kitchens aren't the standard because many French people are happy with just a kitchen table and a stove to cook on;
- In many properties one enters through the kitchen anyway or straight into a reception room with no concept of a hallway; and/or
- It is not on mains water or drainage.

If relevant you may want to adjust your budget accordingly and include a contingency to enable you to remedy some/all of these features. Many people make the mistake of buying something they don't need and is far too big for them for the wrong reasons, possibly because they equate it to what they owned in the UK. Yes you can expect a lot of visitors, particularly in the year or so after you move but thereafter? Ask yourself who is going to visit and how often? With the best will in the world your children may only visit a couple of times a year and having a number of rooms permanently set aside for them or friends in anticipation of a visit is foolish. You will pay more in *Taxe Foncière* and your heating bills will be higher. Be realistic!

If you are not intending to work or intend to carry on working back in the UK then I suggest you can skip over the rest of this section and continue reading from Section 3.3.

3.2.3   Work or play?
There is an old adage *'Do a job you love and never work a day in your life'* that holds true. Consequently many people turn their dream/hobby/passion or something they like doing into a business so it will be more enjoyable for them and won't seem like going to work

The Fundamentals

every day. If this is you then you will already have firm ideas of what you want to do, so ask yourself:
- How often do you want/need to work, will it be full/part time i.e. will it provide your income or just pocket money?
- How much income do you need and for how long?
- Will it be an entirely new venture or do you plan to takeover an existing business?
- Will the business be integral to or separate from your accommodation?

Unless you are thinking of a purely service based offering you will probably be looking to buy an existing business that is for sale or to start your own. The question here is *'Do you have relevant expertise in your intended enterprise or just want to give it a go?'* Either way there is some necessary groundwork to carry out first and understand that if you are just *'giving it a go'* you will have a steep learning curve.

If relevant, initially consider your relationship dynamics, if one of you is organised and the other haphazard, one quiet and one an extrovert, one a night owl one an early bird, one a completer-finisher and one a resource investigator, one who is adept at time-management and the other a butterfly then you will be in for an interesting journey once the initial novelty of your new surroundings has worn off and it no longer feels like a holiday and you are working together each day. So consider what you intend to do very carefully.

It maybe you decide to setup something once you have been living here for a while in which case you will have a head-start when it comes to advertising, knowing the competition/market etc.

3.2.4 Options

If you are thinking of offering some kind of professional services and your profession is a regulated one and one which in the UK it is necessary to have a qualification for, then check that qualification is relevant in France (by say contacting an applicable French Professional body) before you start trading.

Perhaps you are thinking of setting up/offering a different kind of service business, internet buying and selling that won't require you to hold inventory or one that doesn't necessarily require specific premises? A lot of people with the requisite skills, i.e. conversational French consider teaching English in which case your entry level costs are minimal and I suggest you can skip to Section 3.3.

3.2.4.1 *Takeover an existing business*

If you are looking at properties that have or are part of an established business then there will be mention of this in the paperwork that you get through from the Estate Agent and you will be readily able to see if it satisfies your *'What'*. Through subsequent questioning of the agent/ owner and dependent on your own financial position you will likely get a rough idea of the turnover etc. but it is unlikely you will get to see any detailed figures or the actual books until you have made an acceptable offer. Be sure to carry out your due diligence thoroughly and in the meantime you can always propose a *'Condition Suspensive'* (See section 4.9.4) to cover off your expectations in this regard.

The Fundamentals

3.2.4.2 Decide to start a business

So you have had an idea for a business. Is this a long-held dream or something you feel you have to do to supplement your income?

It seems that many people decide almost as a default to open something in the hospitality arena, *'oh we'll run a* Bar, B&B, *Chambre d'Hôte or a Restaurant'* whether they have previous hospitality experience or not. If so can you live with the constant intrusion of people in your house, can your children, animals? If you have no experience of this then think long and hard about whether you are cut out for being continually cheerful day after day, or even, if you are offering evening meals, whether you are prepared to eat with different people day in day out.

You might be skilled at renovating property and reselling it in the UK but in France it is a very different market place, there are different product costs, rules and regulations, timescales and wiring standards to consider, particularly dare I say if you employ French tradesmen, this is not the UK!

If your proposed business is completely alien to anything you have done previously, do your homework and research it in depth, particularly the legal side of things, licences, registrations etc. Have a clear business model in mind and before you embark on anything further ask yourself honestly whether you will be out of your depth?

Consider that in the rural areas, even in largish towns, do not be surprised to find that most business's close on a Monday and apart from restaurants not much is open on a Sunday afternoon either, as this may impact your cash flow projections.

Once you arrive are you intending to integrate or just create/join an expat bubble? If the former you will need some French language skills and business or technical terminology is different to everyday French.

You might have just decided that you want to setup your own business. All I can say is **don't jump into it** as Napoleon was alleged to have said:
On s'engage et puis . . . . . on voit? or *'We commit and then we see'*
this is not a strategy likely to guarantee success, he may even have employed it at Waterloo? Don't make that mistake.

You only have to watch such programmes as Channel 4's *'A New Life in the Sun'* to see that many people set out on a path that clearly isn't thought through as it doesn't provide enough income for them and they have to diversify or change the scope of their business to bring them the standard of living/income that they want once reality bites. Businesses naturally evolve but you want to do that organically and when you are ready, rather than be forced into it by adverse events. I have to say that the programme has provided me with a number of useful learning points for inclusion in this book although it beggars belief what some people will do and the risks they take, but then again following sensible couples doesn't make for good TV.

From a financial perspective if you have ready access to funds all well and good. If you are looking for a loan or a mortgage then commercial funding may likely depend on the actual property you choose although if you are lucky you can secure an Agreement in Principle upfront.

The Fundamentals

3.2.4.3   Hand's On from a Distance

Of course there is another option I haven't discussed so far and that is retaining a/your UK business when you move to France. Chronologically it deserves to be somewhere in Section 6 but I'll deal with it here as it may influence your choice of 'Where'?

Prior to our move Joanne had decided to retain her small retail business in the UK for at least a year to see how things worked out being *'an absent owner'*. In the event she kept it another two and a half, before finally relinquishing the reins and selling it in January 2019. Until then she regularly flew back to the UK for a week every 6 weeks or so, which she could easily do pre-covid. Of course she needed to be flexible with travel dates as she was at the mercy of the airline's fluctuating prices.

But what did she do in the interim to keep her *'hand on the tiller'*? Well. she:
- Had reliable staff who were empowered to make orders as required;
- Had video chats with them on a regular basis and conducted virtual tours of the shop and the shelves to see how products were selling;
- Had daily sales reports sent to her so she could monitor the financials;
- Arranged for 'reps' to visit during the weeks she was back in the UK;
- Still attended the large bi-annual trade fairs in Birmingham; and
- Was available at the end of a phone/videocall as needed.

On her trips she admitted to missing home once she had been gone 3 or 4 days but the weeks back also provided her with an ideal opportunity to catch up with family and friends that she might not otherwise have seen, and with her regular customers.

If you have a small UK business that you want to keep on after your move here then you need to understand how it will function without you and make communication and travel arrangements accordingly. We were lucky because we still had a car based at our small UK house that was only 20 minutes from Stansted and the business was in between the two, otherwise Joanne would have had to factor in both car hire and hotel accommodation on each trip as there is only many times you can ask family/friends for lifts or stay with them.

My assumption here is that if you have a medium sized business you will have an integrated IT system which will make keeping track of things far easier.

3.3   Work out your 'Where'?

We have now established the 'Who', 'Why' and 'What' behind a move, time then to look at the 'Where'? I'll start with some country facts.

3.3.1   National Differences

3.3.1.1   Head of State

The basic difference between our two countries is that whereas the United Kingdom is a constitutional monarchy with the monarch as the Head of State and Church (Defender of the Faith), France is a Republic headed by a President. The French national *'motto'* is the well-known *Liberté, Egalite, Fraternité* (liberty, equality, fraternity) and stems from the time of the French Revolution towards the end of the 18th Century. However in recent times it could be supplemented with *Laïcité* - Secularism. In France there has been a legal separation of church and state since 1905 when the *Loi de Laïcité* which allowed freedom of worship irrespective of which religion or denomination wishes to do so was passed.

The Fundamentals

3.3.1.2 *Parliamentary System*

Both countries have what is known as a *bicaméral* legislature with two distinct parliamentary bodies/houses. In the UK the lower chamber or House of Commons consists of 650 MP's elected every 5 years and an Upper House known as the House of Lords, an unelected chamber with some 800 members either hereditary or appointed peers. All of whom sit collectively in the Houses of Parliament in London.

France's lower house or *Assemblée Nationale consists of 577 Députés* who are also elected for 5 years and meet in the Palais Bourbon; and the Upper House or *Sénat* comprising 348 *Sénators* who are each elected by regional councillors or delegates from municipal councils in their *département* for 6 years, and who meet in the Palais du Luxembourg, both of which are in Paris.

3.3.2 Geography

France is a large and diverse country and still the most visited country on the planet with around 90m visitors in 2019. Not only that, France is much larger than most people realise! It is some 1,000km (600 miles) from north to south and approximately the same from east to west, which makes it the third largest country in Europe (after Russia and Ukraine), and it covers an area of 551,500km² (213,000 square miles) whereas the whole of the UK is only 242,500 km² (93,600 square miles) and France is approximately 4 times the size of just England and is the second most rural country in Europe after Poland. In June 2021 a survey by the French National Statistical Office found 1 in 3 of the French population live in a rural area.

Not only that but its woodland cover is much greater. In France there is c28% tree cover whereas the UK is only about 12% wooded. If you work through the maths France has 5.3 times the amount of woodland as England given it is 4 times larger

3.3.3 Administration - Regions

Within this overall expanse are 13 relatively recently created (January 2016) regions, combined down from the previous 22. Seven were new and created through an amalgamation of a number of the former regions, vis:

- Bourgogne-Franche-Comté   (Bourgogne and Franche-Comté)
- Grand-Est   (Alsace, Champagne-Ardenne and Lorraine)
- Hautes-de-France   (Nord-Pas-de-Calais and Picardie)
- Normandie   (Basse-Normandie and Haute-Normandie)
- Nouvelle-Aquitaine   (Aquitaine, Limousin and Poitou-Charentes)
- Occitanie   (Languedoc-Roussillon and Midi-Pyrénées)
- Rhône-Alpes   (Auvergne and Rhône-Alpes)

In addition 6 former regions retained their names and are as follows:

- Bretagne;
- Corse;
- Centre;
- Île-de-France;
- Pays de la Loire; and
- Provence-Alpes-Côte d'Azur.

The Fundamentals

As you would expect a country with such a size encompasses much diversity from which to choose where to live, e.g:
- The rocky outcrops of Brittany and its Gaelic roots in the North West;
- Champagne country with its history of the crowning of French Monarchy in the North East;
- The towering Alps in the East;
- The volcanic Central Massif;
- The riviera coast of the South East.
- The rugged Pyrenees and the foothills of Basque country in the South; or
- The gorges and footsteps of cro-magnon man in the South West.

3.3.4 Administration - Départements

In the UK our system of Local Government is primarily shire or county based supplemented by districts and parishes, France does not have counties but is divided into administrative units called *Départements,* of which 96 are on the mainland and 5 in overseas territories.

(The latter are historically known as DOM-TOM - *Départements et Territoires d'outre-mer*). These *Départements* do not have such a long history as the British shires or counties. They came about during the revolution to help impose Parisian control on the provinces. Unlike their UK counterparts they are almost all of approximately equal size, that size being determined by the distance a government official could cover in a day by horse from the *Département* capital. They were nearly all given deliberately neutral names, taken from local rivers or other natural/prominent geographic features which was all designed to suppress regional identity. However there are today, somewhat confusingly, six *Départements* which include the word "Loire" in their title, as well as two with "Loir" and one called "Loiret".

The Fundamentals

Today, each of these local government areas is headed by a *Préfet* and administered by a *Conseil Général* based in a *préfecture*. Departmental *Préfets* are representatives of the National Government at a local level and as such are a direct representative of the Prime Minster. They are appointed by decree of the President on behalf of the Prime Minster and the Minister of the Interior (equivalent to the UK Home Secretary).

Within each *Département* are multiple *Communes*. A *commune* is the smallest and oldest administrative division in France (apart from any *arrondissements* in large municipalities) and there are over 36,000 of them. They vary enormously in size (both in square kilometres and population) from something the size of Paris to a small hamlet with a handful of residents. They were based on extant villages and they all have names. They are governed by elected officials and a town council (*Maire* and a *conseil municipal*) with wide ranging autonomous powers to implement national policy.

Maire's are paid according to the size of their municipality as that impacts the amount of work they have to do for it and so it is not always a full-time job. The payment ranges from some 600€ per month for a small commune of less than 500 inhabitants, through c2,500€ per month for around 15,000 people up to over 5,500€ per month for more than 100,000 people.

Around 200,000 British people live in France, the *Corrèze* where we have settled is a small Department 82nd in terms of population (2013) and 55th in terms of area/size. It is a very green department and we in the west of it are surrounded by apple orchards but the area is actually responsible for providing more than $1/6$ of France's annual raspberry crop.

The Fundamentals

3.3.5 Narrowing it Down

You might already have an idea of roughly where you want to move to, at least at *département(s)* level, but failing that you will know whether you want town or country. You might base your choice on an area suitable to pursue your favourite leisure activity, hobby or passion, e.g. so you can easily go Canoeing, Climbing, Cycling, Sailing, Walking, Wine tasting etc? As previously stated some of you may intend to carry on working back in the UK in which case your '*Where*' needs to give ready access to your intended commuting route, be it by Airplane, Road, Train. Although you can still choose a (semi-) rural idyll.

A French based business on the other hand requires a different thought process. Obviously what you want to do will have a bearing on/influence where you move to. If you are thinking of something accommodation based then accessibility to your target audience - good roads or proximity to an airport or high-speed train line will be important, as will having some local features for your guests to visit. If you are thinking of something recreational like canoeing, cycling or pony trekking for example then you need to have the appropriate geography on hand. If you are thinking of a retail business as opposed to something web-based however you will need sustained footfall and you won't get that in a rural location as that comes from something more urban.

3.4 Location, Location, Location

This adage is certainly true when you move to foreign climes. What do you want? A rural idyll, edge of civilisation or the middle of town?

By comparison to England, France is a huge country, over 4 times the size and what looks close by on a map may not be in reality. Remember that what is attractive in the height of summer might not be in the depths of winter or indeed vice versa, but if it appeals in winter then you are likely to be happy in summer. Staying somewhere that requires you getting in a car and taking a 15-20 minute drive to the shops may be suitable for a couple of weeks holiday but you will soon get bored with it on a full-time basis particularly if you get back home and realise you've forgotten the milk! Be aware also that outside of the big cities/towns public transport is few and far between and taxis are prohibitively expensive.

When you come from a typical housing estate in the UK the prospect of the nearest neighbour being half a mile away is extremely attractive, but in reality what if you have an accident or need help, are just missing human contact and want to chat over the fence, or are snowed in and need some basic provisions? Will it still appeal/seem practical then? Similarly If the house is in a wooded valley or faces North work out whether it will get any sun during the winter months or if you see any, ask the neighbours or the vendors as it may colour your thinking.

When I talk about location I am not just talking about which area of France you want move to, I'm talking about what defines your ideal property, not just the house but the other factors that will impact your new life. For example when we were looking at properties the main box that we wanted ticking was as follows:
- Close to (walking distance)/on the edge of a town/village.

As well as ready accessibility of a:
- Bakery;

The Fundamentals

- Bank;
- Bar;
- Dentist;
- Doctor;
- Petrol Station;
- Supermarket; and
- Vets

and relatively easy access to an Airport and a Train Station if we needed them as that would cover all our requirements. We liked the look of our house from the details but fell in love when we viewed it despite knowing nothing about the area, although it turned out to be a hidden gem, with facilities to suit us and any visitors we might have in a village close to a town. As such we were extremely lucky in that we have all of the above and as added bonuses we have a (private) Ambulance station HQ, a total of 3 other Banks in town (with 5 ATM's in total), 5 Garages, 4 Hotels, 3 Restaurants and 4 other Supermarkets within a 12 minute drive, a Chateau and a Racecourse nearby as well as a National Stud with a multiplicity of free equestrian events throughout the year and a Fire Station, not bad for a town of just 1,800 people. As bonuses the Doctor, Dentist and Vet all speak some English and from the house we have stunning uninterrupted views of the (sometimes) snow covered Western edges of the Massif Central (*Les Monédières*), not a bad office to be in!

We also have a local Rugby Club that plays to a reasonable standard (in addition to a professional team in Brive, a short drive away) which ticks my own personal box. However flexibility is keynote, as it is in many areas of life. So your location (as well as a lockdown) may even make you rethink your shopping habits and rather than nip to the shops every day you may find a weekly shop more convenient because the supermarket is too far. Either that or you may simply do without until a larger shopping trip beckons?

Define your search area – else it will complicate any viewings.

3.5 Personal Choice

I can understand that you might ask, why choose France to go and live in as opposed to that other popular choice of Spain? Well, for me the sun-scorched concrete jungle of the majority of the coastline of the Costa's allied to the little Englander mentality there held no appeal whatsoever. We didn't just want sun, sun and more sun, some seasonal variation was preferable and we wanted to experience the varied colours of spring and the russet hues of autumn which we have in spades in the *Corrèze*. The inland, more mountainous part of Spain did appeal but I don't speak the language, whereas at least I had prior experience of France and French living and France is better connected to different parts of the UK through the many regional airports and low cost airlines. Yes French bureaucracy has a bad name, and there are over 5.5m employees *fonctionnaires* in the inflated public sector yet from what I hear and read I still think it bears favourable comparison with Spain where timescales for getting simple things like licences. permits etc take an age. What is more France scores well on many indicators of well-being compared to most other countries in the OECD Better Life Index where it is above average in terms of civic engagement, health, housing, income and wealth, security, social ties and work-life balance. Consequently we have been lucky and *'living the dream'* since 2016.

Finding 'the One'

4. Finding 'the One'

By now you should have established your *'Why'*, determined your *'What'*, worked out your *'Where'* and know whether you want to run a business or not. Consequently you are now ready to try and find *'the one'*, as the *'When'* of your move will ultimately depend on finding it.

4.1 Decide your strategy

Now you know these factors are you an impulsive or pre-meditated type? By that I mean are you the sort that once you have the idea you just want to get on with it or are you more considered, more measured, and take your time to research and plan out your moves?

4.1.1 How are you going to sell your UK Property?

By this I mean think long and hard about whether you want to embark on a complex overall transaction that ties a UK based sale in with a French based purchase or whether you want to or are able to stage them. For a start you are dealing with two different legal systems and the fact that by comparison the English system is back loaded, i.e. exchange of contracts generally happens a few months into the purchase whereas the French system is front loaded with the *Compromis du Vente* coming soon after the cooling off period. There is also the question of cost, phasing everything to tie in is clearly quite complicated, you will need bi-lingual UK Solicitors and you will pay out more in fees to enable it to happen.

4.1.2 How to find your French Property

Are you happy uncovering properties and finding out information about them on the internet or are you a more touchy feely sort of person wanting to examine them close up in the first instance?

Beware coming out without a clear focus, just because you have fallen for France isn't enough, otherwise you will find yourselves pulled from pillar to post looking at all manner of properties without having a clear idea of what you want or what will work for you. Especially if you just book a couple of days out with a single agent and ask them to show you what they have in their portfolio (that meets your basic criteria).

It is easy to get seduced by the size of properties. The typical grounds on offer with rural properties here by far and away exceed what you might expect for your budget in the UK and it is easy to underestimate what you are potentially buying. If you are sports minded then you can easily get an idea of comparable sizes; Wembley as marked out for soccer is around 0.72 ha (1.8 acres) whereas Twickenham with its larger pitch and dead ball areas extends to 0.88 ha (2.18 acres) and an international cricket stadium typically has a minimum 1.7ha of a grass field, or 4¼ acres. Do not take on more than you can comfortably manage. You want to be a Human Being not a Human Doing so you do not want to spend all your time working or paying someone to do it for you, you want to be able to get out and enjoy your new environment, after all that is why you want to move here, right?

4.1.3 Research in Depth

There are plenty of avenues to follow that will assist in your research depending on how much time you have available (we had more than most as our UK Property Sale fell though twice thus extending the time we had before we moved out). For example:

Finding 'the One'

- Holiday to/visit different parts of the country to aid your decision;
- Attend Property Shows, not so much to look for properties themselves but for all the other exhibitors that attend; Banks, Currency Exchange Companies, Estate Agents, Language Learning, Companies, Multi-lingual Solicitors, Removal Companies, Tourist Boards etc. and also to sample the various regional food delicacies and attend the extremely informative range of seminars offered;
- Look online for the above types of enterprise; Make contact with them & try and understand the business rules and regulations etc. that apply to any business you propose establishing;
- Subscribe to relevant magazines; and
- Subscribe to relevant newsletters, estate agent or otherwise.

4.1.4 Rent before buying

Once you have decided on the area you want to move to, something to consider if you are able, depending on the money you have available and the commitments you have in the UK is to find somewhere to rent in that area. Out of season you should be able to rent a holiday home or a *Gite* for a relative song compared with doing the same at the height of the summer. So doing will enable you to live and breathe as a local, to examine what facilities are available in the wider area, uncover what will be going on in July and August – many French villages come alive in the summer months with night markets, fayres etc. and become familiar with what may become your local bar, *bibliothèque*, *boulangerie* or *supermarché* and instinctively know if it's right for you.

4.2 Ask questions to narrow down your search

The amount of information that you get from estate agents *Immobiliers* is as varied as it is in the UK, some are better than others and you will soon have your favourites. The main difference is, that in the UK, unless you are relocating it is relatively easy to find the property whose details you have been sent as you can then drive by as part of your preliminary assessment. In France it is a little trickier. There are two reasons for this, one is that the addresses are a lot vaguer in some instances, simply naming a house in a commune doesn't give you, the house hunter, much to go on, and the second reason is that agents don't necessarily like pinpointing the property on a map as they are quite protective of their right to show you round.

Next is the habit of giving room sizes expressed in square metres. A 16m² bedroom sounds attractive but this obscures say a usable 4m*4m room from one that is 8m*2m and far less practical. Note that a room of any size can be described as a bedroom even if it has a sloping ceiling providing there is minimum headroom of 1.8m. Allied to this is that a large number of older French houses have rooms leading off of rooms, particularly bedrooms. Whilst this might be acceptable if you have a young family it clearly won't work as the premise for a B&B or operating *Gites*. How do you get round this?

Well simply ask for a floorplan, that way you can see whether the internal layout will work for you and if for example the main bedroom is over the kitchen or the lounge you might not view that as desirable? We only encountered one (British Owned) agency that routinely gave floorplans as part of the details they provided. Even if they are not to scale they give you some indication of proportionality. You'll likely be told that they

Finding 'the One'

don't produce them in which case ask the agent to hand-draw one and send that across, and we were never told 'no'. The thought of a commission from a possible sale will motivate them.

Note I am now aware of a couple of other (English) agencies who sensibly offer floorplans to their properties, so shop around.

Also ask for more photographs (than the ones necessarily on the agents website). Attractive sounding bedrooms may have chest high beams running across them – something you might tolerate for a week's holiday but not living there full-time.

During our internet based research on potential houses to ultimately go and view, we developed a list of some two dozen questions or so that we sent to agents when talking to them about one of their properties. From the responses we were able to discount a vast number of houses and so greatly simplify our viewing trips. See Annex A for further insight.

4.3 Cadastral Plan

In France the equivalent of the UK Land Registry is the Cadastral Plan. This was first created in the Napoleonic era to assist with calculating land tax and is now ultimately maintained by the French tax authority, the *Direction Générale des Finances Publiques (DGFiP)*. Basically all of the mainland *Départements* are divided up into numbered plots on which ownership of the land is based and are shown graphically (although they do not provide details of the owner of a property or (necessarily) all the land parcels in a single ownership). It is helpful to home buyers because it shows individual buildings, the relative size of the plot and the place name *lieu dit*, of the property together with the specific cadastral numbers to which it belongs.

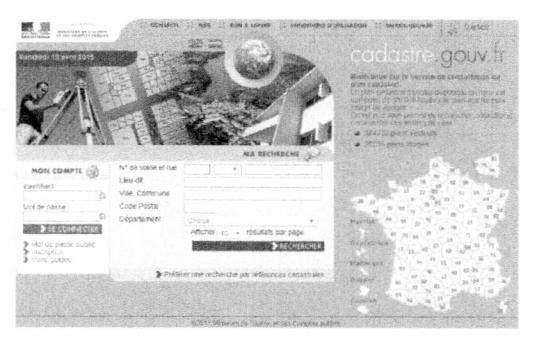

Another note of caution here, the cadastral plan does not show precise boundaries between neighbouring properties so consequently it doesn't provide a conclusive legal definition, although if required you can establish this through a formal land survey. The only person who can redefine a plot is a *géomètre* and they are not cheap (they are also hard to find as there is a shortage of them in France). If you know the basic property details then you can readily access the Cadastral plan, (See Annex C for more information).

The website is easily navigable and is available in English, French and Spanish. The initial display is a map of France, you can then zone into a specific *Département* if you want or enter the *lieu dit,* the Commune, Town or Post Code. Your search then returns a list of up to

Finding 'the One'

10 *Parcelles*. Conversely if you get sent the details from the Estate Agent you can confirm them here.

The cadastral plan and the *Parcelles* that it shows is very important because of some of the idiosyncrasies of French properties compared to those in the UK. Three examples from houses that we looked at spring to mind all of which had on the face of it had a reasonable amount (in excess of one hectare) of land attached. Consequently beware of houses:

1) With land or buildings on both sides of a road.
   Sure you can '*drive*' the road using Google Maps before viewing if you are lucky but that will not necessarily show you how busy it is. If you have to keep crossing the road to get to another part of your garden or garage you need to consider how safe it might be so to do, not just for you but for your children, your animals, friends etc.
2) With land that isn't contiguous.
   You read that a property you are interested in has a certain amount of acreage with it but either when you get there or if you check it out beforehand using the *Cadastre* you find that one or more *Parcelles* are actually someway distant/down the road. This may inhibit your access or equally make the property seem less attractive depending on what you are looking for.
3) With inset land that doesn't belong to you.
   We looked at one property that had a one acre field separated from the bulk of the garden by a smallish copse, consequently it wasn't immediately visible from the house. In this field there was a large rectangle of land stretching inwards from the adjacent road that actually belonged to a third party. Immediately we started thinking about Alfie's safety. Would this party allow us to fence along the road and put a gate in for their access, what if they were in the habit of just turning up to mow this land and Alfie saw/heard/smelt them? He is extremely protective and the problems it might cause didn't bear thinking about. Equally we saw another property with a large tract of land surrounding the house and running down to a busy road which actually had a small square cemetery plot within it whereupon we were told that there were regular visitors to same.

4.4 Trying to Establish a Fair Price

Compared with the UK house buying perspective there is a missing part of the jigsaw when it comes to buying a house in France. For over 25 years now it has been possible for potential purchasers to access HM Land Registry '*price paid data*' which contains the sale prices of all properties in England and Wales that have been submitted to HMLR for registration. This enabled one to see how values had changed over time, although obviously one couldn't see the property's actual condition. Yet in France there was no direct equivalent. Consequently one was pretty much in the dark when it came to determining property values and one paid what one could afford and/or what one thought was reasonable (compared with say something similar back in the UK).

Until recently this information could be obtained but only by paying a *Notaire* for information but new laws aimed at introducing greater transparency to the property market mean that one can now get relevant details of property sales in the last 5

Finding 'the One'

years from a map of the area in question through means of a Government site. (See Annex C for more information).

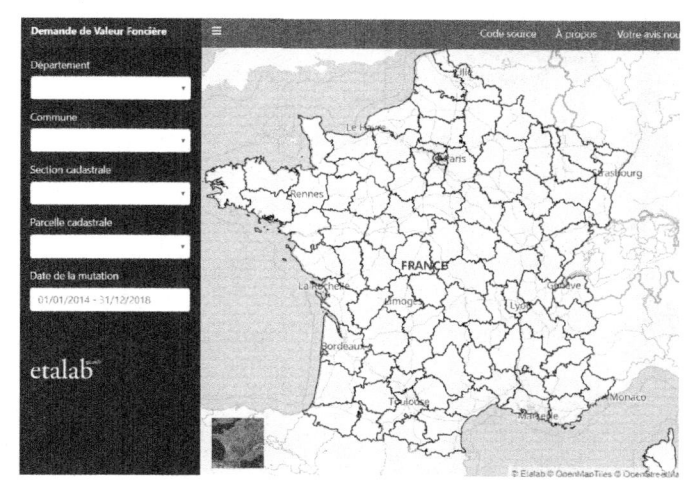

This will enable you to build up a picture of what you think the house is worth, after that it is as much a lottery as house buying is in the UK.

4.5   Reconnoitre Potential Areas

If practicable carry out a preliminary recce of areas you've seen property advertised in around your *'where'*. Post 2012 we had a week's *gite* holiday in *Belves* to confirm our liking of the area and in our case simply driving around from Toulouse to Bordeaux and 600 miles in between (and experiencing 4 seasons in one memorable day) circling areas on the map that looked lovely and crossing out areas to avoid paid dividends. Unless we had done this we wouldn't have necessarily known about the Nuclear Power Station at Golfech (some 25km SE from Agen) as that is visible from, and to our thinking, a blight on a large swathe of the adjacent countryside. Keep in mind that without a visit you won't see that large electricity sub-station next door, the run of electricity pylons, the quarry or that TV Mast opposite because the property details certainly won't mention them nor show them.

As I have already said France is a big country, you need to be fairly systematic when it comes to looking at property otherwise you will spend a long time in the car driving backwards and forwards. We knew the Dordogne was a big department, the third largest in France, and one with a complex and diverse climate and topography but even so to this end we did not help ourselves because as a result of our recce' we expanded our search from the *Belves-La Bugue* area and started requesting details about houses in the wider *Dordogne* area before including *Tarn & Garonne* and *Lot & Garonne*. You'll notice the *Corrèze* didn't feature!

n.b. Somewhat confusingly the *Corrèze Département* features a town of the same name!

Finding 'the One'

4.6 Your Viewing Trip(s)

4.6.1 Doing the Groundwork

When you first start requesting property details you will likely cast your net over a wide number of agents. Don't be shocked if you find that the pictures from French agents include such things as a bicycle in the kitchen
or an ironing board full of clothes in the lounge. It is just that they seem to have a different quality threshold for pictures than agents in the UK.

With my professional background we didn't just decide to view houses because we liked reading their details, I developed a grid to effectively score the different types of house based on what was important to us (See section 3.4). We then ranked the properties according to their score. Then using their location (or at worst commune) I plotted the highest scoring properties on a map and worked out the best routes between them along with getting an idea of travel times. At that point I contacted agents and said we want to view this house on this day and ideally around this time, allowing say an hour and a half to two hours per property depending on its size. It sounds very directive but the agents fell in with this approach and very few rejected it.

N.b. When buying/comparing/doing your research check that property adverts mention FAI/HAI (See Annex B) as it means agency fees are included so you know the total amount you are paying.

Understandably in recent months (in light of the coronavirus pandemic) the temptation to undertake a virtual viewing has increased but I would urge caution in making your decision purely based on one. Remember you will only be shown what the owners/agent want you to see. You need to physically visit not just to see the property but to see for example:

- Whether the noise from passing traffic, or any other local source, is acceptable;
- If there is a church nearby as that may impact any modifications you want to make;
- Exactly what may go on in or around that next door building or anything else out of the ordinary that may show up on an aerial view; or
- Any evidence of woodworm or pick up on any damp smells.

Stay flexible. We had to change an entire afternoon's plans and cancel a couple of viewings on our first trip when we were caught up in a farmer's protest that blocked roads and caused us to reroute. That's when you find one's old map-reading skills coming to the fore in a hire car with no SatNav!

When you are out and about viewing, particularly if you are travelling to somewhere you have arranged privately, trying a drive-by or trying to locate a house name in a commune; if your SatNav can't make head nor tail of the directions you have been given remember if you get to the main village in the commune go in and ask for directions at the *Mairie*. They will certainly know where the houses are.

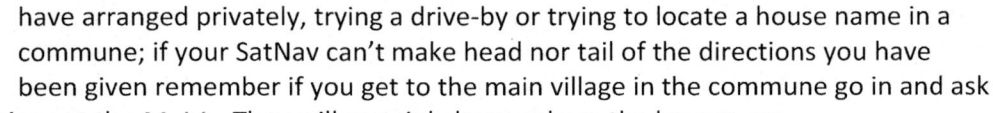

Obviously another approach is simply to book a couple of days out with a single agent and spend time with them looking at all the properties they may deem suitable for you. We did this on a couple of occasions and it did introduce some potential candidates into the mix. But if you happen on an agent make sure they are registered with an official body. An agent may ask you to sign a '*Bon de Visite*' when you view a property through them. Don't worry,

Finding 'the One'

all this means is that if you ultimately decide to buy it then you are saying you will do so through them.

Once you have a target property(s) in mind bear in mind the housing market in France is quite different to the UK, houses are sometimes on the market for many months, consequently when you ask to see somewhere you are rarely told you have to wait. Even with what are in fact holiday homes (*maisons secondaire*) there is usually a local person who has a key and looks after the place for the absent owners who could give you/agent access.

If you are viewing more than one property in a day/trip it's a good idea to make some notes when you leave each one so you don't get confused when discussing/reviewing them later, believe me it easily happens. A better idea is to use a portable Dictaphone or a voice recorder on your phone to record your immediate thoughts.

Don't underestimate the value of a good estate agent. The good one's obviously want you to buy from them but to be happy doing so, they shouldn't introduce you to properties that don't meet your main criteria (certainly not without explaining so first, thus giving you the chance to say No before wasting time going to see it). If you are lucky they also may not just sell you a house but recommend a *Notaire*, help you organise a Bank Account, change the name on your Electricity and Water bills etc.

4.6.2 Sorting the 'Wheat from the Chaff'

When assessing a property, particularly if it has a significant amount of land attached compared with what you are used to in the UK, it is easy to get carried away with the house and its grand sweeping vistas but remember you need to be able to manage the grass or pasture. What is more you will need a plan for when you are older and possibly not as physically capable as you once were? A note of caution here, French Agents are aware that one of the attractions of their properties to English buyers is the comparative amount of extra space so they almost always start you outside in the garden/grounds which you invariably think are wonderful until you go inside. It is then you may realise that you can't live with the beam across the bedroom or the staircase behind the door and wish you had gone inside first but it is your decision.

Once you think you have found '*the one*' as in the UK try and see the house or at least pass through the area at different times of day to find out how busy that lane/road is. Is it a shortcut to the factory/school/supermarket etc? Would you be irritated by the floodlights from the sports field etc. There is a government site that will help you by highlighting various risks including those from earthquakes, flooding, radon gas, subsistence etc based on street address. (See Annex C).

Similarly if internet access is crucial to you/your proposed business there are internet resources available to display a map of fibre-optic deployment in the country down to individual house level as well as a site where you can enter an address to see the connectivity speed in a particular area before you commit to moving there. (See Annex C).

When you come away from a visit with a good feeling you know that you are nearly there. But in your assessment, or even comparison against other houses that gave you an equally

Finding 'the One'

good feeling, be objective. Don't be seduced just by the electric entrance gates, a great garden or a super swimming pool even though they may be to aspire to in the UK, but make sure that there is a way of operating the gates (e.g. unbolting the motor arms) if there is a power cut otherwise you'll be trapped in/out of your dream house unless there is a pedestrian gate alongside. The garden will need regular maintenance, mowing, planting, weeding etc. the swimming pool will need regular maintenance, chemicals, cleaning and if it is heated (and outdoors) then solar would be preferable to keep your bills down.

There is only so much you can look at/remember when on a viewing trip which is where a notepad/voice recorder helps so an unexpected bonus for us after we moved in was to find a considerable number of fruit trees around the garden, Apples, Cherries, Gooseberries, Kiwi's, Pears, Plums, Raspberries and Strawberries as well as an inordinate amount of Blackberry Bushes in the hedgerows, together with Hazelnut, Horse Chestnut and Walnut trees to which we have added Fig, Nectarine and Peach trees and for my birthday a couple of years ago I received a present of a small Kumquat tree which flourishes here thanks to the climate. Equally you may find that your vendors have left small items of furniture/tools etc that you can utilise once you have moved in.

4.6.3 Avoid the 'Pig in a Poke'

A word of caution if the person you buy from claims to be a builder, you have to take them at face value, but take your time viewing the property. The last thing you want is to buy from someone who spent years learning their trade at *'Bodge-it, Coverup and Scarpa'*. You may not spot problems when viewing what you believe is *'the One'* and things like missing/upside down architraves or skirting boards, offset tiles in the kitchen/bathroom/ensuite or poor internal finishing could give an immediate visual clue but what about the things under the surface that take time to manifest themselves? Don't give undue weighting to the fact that it was a builder's house, as with many things it is simply a case of buyer beware! We later found out our vendor had replaced the front door with its predecessor, it looked the same as when we viewed the house but it had a dodgy lock. In all, his lack of expertise as a builder (which he said he was) was surpassed only by his lack of prowess as an electrician.

As a result of recent changes I would also suggest you stay clear of anything with an oil-fired heating system (See section 1.3.6.3). Consider also, when buying in towns that you may be forced to renovate the façade of your building at your own cost, particularly if it is not in good shape, e.g. in 2021 this was enforced in certain arrondissements in Marseille.

4.6.4 A Place to Stay Whilst Viewing

As an aside, if your viewing takes you to the *Corrèze, Dordogne, Haute Vienne* borders and you want to stay in a *Chambre D'hôte* in a former medieval village, one of *Les Plus Beaux Villages de France* then get in touch with me and I'll pass on the relevant details of two sets of friends locally who each run one and you can check out their reviews online.

4.7 Perseverance is the Key

If you are lucky the house whose details you have fallen in love with will become exactly that, your dream home. If however it isn't, for any number of reasons, and none of the other properties are either, do **not** get despondent, the right one is out there, you just have to find it.

Finding 'the One'

Once we had finally exchanged contracts on our English sale we made three separate viewing trips in all. One the week before we downsized in England, the second the week after, and at the end of that we were quite despondent and had wondered whether we would ever find a home in France. Yet we still had two high scoring potential properties to view. One had been out of the way geographically from the area of our second trip and the owners of the other had been on holiday and it had taken time for the agent to source a key, when they did we were a good 3 hours' drive away from it and with other properties to view at the time so they kept it until we could return on another occasion.

That third trip was 3 weeks after downsizing during which we drove down from Essex as opposed to hiring a car from Limoges Airport. We visited both of those houses and a few others besides and it is the trip where our perseverance bore fruit. By the end of it we had visited 48 properties in all, returning to 2 of them so had 50 total visits in 13½ days of viewing and driven a total of some 4400km. Our *'one'* which provided the *Cri de Coeur* was number 47 (the 49th visit), **perseverance does pay**!

If however you find *'the one'*, fall in love with it and your plans involve say opening a B&B, Campsite, or business from scratch, then don't assume that you can despite what the agent says. The land may well have planning considerations attached and *'Change of Use'* may either not be possible or if it is you may find there is an unexpected price-tag to go along with it, so either check it out before you make a formal offer to buy or draw up a relevant Condition Suspensive (See section 4.9.4) before embarking on the sales process. My former industry had a well used saying, 'Don't assume, it makes an Ass of U and Me'. **Don't let that apply to you**!

4.8 Transport

One of the joys of coming to France in pre-lockdown days was the multiplicity of regional airports to fly into but be wary of choosing *'the one'* based purely on its proximity to such a local airport as there is a danger you will become over reliant on it. The problem being that the low-cost flight business is a fickle one and should the particular carrier decide not to serve that area anymore you don't want to be stranded effectively in the middle of nowhere with only a car to get you back to the UK or get your visitors to you. This will also impact on any business you run that relies on people coming out from the UK.

Be careful if you go down this route as another common problem is that sometimes a service is moved to another airport in the UK which is not as convenient for you to go back to, or for your family and friends to travel out from. Try and choose a location that gives you some flexibility in your travel choices.

4.9 The French Sales Process

Hopefully your viewing trip(s) bear fruit at which point you will engage with the buying process so I can't conclude this chapter without a mention of certain parts of the French Sales process. I do not intend explaining these steps in great detail but will comment on certain aspects of it based on our experience that you may not be aware of.

> My disclaimer here is that as I am not legally qualified you should check all salient points with the relevant professional.

Finding 'the One'

4.9.1 Offer Secures

Should you be lucky enough to find *'the one'* be aware that one difference with the French house buying process is that if you offer to buy at the asking price (even verbally) then providing the terms are clear, a contractual commitment arises and the Vendor is obliged to sell the property to you. True gazumping is actually banned under French Law but the quicker the draft sale contract is prepared the better.

Do not expect your purchase to be easy just because you might happen to be buying from English people, conversely do not expect it to be difficult because you are buying from French people. We bought ours from the Englishman that *'built'* the house he was living in and thought we would be ok. What we didn't know was that he had serious delusions of adequacy as to his building prowess or lack of – whatever his problem the solution was expanding foam! People are people at the end of the day, some are good and some are bad. We found out the hard way.

Remember that any price you see advertised may not include taxes or fees and you need to allow for legal costs on top.

4.9.2 Cooling Off

Once the contract for the Sale and Purchase has been prepared then French law allows the buyer a ten day cooling off period in which to withdraw from the purchase for no reason without penalty.

4.9.3 Notaires

The property sale that you are progressing towards is handled by a *Notaire*. These are public officials appointed by the Minister of Justice and it is mandatory for anyone selling a house to use them. Although appointed by the state they are not paid by them, rather they are paid for by their clients according to a scale of charges laid down by the state for the services that they perform. Incidentally they normally charge you an over estimate of the fees involved - *Notaire*, Land Registry, Stamp Duty etc. (on average 7-10% of the purchase price), payable in advance. Any balance is returned after the sale has completed and all appropriate paperwork has been registered, usually some months later.

They are not the same as a Solicitor that one would use in the UK as they are concerned purely with ensuring that the process is followed correctly and consequently do not work for either the Vendor nor the Purchaser. I did not feel entirely comfortable with this approach and so appointed my own *Notaire*. In such cases it does not cost any more, the two *Notaires* simply split the statutory fee between them.

If you are lucky your Agent may recommend a *Notaire* who speaks English which clearly simplifies things but you are obviously at liberty to engage a translator and take them along to any signing (at additional cost to you of course). Equally you could employ a UK based bilingual solicitor to work on your behalf and liaise with the *Notaire*.

Be aware! Sometimes an agent may insist that the sellers want to use the *'family Notaire'*. This is a red flag for me because *'family Notaires'* can sometimes paste over the cracks for their long standing French clients.

Do not be persuaded to bypass the use of a *Notaire* in favour of an Estate Agents contract, if you are not happy with the process then by all means choose your own *Notaire*. Arguably

Finding 'the One'

one of the most important jobs that a *Notaire* performs is to notify the buyers if the person selling the property has gone bankrupt, as without it the buyer runs the serious risk of losing a property that they had bought in good faith. As once bankruptcy has been declared any property is deemed an asset that can be used to pay off creditors which will be to your detriment. They will also check any extant guarantees on building work done on the property within the last 10 years as all reputable builders have Decennial insurance.

Equally, don't think about trying to agree a private sale with the buyers (to avoid the agency fees) as unless the sale has been advertised privately from the outset it rarely works out as the *Notaire* will be in touch with the agent as part of the Sale Process and will hold up the transaction until the agents have received their fee!

Incidentally in certain circumstances you can buy a property directly from a Notaire, but you will still pay commission like with an Estate Agent!

4.9.4 Condition Suspensive

As the Sale and Purchase agreement is being drawn up you as the buyer (and indeed the Seller) have the opportunity to include certain conditional clauses within it, these are known as *Condition Suspensives*. For example the common types of inclusions might be that the purchase is subject to:
- You, the purchaser obtaining a mortgage for the property;
- A satisfactory outcome of a House Survey – although I suggest that this would need to be defined in greater detail as *'satisfactory'* means all things to all people; (Note that surveys before purchase are by no means as common in France as they are in the UK);
- Confirmation of a particular boundary issue;
- Obtaining specific planning consent;
- The purchase (or sale) of adjoining or constituent *Parcelles* of land; or
- That the Vendor includes the land tractor/mower in the actual sale.

Basically any significant thing that you want confirming before you agree to buy the property, your agent or *Notaire* will be able to advise you on what is a suitable inclusion. If whilst looking around the property you see something that isn't mentioned in the property details and that you expect to remain, i.e. for you to acquire as part of the purchase, then I suggest you propose a suitable condition. We expected the satellite dish, some internal light fittings as well as some 8m^3 of wood stored under the veranda to be included with the house; they weren't, and we hadn't thought to make them a condition of purchase!

If the agent tells you something that isn't on the details and you think it is important then ask the *Notaire* to include it. Otherwise the agent could plead ignorance and they would likely win on that basis in court because if the agent argues that the vendor did not tell them, they would not be liable. Where things have been included the agreement will also state the date by which a condition precedent must be fulfilled. If it is not satisfied by this date the Purchaser or Vendor can withdraw from the deal, although it will be subject to the detailed contract conditions.

As a buyer one can't use conditional clauses as a way of simply gaining more time to decide whether or not one wants to proceed with the purchase!

Finding 'the One'

4.9.5 SAFAR

It was the involvement of SAFER (*Société d'aménagement foncier et d'établissement rural*) in our sale that came out of nowhere as far as we were concerned. We only became aware of their potential involvement in our purchase when we were gathered for the signing of the *Compromis du Vente*. (See section 4.9.6) SAFAR is a body you will undoubtedly encounter if you are looking to buy property in rural France. The reason being that this government agency has the right of first purchase (*droit de préemption*) on most rural property with land or any property with Agricultural status that comes onto the market in France. Even worse SAFER now has the right to split up the property so as to only take some of the land. Previously, they had to take all and pay the acceptable selling price. The principle behind this is to assist young farmers and help them become established as well as to rearrange agricultural assets into more viable entities. The agency also has some rural & environmental development obligations where they might enforce their right to help local councils or other public bodies.

Notaires have an obligation to notify SAFER of all sale and purchase contracts, after which the agency has two months to decide whether it wishes to use its right of pre-emption. So although you may think you are on the threshold of moving to France when you sign the sale contract with your seller, in practice you have to wait until SAFER have had an opportunity to buy before you can start counting your chickens!

In practice, the vast majority of rural property transactions go through without SAFER showing any interest, although clearly those properties where such agricultural interests are obviously involved do merit close scrutiny. If they decree that they are interested it does make life difficult & can blow a hole in your plans as it can result in the Vendor withdrawing the sale or being required to sell to SAFER who have an automatic right of purchase if they accept to buy on the terms of the sale contract. The local *préfet* fixes the plot size triggering any SAFER pre-emption every 5 years.

Do not despair, if time is indeed of the essence you cannot circumvent the involvement of SAFAR if they have a pre-emption right in your potential purchase but you can speed it up so you know the outcome much quicker. As of Summer 2021 a payment of 380€ will get you an answer within one month rather than two, 480€ a response within 15 days, or 660€ for a reply within 72 hours, and you should instruct your *Notaire* accordingly.

4.9.6 Exchange and Completion

Basically what we in the UK call Exchange of Contacts is called the *Compromis du Vente* (CdV) in France and it happens towards the start of the overall process, a discrete period after the end of '*Cooling Off*' rather than the end; and what we would call Completion is known as the *Acte du Vente* (AdV).

What surprised us was at different times in both the *Compromis* and *Acte* stages whilst sitting in the *Notaire's* office both Joanne and I were asked to copy out various paragraphs **in French** to include in said documents and this was completely unexpected. A somewhat strange spidery text ensued from both of us as these days most writing is done at a keyboard and other than application forms I cannot personally remember when I last had to write out anything more substantial than a couple of

Finding 'the One'

sentences. What is more we then had to initial the bottom corner of each page before signing at the end. All in all a far more extensive involvement in the contractual side than one would expect in the UK and in our case quite nerve wracking. Not just for the legalities of what we were getting into but knowing we had a tight timetable to meet to catch our flight home as we hadn't allowed for any of the extra time required for writing things which had eaten into our contingency.

> If you barely write anything these days then spend a bit of time making sure that what you do write is legible so it doesn't cause problems on the day.

Where the process is similar to England (I can't speak for Scotland) is that when you sign the CDV you will usually need to pay 10% of the agreed purchase price to the *Notaire* as a deposit, so make sure you have the appropriate amount in Euro's available to do this. If you pull out for any reason other than a Condition Suspensive after that point then you are likely to lose this amount. Once the CdV has been signed off the *Notaire* will start the appropriate searches.

Usually once a completion date is mentioned everyone is happy but bear in mind that before definitively agreeing to the *'When'* you need to check with your removal people first as International removal companies likely want upwards of 2-weeks' notice or more, particularly in the summer months and you will invariably need to fit in around them unless you go down the temporary storage route. The *Notaire* will likely expect to have the balancing payment on your purchase cleared in their account 2-3 days before completion day. They will sometimes conduct the final signing – AdV – at the house. That gives the potential purchasers a chance to look round and ensure that everything is as they expect. Our *Notaire* was happy to do that but the attitude of our Vendors when he met them at their *Notaire's* for the signing of the CdV was such that he insisted they travelled to his office, which was 1½ hours' drive away. At the time we didn't know any different but in retrospect wished that the signing would have been at the house as any obvious problems/differences in expectations are immediately apparent and can be clarified 'face to face'. To conclude you will be given an *'Attestation of purchase'* which will prove that you are the legal owner of the property because copies of the actual deeds are not sent through until some months after the purchase.

Preparation

5. Preparation

So now after all your hard work, ok and possibly a little luck, the reality of you moving into *'the one'* is edging closer and the sale process is ticking along. On the assumption that you will be ready to move once it finishes, i.e. you are not waiting for anything to happen in the UK, what can you usefully do to simplify your transition? Obviously if you are just retiring and not planning on setting up a business then after the ADV you move in and have a happy life, albeit that you will probably have redecoration and maybe some minimal redesign schemes in mind so continue reading from Section 5.2. However if you plan to use the premises as a business then your hard work is just beginning as you now know definitively what type of property it is you are moving into assuming no last-minute hiccups with family, funding, the legal process or SAFAR for example.

Have a clear idea of what (if any) structural changes and/or additions you want to make and decide whether the internal layout will work for what you have in mind for you and any staff you think you need. Think about any (re-) decoration you want to do and get a sense of both costs and timescale for what you envisage. At this point too it would seem prudent to start to formulate your business case that really has no relevance if done earlier. Before putting pen to paper/spreadsheet you need to think both holistically and specifically although not all of what follows will be relevant to your situation.

If part of your plan in moving to France involves setting up a business then things are undoubtedly a little bit harder under the current regime. If your finances will allow you to move here and live for a while you can then research your proposed business in person and take longer doing it than making enquiries by internet or waiting for various viewing trips or holidays to come to fruition. It is simpler because on arrival you obviously don't have to furnish the authorities with a business plan to get your visa and you can move here, albeit with a different visa, and take your time.

> n.b. Any expat with a WARP card is entitled to undertake a professional activity in France once they have registered the business. Not so for anyone else.

5.1 Develop the dream

Do you know the business or are you buying it because it's a bar, B&B, restaurant in the area you know or because that's what you want to do or have always dreamed of doing? The type of business that you want to establish may be based on prior experience or simply by *'taking a leaf out of Napoleon's book'* to setup a Bar, B&B, Café, Camp/Glampsite, Lifestyle Offering, Recreational Enterprise, Restaurant, Retail Outlet, Retreat/Wellness Centre or Wedding/Event business etc.

It is unlikely you will be establishing a business for fun, it will be for financial reasons, so after the excitement of deciding to run your own business you should aim for a quiet moment of reflection to sit down and ask yourself *'what does success look like'*? It will give you a clearer indication of what you need to achieve.

5.1.1 Considerations

So, you are planning on moving to a new country and opening a business; with my analysis and project management background I would focus on the detail and planning side before I start, just like we did when planning our viewing trips. After all if you fail to plan you are

Preparation

planning to fail, but this might not be an approach that suits you, after all you *'pays your money and takes your choice'*. But you should at least take the following considerations into account and read the rest of this sub-section as I believe your case will be stronger if you do. My reasoning being that you don't want to get part way through setting up your potential business before (and borrowing from my former profession) discovering one or more OSINTOT's (the Oh s*** I never thought of that) which could derail or seriously hamper your project.

5.1.1.1   *Market Research*

Once you have decided on what type of business you want to start you should do some Market Research (however basic) before committing, as any successful entrepreneur will tell you about the importance of market research and knowing your target audience. Because why would you think that arriving somewhere and setting up your idea for a business would automatically be a great success without first checking out whether there's any local competition, what the demand would be like or even whether it's possible to get the appropriate licence or registration? Given internet resources these days there is really no excuse for not doing this. So:

- Can the market stand another entrant?
- What is/will be the USP that differentiates you from your competition?
- What about advertising, where is your target market?
  Do you just intend catering (no pun intended) to Brits or do you want to appeal to the domestic market, Belgian, Dutch and German holidaymakers as well?
- Remember that some business is seasonal.
  After the *Rentrée (*See section 9.60) many places close down and some villages become ghost towns, don't rely on sustained footfall unless you want your cash flow to fall off a cliff, particularly if you need to keep the cash flowing (inwards) during winter.
- Model different scenarios before you start, don't just blindly assume that there is a gap in the market or customers will flock towards you and *'because you build it they will come'*!
- Ideally as part of your preparatory work, visit your local Chamber of Commerce who will give you advice on what steps your intended business needs to go through, and what paperwork will be required.
- Can you get whatever licences are necessary before committing, or at least try and make it a condition suspensive (See section 4.9.4).

If you intend buying an existing business.
- If practicable visit your business as a customer before buying as you will get an idea of the clientele and the footfall. Then you can make a rough budget for any changes you are thinking of making before making your offer and tailor it accordingly.

5.1.1.2   *Financial*

- Are you buying the business unseen, purely on the basis of its financials and/or its location and what you know of the area, or have you been a customer and have personal knowledge of its operation?
- Plenty of people develop what becomes a profitable business but there is a difference between making an annual profit to live on and making a profit such that

Preparation

it pays back the amount of investment you made to start it on the first place. What profit level and Return on Investment (ROI) are you comfortable with?
- What is/will be your Break-Even Point?
- Don't have unrealistic expectations as regards turnover or your working week etc.
- Think seriously whether you have the funds you need? Funding a property purchase is one thing, funding a business on top/as part of it is entirely different. Are you going to be using equity from a UK based property sale/pension/savings/borrowed money. If the latter and you plan on using the credit card route ask yourself whether funding any setup work etc. on a credit card is (really) a good idea as that will place added pressure on you to start trading? Interest charges are punitive and doing so will guarantee headaches.
- Do you need to take out a mortgage or bank loan and if so are you comfortable with the level of repayments?
- Remember when building your Business Case that when it comes to Restaurants, particularly in a holiday area, that tourists tend to walk in rather than book which makes predicting footfall difficult.
- Do a simple sense check on the viability of your idea. If your business involves say making candles or soap which you will sell for 2€/unit with a 1€ profit and you want an income of 30,000€ do you have the time/equipment to make a minimum of 30,000 units? This rule works equally well with restaurant covers/room lettings if you factor in the average profit per meal/room and the days you intend to open.

If you plan to run an accommodation based business
- What occupancy rate do you need to achieve the level of income you require?
- Be aware! Some friends of ours decided to utilise their spare room as a B&B during the summer to bring in some extra cash. After registering and getting the relevant licence they were somewhat shocked to receive an invoice for 140€ per TV* (which includes any in a shared space - so if guests have to walk through your lounge to get to the dining room that will count). This levy applies equally if you intend opening as a *Chambre D'hôte*. In their case it differentiated their offering from the local competition so they reluctantly paid it, particularly as owners can be subject to unannounced/anonymous inspections, but it was an unexpected cost.

* This is separate to the *contribution à l'audiovisuel* in your *Taxe Foncière*.

Bear in mind however should you be thinking of buying a property with a *gîte* which you'll be renting out, be aware that when you come to sell the property the *Notaire* will apply Capital Gains Tax on the *gîte* part even if the house was your main residence. He'll calculate the size of the *gîte* in relation to the property and apply a rate of CGT on that proportion. The same applies if you want to operate all or part of your house as a *Chambres D'Hôte* or indeed running any other business activity from your new home then be sure to understand the CGT implications for when you sell it. The crux is if you commercialise a part of your house for paying guests that part is liable for the CGT.

5.1.1.3 Planning
- Timescale, be realistic with any deadlines.
  Any deadlines will be self-imposed, ask yourself do you need them? You have

Preparation

potentially come to France to retire so ask yourself, *'do you have the time, energy and commitment to run a business'*?

- As part of any changes you want to make ensure that any new/replacement equipment that you buy will fit both in the building and its proposed resting place to avoid nugatory purchases or creating extra work for yourself.

5.1.1.4 *Practical*

- If you are planning/intend to take over an existing (and profitable) business consider that it may be that purely because of the personality of the existing owner. Are you as extrovert, funny etc?
- Be realistic, business are for sale for a reason, understand the vendors motives?
- If your intended business is a '*B&B*', *Chambres d'hôte* or *Gites*, are you happy actually working 12/14 hour days 24/7 and don't forget you are effectively on call for any problems that arise let alone potentially playing '*mien host*' all day every day. Where is your Work-Life balance there? Is this why you want to move to France?
- If you plan to run a bar/restaurant will you be allowed to setup and serve to tables on the pavement outside?
- If it is a totally new venture in which you have no prior experience, e.g. hospitality or a restaurant, how will you know what equipment is necessary let alone what range of products to order as it is not easy to build a professional kitchen? Ask yourself how long are you prepared to operate outside your comfort zone?
- If you intend renting say bicycles, go-karts, jet-skis or rely on motorised dinghies, boats etc you need more than basic mechanical knowledge to keep your show on your chosen road without paying a fortune to local mechanics.
- Are you going to be able to keep rentable items secure.
- Is your proposed business going to add value to your Commune?

If you plan to run an accommodation based business

Our friends farmhouse near Belves where our journey effectively began had been extensively renovated, was 'L' shaped and their accommodation could be easily separated from the rest of the house by locking a communicating door such as you would find in hotel suites. Their property also had two separate driveways and entrances, that way they could holiday there without impinging on any guests.

- Does the layout of '*the One*' lend itself to separating out your accommodation from your guests? At least that way if you find interacting with them morning, noon and night a bit too much you can retreat to some quiet space. If they share/have access to your kitchen, lounge etc. at all times then you might start to feel overpowered, especially if you are new to hospitality.
- Are you planning to offer guests TV, just English or European channels as well?
- If you intend catering for children have you factored in sufficient equipment and/or toys to keep them occupied?
- At the outset decide whether your business will accept animals, children or disabled guests as there could be additional costs, both initial and ongoing associated with hosting these?

Preparation

- Would your dog(s) tolerate guests bringing theirs, or what if they decided to bring their cat, conversely what if you have a cat(s) would it/they tolerate dogs? Although the latter may not tolerate it/them?

5.1.2 Develop a formal business case

So you have now worked though these considerations and want to press ahead. Even though you may be funding your business with valuable equity made on your English sale or a lump sum from your pension fund rather than through a mortgage or bank loan, don't let it burn a hole in your pocket. Think carefully, are you really prepared to gamble your hard earned house equity, life savings or pension on this venture, additionally, depending on your circumstances is your Husband/Wife/Partner and/or your children fully committed to this course of action? You have responsibilities to them, ask yourself is the potential selfishness on your part sacrificing their future? Harsh words I know but one sometimes needs a reality check and better your balloon is burst when you still have your feet on the ground if that's not mixing metaphors.

If you are borrowing money from a financial institution then they will likely as not want to see a formal business case but I would strongly suggest that you develop such a case even if you are using your own money and particularly if the business you are thinking about creating involves a significant (5 figure) financial investment to establish and/or needs specific premises to operate from. If you intend to open a B&B, Bar, *Chambre d'hôte*, Restaurant or Retail Business I would suggest that a Business Case is far more important than if you plan functioning as a personal service like operating as a fitness instructor or teaching drawing, English or painting etc. although if this is the case do at least produce a cashflow forecast and then you can skip to section 5.2.

5.1.2.1 *Start with setting a Budget*

If you are opting to start a business don't let your heart or more importantly the sun rule your head. Without intentionally knocking anyone's entrepreneurial spirit I am staggered when watching TV programmes about people escaping to the continent to start a new life and/or business as to how many of them just stumble along without a clear plan and the Napoleonic attitude seems to prevail. Seemingly happy to commit their life savings, or all the money they have made on a UK sale, or their pension into a new venture without any clear focus let alone anything like a contingency plan. It seems pretty certain that most of them act on a whim, seemingly devoid of any common sense which has long since flown out of the window. As a result many go through a phase of living '*hand to mouth*' which is not ideal for anyone if you are trying to make a new life, particularly as the early days may well be tough as you will want to reinvest the profits to help grow the business.

When setting up your business make sure you have an adequate budget/buffer. To my mind as well as any refurbishment/renovation costs ideally you want to be able to live here in France for 6-12 months without the unnecessary pressure of needing the business to deliver an income to keep you afloat. You only get one lot of life savings, lump sum from a house sale, pension or a redundancy package etc. invest it wisely and don't squander it. Don't cut your timings too tight and give yourself impossible deadlines (for completing a renovation say and/or setting an opening date for a business) you don't need the added pressure particularly it is of the financial kind. Having to open by

Preparation

an arbitrary date to start cash flowing might motivate you at the outset but is not a great recipe for a quality build.

5.1.2.2 <u>Allow for Contingency</u>

You might think this over prescriptive but curb your enthusiasm for a moment. Having now set your budget scale it back along with the amount of work you anticipate doing by 15%. If the building is old, the work complex or you are risk averse, consider making this 20-25%. A lot of my later professional assignments included elements of building refurbishment and I know that there are many '*unknown unknowns*' out there and if you don't have the funding in place to deal with them you will come unstuck. This is reinforced by any TV programme that features building/refurbishing property as they regularly run into unforeseen problems that result in extra costs and work being needed. So scale back your ambition and curb your initial enthusiasm as there is a lot of hard work ahead. You are setting up a business so be professional about it. You don't want to have to compromise on either content or quality just so you can start trading to get an income flowing because you haven't funded it properly. If you come up short then you could potentially consider looking for Angel investors or perhaps take the crowdfunding route but each of these paths needs to be fully thought through? You certainly don't want to move out of your home into a caravan in high summer just so you can start receiving guests because work isn't finished. In the unlikely event you get to the end of your fit-out with this contingency fund untouched then you will have a head start on funding the next tranche of work.

5.1.2.3 <u>Get into the detail</u>

As regards the actual Business Case don't be overly prescriptive but I sometimes had to write these for a living and they included some really heavy duty (multi-million £) ones, so I know the process you go through to write one makes you look into the detail of your proposed venture from a number of different angles and introduces some rigour and structure into your thinking after which you will have a much better understanding of its' viability such that whims no longer have a place. Is your idea sufficiently well developed to get an advance?

There's no right or wrong way to write a business plan. Tactically you could do worse than having options to cater for all (major) contingencies but don't suffer from '*Paralysis by Analysis*' from over thinking it. What's important is that your plan meets your needs, and/or the needs of the institution you are trying to persuade/convince to advance you funding or get you a visa. Indeed they may advise you of the prescribed format, if not then you can find plenty of advice about them online. If you decide/need to employ staff to help in the business, factor that in along with any necessary training and make sure you include statements about the acquisition of relevant equipment (if you are serious don't use domestic equipment as it will not last, buy professional gear), furniture, inspections, installation, insurance(s), licences etc. Itemise all your anticipated setup costs and investigate equipment lead times. Ideally your business model should not rely on a single source/income stream and you need to ascertain what ROI is acceptable to you and over what time period and what your break-even point is? It seems that many people haven't got a clue and just meander on.

Preparation

5.1.2.4   Follow up with a Cashflow Forecast

A solid cashflow forecast is necessary if you intend to run a more complex business, indeed it may well be required by any potential lender, but base it on realistic assumptions rather than optimistic ones, you are only fooling yourself otherwise.

5.1.2.5   Get an independent review

Once you have drafted them get someone independent and who is business minded to impartially review them before submission. Do they bear scrutiny in the cold light of day or is it really a pipedream where your equity, pension or savings will dwindle away? If there isn't anybody you can think of/trust with this activity then play the *'what if'* game and do it yourself, i.e. ask yourself what (happens to the business) if:

- We don't get the required planning permission/licence(s) or we don't get them in time to start?
- Our neighbours object?
- Our renovations/refurbishments take twice the time that we planned?
- We fail to open when we expect to?
- One of us falls ill for a period of time or has an accident?
- Our main assumptions don't materialise/fail?
- One or more of our staff resign or we can't find staff with the requisite skills?
- A competitor opens nearby and/or undercuts us?
- We damage our car/van and it is off the road for a period of time?
- The exchange rate declines?
- Turnover isn't maintained to the level we require?
- We can't make enough money during the summer to see us through the winter?
- We run out of contingency funding (is our project phased?)
- Our website crashes (and for a prolonged period)?
- Our website isn't driving the bookings/interest we need?
- We get a bad review(s) on our booking site/TripAdvisor?
- There is a prolonged period of bad weather?
- There is a water shortage?
- There is a prolonged period without electricity?
- There is another pandemic?
- Our closest regional airport closes/low cost carrier pulls out?
- We lose our sense of humour? etc.

Clearly not every question will be relevant to your proposed enterprise but I'm sure you get the idea. Why? Because you would be foolish to go into any entrepreneurial venture without considering the implications of at least some of these situations. You should have a Plan B, and ideally a Plan C too as fallback options though don't over-elaborate to start with. My former industry cited the KISS principle when evaluating work – Keep It Simple Stupid! As a result you will determine whether your business plan is robust enough to cope? If it passes this type of scrutiny you should be in good shape to talk to any potential lender as it will help your application if you can show you have considered these options.

Preparation

5.1.2.6 If you want to be thorough

If you reach this point and are confident of success and really want to be thorough you could draw up a Discounted Cash Flow (DCF) to estimate the value of your investment based on projecting how much money it will generate in the future, i.e. it's about the time value of money. If you are interested then look it up as how to do it beyond the scope of this book.

How prepared are you for the challenges ahead? Take your time and think carefully. One of the reasons you possibly moved here for was to escape the daily commute and the stress of everyday life, do you really want to reintroduce that with a poorly thought out plan that spends all your cash reserves and requires you to start trading to bring in financial reward on an unrealistic date? Make sure you don't underestimate the time it may take to get planning permission or appropriate licences for your venture, or even the cost of materials which will be guaranteed to be more than in the UK/you are used to. Ensure you understand the implications before you propose an opening day.

5.2 Improve your language skills

5.2.1 Regulation

Linguistically the French language is regulated by the *Académie française*, founded by Cardinal Richelieu and dating from the 17th Century it is the official arbiter of the French language and it determines the standards of grammar and vocabulary that are acceptable. In so doing it introduces new words and updates the meaning of others although some say its' role is to resist the introduction of English/American English words into the French Language. It is effectively a linguistic jury, and is a group of 40 peer-elected academic members, commonly known either as the immortals *Les Immortels* or the forty *Les Quarante*.

The Académie itself has 40 numbered seats and potential members apply for a specific seat number. New members are then elected for life (by the other members of the academy) on a simple majority of votes, but they can resign or be dismissed for misconduct. Being a member is not cheap, once elected they have to pay for their own green gold-braided official uniform, *l'habit vert,* together with its ornate sword and cocked hat that they wear at formal ceremonies, and the cost of this uniform runs into tens of thousands of euros.

5.2.2 Rationale

Look at it this way, now you have moved/in the process of moving here you are not on holiday where a few basic words/phrases will get you by, you have chosen to live in France so isn't it somewhat arrogant to think that you can get by just by using English? Why move here and expect it to be like the UK, it will be different, embrace it, isn't that why you came? You will need to be able to communicate, so as a common courtesy please try and learn some basic French. Why not start by writing your shopping lists in French?

I accept that people buy properties for all sorts of reasons but we have met many long-term residents who barely speak any words of French. Of course those people are happy to live in an artificial bubble, watching and reading English TV and newspapers, using mobile British Hairdressers sticking with British friends and not making the effort to learn nor speak French, having their browser set to permanently translate and just rely on their neighbours. They obviously have a different wiring diagram to me. Consequently this does not sit well

Preparation

with me. One does not have to be fluent but I think it only right that if you freely choose to live in another country that you should be proficient in some aspects of the language, so I would implore you to spend some of the time learning/improving French. Do not become one of those stereotypical *'Brits abroad'* who expect everyone they meet to speak English and when questioned by a local just speak louder and in so doing give the rest of us a bad name. Equally I have no time for those Brits abroad who complain loudly that it/the food/the weather is not like it is in England, but then I'm sure those type of people wouldn't be reading this book! After all if you were still in the UK and for example some Albanians or Laotians moved in next door you wouldn't necessarily speak to them in their native language and you would expect them to know some English wouldn't you?

5.2.3 Stickers

Once you know your move is happening, or even during your search if you are truly committed, put stickers/post-it notes on various items around the house with the French description for the item to get you used to thinking differently.

In the build up to the exchange of contracts on our English Sale I placed stickers all over the kitchen to familiarise ourselves with the French names for every day appliances etc. just to get us started.

5.2.4 Basics

5.2.4.1 What to pronounce and when

I do not intend this guide to be a French language textbook. Suffice it to say that French like English is not a phonetic language which simply means that they have some letters that aren't pronounced and others that can be pronounced in different ways. Further they don't stress certain syllables within words unlike in English. There are also liaisons where consecutive words flow without an emphasis on the initial vowel, hence it is not so much *vous avez* but *vousavez*.

In French the basic rule is that final consonants are not pronounced although there are many exceptions, notably B, C, F, K, L, Q, and R. The word **CaReFuL** can help you remember (hopefully) the most commonly pronounced of these and I have found that a**Qua**B**i**K**e** helps with the others – look again ignoring the vowels if you are confused! As to the exceptions, they will come in time, listen and learn!

The other confusing aspect for anglophiles is the apparent arbitrary designation of words as either masculine or feminine. English has words with multiple meaning depending on context but in France it sometimes changes with gender, e.g. *La Poêle* is a frying pan but *Le Poêle* is a woodburning stove.

5.2.4.2 Simple Phrases

During your life here you will undoubtedly need to answer your telephone, ask for or query something at customer services, explain something to someone if things happen, make appointments at the doctors or the garage, setup accounts, understand bills and what about being able to give basic directions to your house for delivery drivers? There is always the concern that your (linguistic) partner has an accident at home then you will need to call the emergency services for an ambulance. So isn't it respectful to at least attempt to learn?

Preparation

You may be out in the car and it breaks down or you have an accident or perhaps you need to ask for or are asked for directions? Doesn't it make sense to have a few simple phrases in your armoury? It is a good idea to keep a pocket (or larger if you wish) dictionary in the car to help in those matters.

Yes I agree it is difficult for most of us to get our Anglo-Saxon heads around such things as the ubiquitous *On*, the implicit masculinity of the language or putting the noun before the adjective (apart from a few exceptions your French teacher will explain to you) and making sure the adjective matches the gender of the noun but persevere; and don't just learn words, learn some simple phrases that will help you along the way, nothing complicated just maybe things like:

- Can you please repeat that more slowly;
- Can you send that to me in an email
  (at least getting it in writing means you can translate it in your own time);
- My car has broken down and I need assistance/recovery;
- Can you ask him/her to call me;
- I bought the wrong thing/it doesn't work, can I change it;
- I need an appointment today/this week; and
- What happened/happens/is happening now, etc.

As your confidence grows you can build on these. In particular if you are making a telephone call I would strongly suggest you write out a script in advance so that you don't get flustered or confused over tenses, particularly if getting connected to an answerphone because generally you feel more confident if you are in charge of the conversation.

If you are planning significant decoration/renovation of your property then it would be worthwhile learning the names of the basic materials or tools you will likely need.

5.2.5 Practicalities

One of the biggest problems you will have, depending on the location of *'the one'* and where you eventually settle, will be continuity. It's all very well having regular lessons and/or using Software/*'Apps'* to learn from but if you don't speak the language every day, and I don't mean the regular boulangerie visit or supermarket trip as the dialogue in those outings is quite prescribed, *'two croissants and a baguette please'*, *'do you have any carrots/peas'*, *'can I change this for a smaller/larger size'* etc? I mean meeting/visiting neighbours or working with people and being exposed to it for multiple hours each day where the conversation is unrehearsed and unscripted rather than for an hour or so a week then you will find it much aqua Bike harder to pick up. Listening and understanding the nuances of pronunciation takes time and practice. If you have accommodating neighbours then ask them to correct you as you practice, you may find that they want to practice some English at the same time?

As regards listening, something else to factor in and something you may not previously have considered are regional French accents, the *'écouter et répéter'* approach from school or from some software will leave you lacking when you encounter the thick variety of regional French accents. In reverse, accents, or in general the majority of expats failure to use them or at least attempt them are the major reason why a French person will not understand

Preparation

you! This may also be why when you make a telephone call with your best rehearsed French the person at the other end responds in English because they can tell from your accent, or lack of it, that you are not a native speaker. Sometimes it's reassuring when you call somewhere if they recognise you are English or say do you want to speak English but it won't help you in the longer term, try and at least introduce some French into the conversation, maybe answering their questions with your possibly limited language skills, they won't think badly of you for trying.

5.2.5.1   Papers or People

Reading a newspaper can help, but a word of caution here, the journalistic language and phraseology in both online and printed form is so different from both everyday French and what you would encounter in an English newspaper, so don't feel disappointed if you don't find it easy.

If you meet your children and other parents at the school gate then your language will slowly improve over time as it will if your children go to or have friends come over after school. If you don't have that luxury then your local coffee shop is a good place to go on a regular basis.

5.2.6   Online Resources

There are many online resources out there to choose from, pick something that works at your pace but try to devote at least 10-15 minutes each day to acquiring new words/phrases. Unless you are a language graduate it is unlikely to come naturally so you need to work at it all the time. Believe me the great feeling you get when you have just been into the garage to book a service or made a (cold) telephone call to arrange/ask something and not a word of English has passed your lips is reward itself. Even after 5 years now I still try and learn some French every day and take a weekly 1 hour lesson. A bonus of which is my French teacher is an avid rugby man so that has helped expand my vocabulary immensely.

Do not make the mistake of trying to translate things word for word, it doesn't always work. You have to learn phrases and yes basic grammar is important but luckily you will find most people quite forgiving if for example you call something masculine when it is feminine or vice versa, or even that you have put the adjective before the noun as in English; that you have tried makes all the difference. Words alone aren't always enough, try and at least grasp some basic sentences. Resist the temptation of dropping everything into a translation site/app or setting your browser to automatically translate French into English, try and work it out for yourself first before you reinforce your understanding. But remember as the language apps will tell you developing your language skills is about making progress and improving your comprehension, grammar and vocabulary rather that getting everything perfect, you can aspire to that over time!

5.2.7   Ban English

During the prelude to your move as well as once you are established in your new residence it is a good idea to agree to talk French for periods of time. Even with a limited knowledge of French you can both agree to say spend 10 minutes a day, why not start with breakfast, speaking basic French. If one of you has a better aptitude they can help the weaker one in a sheltered friendly environment.

Preparation

5.3 Utilities

There are now well over 100 electricity suppliers in France, it is not just EDF anymore, and there are at least a dozen gas suppliers. As you might expect there is competition for Internet, Telephone and Water provision too. Until you get a feel for things you might just want to take over the existing supply for different services so I would suggest that you arrange this before you move out. To this end you will find suppliers that have English speaking helplines a real bonus and we moved knowing that we had assured continuation of supply of electricity, telephone and internet. Two such useful numbers here are:

EDF	+33 (0)9 69 36 63 83	(Mon to Sat 8am to 8pm)
Orange	+33 (0)9 69 36 39 00	(Mon to Fr 9am to 5pm)

5.4 Re-plug where practicable

In France the electricity supply runs at 230 volts rather than the 240 volts in the UK though you should still find that your appliances continue to work satisfactorily whereas for immigrants from the USA things are more problematic as their supply runs at 120 volts so many of their appliances will not work. On the other hand if your appliance is rated for example as 220-240v or indeed 110-240v then it will work automatically. Also re-plug your extension leads, you might have English appliances/tools but you will need to plug into French sockets.

However the plug sockets and the plugs in France are totally different being essentially two pin, with (Type E) or without (Type C) an earth. You can either plan to use a travel adaptor and it is probably worth stocking up with a few of these in the first instance, or if you can obtain some French plugs from the internet say you could re-plug those items/appliances for immediate use such as a Hoover, Kettle, Lamp or TV etc before arrival to smooth that first day.

5.5 Educate and Inform

People move for many reasons. If you intend setting up a business from scratch, utilising your existing skills in France or even taking over an existing business like a bar, *Chambre d'hôte, Gite* complex or Restaurant then why not use the time before you move to make sure you are aware of the relevant health and safety aspects, laws and regulations that will govern your new enterprise along with the tax implications, as they will undoubtedly be different to what you have been used to. For example, even if you want to offer B&B from your house you have to declare same at the *Mairie* using the appropriate CERFA (*centre d'enregistrement et de révision des formulaires administratifs*) form. CERFA (See section 9.20) is a public body that was created to setup and amend all official documents.

Make sure that your skills and/or qualifications are readily transferable to the French marketplace or undertake/book the relevant training course(s) as necessary. If you are looking to open a business then look into acquiring some business French before you arrive so that you can converse with your likely clientele. As opening hospitality related businesses seems prevalent amongst Britons relocating to France, why not look to obtain some relevant knowledge before you move if you don't have any as learning on the job is not easy.

Preparation

5.6 Opening a Bank Account

By and large and certainly based on our experience opening a French Bank account requires an awful lot more paperwork than in England in terms of ID Documents, Proof of Address and Income etc. so I would strongly suggest that you start to set one up as soon as is practicable.

We chose the worst possible time, two weeks before we downsized and the day before we flew out on our first viewing trip. At least we spoke to the Bank in person at a French Property show but this timing put added pressure on ourselves to open our Account with an English address while we still had various documentary evidence linking us to it.

It didn't help that the queries they had arose while we were away viewing properties and so there was an inbuilt delay in us responding. It also didn't help that they had not seen/opened all the attachments I had put on an earlier email so into the second week while we were back home supervising our packing there were repeated requests from them for material I had already sent them. We suspect that pointing them to the earlier mail (and its associated attachments obviously helped our cause) and things went pretty smoothly after that. Somewhat different to the UK we then had to arrange a time for a telephone interview from a Customer Service advisor before the account was fully opened but that may just be specific to our particular bank not all of them.

5.7 Budget for Everyday Items

From your viewing trip(s) or holidays you will gain an idea of what certain everyday items cost. As you would expect some things will be cheaper than you are used to and others more expensive. So it is a good idea to try and draw up a monthly budget for everyday expenditure so you can keep an eye on your cashflow once you have moved and will help you plan your money transfers (See section 9.71).

If there has been a break from selling in the UK to buying in France don't underestimate what you will need to spend to just get the basic foodstuffs, spices etc installed in your new kitchen. Also don't harp on to everyone about how you can get your avocados, cauliflower or onions cheaper in Asda, Coop, Morrisons, Sainsburys or Tesco's etc, if you do then question why you wanted to move to France. It's horses for courses, some things are more expensive here, accept it. It goes without saying that you are liable to spend more when you have guests staying with you (particularly if any of them have specific dietary needs) and you will certainly have plenty of those during the early months/years and you are also likely to spend more going out and about with them. But also allow for increased expenditure during the summer months. Simply because the days are longer, more things are open, you will be inclined to get out and about more and, depending on the area you live, Summer (Night) markets abound and it is generally a far more sociable time.

5.8 Make Necessary Purchases

As you will now know the type and size of house you are moving from (in the UK) what you are moving to and what is supposed to be there, why not take advantage of the time you have until the move completes to purchase any big item that you know you will need e.g. a new bed, a mower, sofa's or washing machine?

Make sure you have budgeted for equipping your Gite, B&B etc. Notwithstanding my

Preparation

comments about shopping locally (See section 7.7.4) unless you plan to buy over the internet once you arrive it will likely take time for you to become familiar with the surrounding commerce and what is where in your new surroundings, so why not simply acquire anything big before you move? That gives you the benefit of:

a) Using your native language so to do; and

b) The possibility of getting any items transported to France by your removal company; that way any stress caused by not having the item(s) in question immediately available from Day 1 is eliminated. Plus you won't blindly rush into buying something that may prove to be sub-standard.

Similarly with any tech you might need for home or your business.

- GPS Trackers/Computers for Bike Hire;
- Communications devices for motor cycle touring;
- CCTV to protect your home and/or equipment etc.

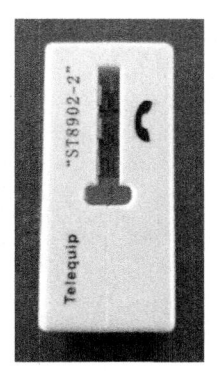

Unless you are moving to a new(ish) property then try to purchase a French phone as the RJ11 jack on any English phone will not fit the older 'T' shaped socket *prise téléphonique en T* that French landlines use. More modern properties have moved to the RJ45 International Standard.

RJ11

RJ45

5.9 Other

5.9.1 Practicalities

Practical considerations before setting off on your new life will include simple things like remembering to read your (Electricity, Gas & Water) meters before you move, forwarding your mail and advising family, friends and certain organisations of your new address, getting your animals micro-chips and passports sorted out etc.

5.9.2 Plan for when you arrive

Some other useful activity before you arrive is to plan out the early weeks here:

- Arrange for any deliveries;
- What you might need to buy?
- What you will do?
- Who you will see, *Maire*, Tax Office etc?
- Where you might go? (from R&R perspective)
- What you need to apply for etc?

Military friends of mine remind me of a suitable phrase covering this aspect of things and it relates to the 7 P's.

(Prior preparation & planning prevents <expletive> poor performance).

Preparation

5.9.2.1 *Handholding*

Something you could consider to smooth the way into your new life is to use a *'handholding'* service. These operations tend to provide things like assistance with Administration, the Relocation itself, Translation and the like. But as when buying most services it is best to be guided by the Latin phrase *'Caveat Emptor'* or Buyer Beware; thus before you are seduced by their adverts and sign up I believe some sensible precautions would be worth taking:

1. Insist on a written contract itemising the work to be done;
2. Agree a time scale and insist it is followed;
3. Don't agree to pay their full fee in advance. Insist on payment in instalments over the period of the contract;
4. They should be based in France, so don't pay an overseas account;
5. Don't be fooled by recommendations from potentially fictitious users on Facebook (it is full of frauds and fabricated profiles). Check out their website, obtain registration numbers and check their veracity with the issuing body or maybe their local *Mairie*;
6. Request weekly updates on progress and work outstanding (the Project Manager in me). If you cannot pick up the phone and get straight through to your handholder or they don't return your calls in a timely manner that should raise alarm bells; and
7. Meet them in person if possible before agreeing anything. You can tell from their body language and the way they conduct themselves if they have an eye for detail and process. They don't have to wear a suit and tie to impress.

5.9.3 Technological Help

If *'the one'* has grounds as such or at least some acreage then consider buying a flashing collar for any of your dog(s). Your canine companion(s) will want to explore and get used to their new environment too and these collars are ideal for keeping an eye on their whereabouts when you let them out after dark, particularly if the house doesn't have/you haven't had the time/opportunity to construct the necessary fences.

Similarly we found it extremely useful to obtain a pair of walkie talkies. That way if one of you gets up early and goes into a barn to do some work or for a walk around the garden or woods then at least you are contactable. Equally if one is off doing some work during the day then they minimise a lot of wasted effort in walking backwards and forwards.

The Move

6. The Move

6.1 Logistics (What & When)

Once you know for certain that you are moving to France then you need to line up your International removal company, although you may well have got some outline quotations in advance to help with your overall financial planning. Your agent or *Notaire* should be able to say what dates it will be possible to sign the *Acte de Vente* which will enable you to plan accordingly in conjunction with your chosen removal company. For example depending on how much work you deem immediately necessary at your new property you may be intending to book into a local hotel for a few nights at the time of the move. All of these factors will enable you to discuss possible dates with your removal company, beware of Bank Holidays, both English and French (See section 7.12 and Annex D) as these may impact your expectations, or cost you more.

Do you know where you are moving to? Strange question I know but at the time we downsized we were still thinking in terms of running a *Gite* business so kept all of the furniture from our 6-bedroom house on the basis that it would all come in handy. Moving it into our eventual 3-bedroom house with no *Gites* not only meant we had more items than we needed but we had paid to keep and insure them in the interim and they all had to be transported across the channel with us. Declutter if possible, use a car boot or garage sale, ebay etc. to help.

6.2 Storage

Potentially a hidden cost to your move. If you sell up in the UK before buying in France then even if you move into rented accommodation it is likely that some or all of your belongings will need to go into storage. The longer it then takes to complete your move and relocate the trickier it becomes both in financial and practical terms. The former because you have to continue paying for both storage and insurance therein and the latter because it is conceivable that you may need to get to things that you currently have stored or like us you store things that you don't actually need.

Most of the International removal companies will provide you with storage as required but they will likely charge you to move your things into storage and then to remove them again prior to delivery to your new home. So if it is relevant or practical so to do, thin them out by selling/donating them.

Also if you have had goods stored you will only be given 28-30 days to notify the removal company of any damage/loss once they have been delivered. That means that once you have arrived you will have to progressively open every single box to check the contents for loss or damage, whether you can fit them inside your new residence or not.

6.3 Practicalities Pre-Arrival

You should find that as part of the Sales Process (See section 4.9 above) your Vendors should have had their fosse emptied, inspected and certificated as such, also if there is a woodburning stove(s) then they should have furnished you, ideally your *Notaire*, with a certificate of the last time it was/they were swept. Practically both things may have been overlooked, deliberately or otherwise, so you may need to arrange these for when you have moved in.

The Move

International removal trucks tend to be bigger than average, make sure that there is enough room for them to both swing in and to enter your driveway and for them to get back out, you don't want to complicate the start of your new life by having the removal men carry everything up from the road to the house, you want them parked directly outside the front door but in any event advise them accordingly.

6.4 Insurance

Your removal company will presumably be insuring your possessions whilst they are in storage and/or during the move itself. But it is advisable to sort out your insurance before you move as you will be much too busy once you arrive. In case you weren't aware French House Insurance is a little different to that in the UK.

6.4.1 Accidental Damage

Probably most importantly there is no such thing as standard accidental damage/all risks cover, unlike the UK. So if you drop a hammer/screwdriver on the sink or the television falls off the wall it's tough and down to you to replace unless your policy covers *accidents de vie*!

6.4.2 Cancellation

Also there are differences as regards cancellation because one cannot be uninsured in France. If you have a policy with a company you have to give 2 months written notice to cancel it rather than just ring up before renewal like we were used to doing. However should you wish to change to a more competitive company they can effect the change for you without waiting the 2 months as they contact the extant company directly on your behalf. (See section 9.57 for more details).

6.4.3 Car Insurance

The principal difference here is that your car is insured not you as the driver. Advantageously in some respects, as in practice anyone driving your car with your permission is automatically covered by your insurance.

6.5 Logistics Post Move

Depending on how long it is between your English sale and French purchase you may well have accumulated some additional goods and chattels that ideally you want with you in your new home. If you plan to drive across this may be your answer, however if you are flying out or you have more than a car load what do you do? You can try and get your removal company to include them, at an acceptable cost, or you could consider one of the many companies that advertise carrying part loads.

A cautionary note here, with 6 months between our downsizing and moving we took the part load option. Most companies seem to base their quote on the volume of space that you are occupying in their vehicle. I chose a company that advertised frequent trips to France then diligently measured everything that we wanted to move and accepted their quote. Despite some communication difficulties at the time our additional goods were eventually picked up the day before we were to fly out to start our adventure. So far so good. A couple of days later I was advised by phone there was a problem. The company then said that our boxes exceeded their weight limits (which hitherto had not been mentioned) and I had to pay extra. Finding out in these circumstances meant that

The Move

they '*had me over a barrel*' and I had no option but to pay up. I had planned to complain to Trading Standards but getting involved in lengthy correspondence when one is in the middle of moving and checking that everything else had been received from storage satisfactorily was imperfect timing so I put it down to experience.

To avoid the same situation arising I would therefore urge you read any small print and/or pose the question as to whether the charges are based purely on volume or whether weight is involved too? That way you will avoid any nasty surprises.

That said however I separately and subsequently agreed a price to transport my ride-on mower across, based on size and weight, with a different company and had no problems whatsoever.

6.6 Moving In

Just as you would in the UK, read the meters and take photos so you don't pay the previous owner's bill. Although if your house doesn't have a meter, you can have one installed at your expense.

If the *Notaire* isn't intending the *AdV* taking place at the house then try and find out what exactly your sellers are going to be leaving behind, the last thing you want to happen is to arrive on the day and find out that the previous occupants either haven't cleared the house as they may have said they would do, or they have simply left a lot of unwanted items behind. Whichever, you will find that this greatly complicates your moving in if your delivery men are outside and have nowhere to put anything, they may not view it as part of their job to remove unwanted furniture/items and you may well get additional/unwanted charges for their extra work.

If you end up moving here in late spring or the summer you might want to set an alarm to get any checking delivery boxes/critical work done before say 11am whereafter you may find it warms up considerably and that the pleasant early morning warmth turns to unbearable heat that makes it too unpleasant to do anything other than retreat to the shade as it becomes far too hot for any form of working.

6.6.1 Opening Accounts

Hopefully many readers are moving to France because they see it as an ideal place to retire and in so doing would hope to be mortgage free. But even so you will have bills to pay once you are here and simplicity would say that possibly the person who is better organised/better with money/with the better French sets them up. On the other hand I know that many households (particularly younger ones) split finances along the lines of the higher earner paying the mortgage and the lesser paying the other bills and you may look to continue that here in France if you don't have the luxury of not having a mortgage. Whatever your situation I would urge you to split the account holders between you both when setting up your dealings with utility companies, for example one of you take the Gas and Electricity, the other Telephone and Water. The reason being is that you never know when you will need ID/Proof of Address in your name and it is a real concern if you don't have any. You will obviously have a Passport but not everyone will have a recent (within the last 3 months) Proof of Address.

The Move

By way of illustration, all our bills were in my name as I set them up having better French than Joanne, but we ran into problems when, after 3 years, she decided to buy a little run-around car, partly to save using our SUV for local trips and also to give her more flexibility on certain days of the week. But we struggled to prove her address when registering the car particularly as Tax and Carte Vitale are usually done on the back of the Monsieur and we had no utility bills in her name and a mobile phone registered in the UK wasn't going to help. We were lucky in that an obliging lady at our local Water Company added Joanne's name to our account, sadly she couldn't reprint an old invoice as they only bill once a year but she did print off a schedule of remaining payments for the year with her name on it and that was sufficient in our case.

6.7 Threshold of a Dream

6.7.1 Prioritise & document your intended workload

You will undoubtedly have a lot of work to do once you move in and it can't all be done at once as you will have a lot of general barge toting and bale lifting to do after your arrival. Create a visible target board of jobs to be done '*post-its*' on a wall or a list on a whiteboard, even using blackboard paint and creating a noticeboard on say the utility room wall will work just as well, it doesn't need to be sophisticated, just to motivate you to continue as you start to see tangible signs of progress. Don't just busk it or take a JFDI (another acronym from my former industry) approach, list out all the necessary work which should give an indication of the Critical Path (longest sequence of activities) and prioritise them, this will be your programme of work. If you are just moving here to retire then continue from 6.8 as the rest of this section is about setting up a business.

If you are buying an existing business and if practicable get/insist on a handover before taking over, that way at least you will get a feel for some of the existing processes and likely meet some staff. Your challenge subsequently is to decide whether to retain all the staff and the existing ways of doing things or change them, avoid too much too soon. Part of this will entail assessing he structure of the building as well as the amount of work to be done before setting a target opening date, with suitable contingency.

If you set yourself objectives/targets borrow an acronym from my former industry and make them Smart! **S**pecific, **M**easurable, **A**chievable, **R**ealistic and **T**imebound rather than fanciful, that way you avoid de-motivating/over-stretching yourself to get something done.

Also create a diary. It is hard to believe that we have, to date, been living here in France for over 5 years, the time has gone by so quickly. What with moving in and getting the house and garden straight, getting to know our way around the local area, and our new found social life it is easy to lose track of what you've done when. Consequently I would strongly suggest that you keep a diary when you come here. Not a '*Dear Diary today I didn't feel that great*' type diary but just a formal note of the key things that you may have done, e.g. bought/installed the generator, fenced the top field, painted the weatherboarding, started the gabion wall etc. So that in time when you look back you start to understand what occupied you and when.

6.7.2 Getting underway

Having now moved in you are on the threshold of making your dream a reality and once funded you can start on making the changes you need to do before you open your business;

The Move

thereby remaining true to Mr Kipling and his serving men, ensuring that the '*How*' hasn't been overlooked.

So what is your personal skillset? Is it something that will allow you to do most of the work yourself? Do you have the appropriate tools? You'll potentially need a list of reliable trades people on hand to keep you up and running should your maintenance skills not be up to it. In particular if you have an ambitious timescale, need certain skills etc. then why not consider asking for volunteer help. There are various organisations who run schemes whereby you can obtain the help you need in return for providing accommodation, food and a minimum wage (See 2.2.3). Equally it is possible to find free general advice about managing your business in France, also in Annex C.

Understandably you'll want to put your stamp on things but take baby steps at first, be wary of changing too much too soon (if taking over a business) or making change for change's sake – remember the French saying *plus ça change, plus c'est la même chose* the more things change, the more they stay the same.

When setting timescales for opening your new business do remember that in this digital age it only takes a bad or scathing review to set you back and potentially finish you before you have started. So don't let your hard work and possibly your dream go to waste, it simply isn't worth rushing things. Set realistic sales targets and revise your cashflow forecast if necessary. Don't start by being too ambitious, phase your renovations if practicable as the early income will help fund subsequent works. Remember the answer to the old saying-as to how do you eat an elephant? In bite sized pieces of course. Part of this will entail assessing he structure of the building as well as the amount of work to be done before setting a target opening date, with suitable contingency.

6.7.2.1   *Professional Advice*

If you expect to earn more than 10,000€ you will need a separate bank account for your work. Obviously a business account will be more advantageous when/if it comes to asking for a loan(s) but it will be more expensive to run in respect of charges. You can just use a simple current account and use that to pay in receipts and pay out for expenses, materials, supplies, wages etc.

If you intend/need to employ staff then make sure you are familiar with the nuances of French employment laws, or find someone who is? You (or any professional advisor you employ) will then have to decide whether to setup your affairs under the Micro-Entrepreneur scheme where you can choose the status of self-employed entrepreneur providing you meet a threshold for your turnover *le chiffre d'affaire (CA)*.

Revisit your local Chamber of Commerce to register the business and obtain your SIRET number (See section 9.106).

By the way, French administration isn't all bad, some friends decided to setup a B&B. They had received their licence and sent off their recorded delivery application to operate as a micro-entrepreneur on a Friday and on the Tuesday got both the delivery receipt back from *La Poste* but more importantly their stamped paperwork back from the Tax Office!

The Move

6.7.2.2 Marketing

Firstly consider your marketing. Have you clearly identified your potential customers, their needs and worked out how you can best satisfy them as the aim of marketing is to stand out and be recognisable? If you are offering accommodation do you intend to use a booking consolidator or setup your own website, or a mix of both (T's & C's permitting)? It will clearly depend on your available budget. Now as someone who worked in the IT industry let me tell you that if you have never setup a website before (when I say website I mean a proper interactive website not necessarily just a Social Media/Facebook page) then pick a proprietary package and get it hosted for you. It is far far simpler and quicker than trying to do it yourself and will provide ready-made and secure links to credit card companies and Paypal for any purchases as well as ensuring your data is backed up on a regular basis. If you do decide/want to setup your own site, firstly ask yourself why? Do you also have the skills to scale it to work on mobile phones and tablets (i.e. develop both Android and Apple versions) as well because you will need an all-round offering.

Of course a big decision is where to locate your website domain: .co.uk, .com, or even .eu or .fr but I guess that will depend largely on where you expect your visitors to come from. They all come with certain restrictions but if you do opt for a French domain then it will need to be compliant with regulations (issued by CNIL See Annex C) as to its' use of cookies (you have to make it as easy to decline any cookies as accept them and your site has to explicitly state what such cookies do), data protection, what information must be displayed etc.

If you are still committed to self-development then include plenty of photos and possibly short video clips on the site, then once you have developed it you must ensure that you allocate adequate time to testing it thoroughly before you put it live.

Subsequently once you have a sound customer base you can think about sending out targeted brochures, emails, leaflets or letters to them, just to keep them abreast of what you are doing, current offers etc.

6.7.2.3 Advertising

Next, whether it is a new or established business you are going to need to advertise unless you hope you will be the venue for an impromptu flash mob. Make sure that you put up clear (outdoor) signage for your business or your site to attract passers-by. You can obviously advertise on your social media or website if you have one. Otherwise one of the easiest ways is through flyers. Flyers can be expensive so keep the artwork simple or print them yourself as you will need to get established in your local area. Like with your chosen marketing activity it will depend on finances and you could also consider advertising your product/service in directories, magazines, newspapers, or on local radio.

As a cheaper less fraught alternative, and if relevant, why not approach your *Maire* to see about the possibility of getting signs to your business put up around the commune? Irrespective, do involve the local Tourist Board so that their staff are aware of what you are offering and can make appropriate recommendations.

6.7.2.4 Next Steps

Think about your product and your presentation of it, would it persuade **you** to drink, eat, hire, stay etc? Are you guest ready? Are there adequate lights, signs, signposts for guests

The Move

arriving in the dark? Before you open for real make sure that you have a dry run/pilot day/soft launch to test drive your operation, exercise your business and to find the pinch points in your processes, either with family/friends or friendly locals either for free or at a greatly reduced price. Take on board their comments and constructive criticisms, as to for example:

- Things/equipment broken/missing;
- What could be done better/improved;
- What doesn't work; and
- Adequacy of signage (Bi or Tri-lingual if necessary).

If you are letting equipment for hire check it all works, ride your rivers, roads, routes etc. to make sure there are no problems. If you have an accommodation offering ensure you have local knowledge and tourist leaflets/welcome folder to support them. Then flush the toilets and run all the showers simultaneously to ensure your plumbing can cope. Switch on every appliance to ensure the adequacy of your electricity supply. Mimic a full changeover day to check you have allowed the necessary time between check out and check in. As necessary produce checklists (bilingual if necessary) to ensure you do things in a consistent and standardised manner e.g. for booking in/out, cleaning rooms, handovers, renting equipment, what to do if guests arrive early etc? New businesses need a dry run to expose potential problems as chaos when operating for real could be crippling. Use such an exercise to ensure that you are familiar with any equipment and if technology is involved be sure you practice and understand how it works before it becomes crucial, and have a backup available if it is too slow, hangs or generally gets in the way. In particular make sure you fully understand how any till works especially how to set it up and/ or change the setup, run the management report function, and how it links to any card reader. Don't leave it to the last minute. If your enterprise involves the offer of food ensure that the guinea pigs make comments that are honest and not sycophantic and that your kitchen has spare gas cylinders if not using electricity.

This will include load/stress testing your Wifi with as many appliances logged on simultaneously as you can muster. Nothing will get you disgruntled guests quicker than advertising Wifi access that doesn't materialise or is inordinately slow.

CONGRATULATIONS are now due on setting up your new venture!

Thereafter, in deference to my former profession I would say that for the first few months of operation your fledgling business regularly reviews its operation to assess what lessons can be learned to both improve the customer experience and its own internal processes and where relevant refine its approach accordingly to improve performance and capability, as learning lessons is meaningless unless you apply them going forward. You can then look to see what actions where will increase margins, and try and negotiate discounts for regular orders with local suppliers.

6.7.2.5   *Once Opened*

You might then want to invite the local *Maire* to formally open your business. Once opened you want to be able to showcase your business to a wider audience as you will want your business to flourish so where possible line up someone within the relevant field to visit and review your venture and highlight your strengths and weaknesses. Niche operations like for

The Move

example running a Canoe Hire, Cycle Hire, Fishing Lake or Retreat business will likely have trade magazines, invite one of the journalists along in the hope of getting a favourable article written. Not only may you see an immediate boost in bookings it will be good material to reference on your website. If you are setting up a B&B, Hotel, Restaurant then try and access a travel company(s) to do the same.

Above all manage your customer's expectations both before they arrive and during their stay, or as I used to try and do in my professional life, under promise and over deliver.

6.7.3 Potential pitfalls

With the best will in the world projects run into difficulties but they can be recovered if you take the right approach. So from a simple Project Management perspective what can you do to keep things on track and achieve your target date whilst trying to balance the competing demands of Time, Cost and Quality? Well for example, if you find:

- Costs Increasing—Reduce the Quality threshold and/or Scope of work;
- Date Increasing – Increase Funding and Resources or reduce Scope;
- Quality Reducing – Increase Funding and Resources, or reduce Scope;
- Scope Increasing – Increase Funding and Resources, or reduce Scope.

But all this depends on availability of resources, both financial & physical.

6.7.3.1 Catering

For those of you looking at an enterprise that involves some form of catering consider that although you may be an accomplished cook in the family kitchen, paying customers are likely to be more critical/discerning. It takes time and a lot of practice to run a professional kitchen and such expertise is not acquired overnight, so such things as consistency, portion control, presentation, timing and reduction of waste may well become an issue. Consider also what happens if the cook has an accident or becomes ill, what happens then? Do you have adequate contingency plans that doesn't involve *'beans on toast'*? Can you/do you plan to accommodate vegans/vegetarians, what about gluten free requirements or allergies?

If hitherto you have not cooked for a living and are worried about consistency, take pictures of the different dishes you offer to act as a reference for you so you deliver them all to the same standard.

Letting *Gites* is one thing, letting *Gites* and providing evening meals etc. is a bit different and you will need a different licence.

6.7.3.2 Property Development

You may be comfortable with the idea of doing a lot of renovation yourself but consider whether your skills are professional enough for your business given how bad client reviews can impact it.

If you really don't have a *clou* about DIY and you need work doing, apart from personal recommendation probably the best way to find a competent builder/roofer etc. in the area is to ask your house insurance company or at the *Mairie*.

If you intend to renovate a property with a view to selling it once completed, or at least within 10 years afterwards then be sure to take out *dommages-ouvrage* insurance. No

The Move

matter how good you are/think you are, without it if serious problems arise within that time period then your buyer may require you to pay to repair it. So the thing here is to keep all your receipts to prove when the work was done. Only claims relating to the *'fitness of living'* are concerned, with any minor albeit inconvenient points the buyer would need to prove that you as vendor were at fault.

As a final point, whether buying or subsequently selling, beware of any hidden faults *vices caches* which exist at the time of the sale and which either aren't obvious but later make the house unsuitable to live in or would have meant that the buyer would either not have bought it or would have changed the price paid to reflect them. *Notaire's* usually construct sales contracts that exempt sellers from these but if they result in work you have carried out then courts are likely to rule that you should have known about them!

6.7.3.3 *Renting Rooms*

Beware, although the legal definition of a *Chambre d'hôte* and a Hotel are similar (they both provide serviced and furnished accommodation for short-term visitors on a payment basis), the former takes place on private residential property (and as such you can't employ/pay anyone) at the home of the business owner, whilst the latter is a commercial premises open to the public. The *code de tourisme* limits the size of a *Chambre d'hôte* to a maximum of 5 bedrooms, accommodating a maximum of 15 persons and because it is one's home the owner is not required to provide disability access/equipment. Beyond this threshold the property is considered to no longer qualify as a *Chambre d'hôte*. In addition to the health and safety requirements, the financial status of hotels is different to that of a *Chambre d'hôte*, as hotel owners have an obligation to charge VAT and are unable to obtain access to the favourable income tax and social security regimes available to *Chambre d'hôte* owners.

Irrespective of one's financial state it could be tempting to try and earn some additional income through renting out a room or two but don't think that you can maybe get an income stream on the quiet to say supplement your pension by letting out a room(s) through AirBnB for example. Reason being that as from the 1st December 2019 any *Maire* in the country can now request details of all properties in their commune listed on rental websites such as Airbnb and Arbritel. In return they will receive an annual list from those platforms containing details of Name, Address, Rental Registration No. and No. of days per year it is available for rental on their websites. Coupled with this those same internet platforms now send the tax authorities income data of which they are aware. So this could reflect on both your *Taxe Foncière* and Income Tax bills as well as causing problems if you don't have the right registrations. Although if you only engage in room letting on an ad-hoc basis and earn less than 760€ it is exempt from tax and does not have to be declared.

Equally because you may already have a Restaurant/Bar etc. don't assume that you can just let rooms out on a B&B basis, you may need an additional/separate licence for this and it may not be automatically assigned.

I would also add a word of caution if you are planning to operate and receive income from letting *Gites*. You may be surprised but the season is a lot shorter than you might imagine and possibly will not extend much beyond July and August at the outset. If it does, fantastic, if it doesn't then that could blow a large hole in your monetary projections. Equally you may find that *'out of season'* hires for a couple/three days at a time appear

The Move

attractive but once you have factored in extra cleaning, laundry and possibly heating costs that these are potentially more trouble than they are worth!

Also any requests for lengthy out of season hires may not be compatible with your licensing, you should take time to check!

Many people (on TV) who are running *Gites*/B&B seem to create a huge amount of stress for themselves on a changeover days, am I being too simplistic to say that having 2/3 sets of linen per bed would alleviate many of the problems, as would part-time cleaning help on the day?

Do you plan to allow guests to bring dogs to your gites/rooms, what about puppies? You may consider yourself dog friendly but what if your guests animals soil bedding/carpets or chew furniture, are you prepared for this?

6.7.3.4   Wedding Events
If for example you are thinking of hosting weddings, will they be bespoke and personalised or just formulaic? Do you have those options available? Is there sufficient accommodation with you/locally?

6.7.3.5   Working Relationships
Apart from not having a business plan the other obvious problem that may arise is if you are working with your husband/wife/partner, possibly for the first time in your lives. The relationship dynamics I alluded to earlier. Allocate roles that you are both comfortable with, that way you won't keep stepping on each other's toes to the detriment of your customers. Be prepared to take criticism, (from clients or each other). If problems arise, don't throw teddy out of the pram or go to sleep on an argument. If you do, don't continue it, swallow your ego and your pride.

6.8   Dogs & Cats

If you are planning to bring your pet dog or cat to France post Transition they will need their own Animal Health Certificate (See section 1.3.5.2).

6.8.1   National Reputation
In many respects France is very dog friendly in that despite the awful reputation the French have about abandoning their dogs when going on holiday I have not yet met a restaurant (including Michelin recommended ones) that didn't allow you to bring your 4 legged friend inside. I don't over exaggerate when I mention that reputation as a shock campaign in 2019 from animal welfare charity '*La Fondation 30 Millions d'Amis*' revealed that the country has the highest number of abandoned domestic animals in Europe, at 100,000 per year, much of this is a result of what they said were impulse buys.

In fact so acute is this problem that Christmas 2020 saw President Macron post a video clip '*starring*' his own rescue dog Nemo, a black Labrador-griffon cross who appeared with the description:
'*My story begins with abandonment..... like me, 100,000 animals are abandoned every year in France*'.
The video discussed abandonment to the soundtrack of Queen's '*We are the champions*' and then went on to explain that in January parliament will hold a debate on a pet adoption bill aimed at combatting cruelty to animals. Its' proposed measures include banning mobile

The Move

sales (those made outside of an animal centre/home) improving conditions at animal rescue centres, punishing cruelty to pets more heavily, requiring pet buyers to be given guidelines for treating their pet well, and compulsory tagging. The video includes the emotive plea *'your pet is part of your family - he's counting on you'*.

The MP who pushed through the legislation is a vet and the new law (which excluded Bullfighting, Hunting or Livestock husbandry on farms) came into effect in Dec 2021 and in addition to that stated above:

- Bans the sale of kittens and puppies in pet shops from 2024;
- Regulates the online sale of animals;
- Introduces a system of certification for buying pets to ensure new owners are aware of their pets needs and to reduce impulse buys;
- Allows for higher fines and increased sentencing for people convicted of animal cruelty or abandonment;
- Ends commercial exploitation of wild animals and bans acquisition or breeding by December 2023;
- Ends wild animal presence in circuses by 2028; and
- Bans mink or any other form of farming animals for fur.

6.8.2 Our Boys

We certainly see our boys as part of our family and it seems that a lot of people when they move here decide to rescue a dog so if it helps I'll document our experience with this. Joanne got Alfie as a puppy but after we moved here we wanted to get him company of his own kind and as I wasn't working I now had the time for a buddy, so once we had settled in we started to look at various adoption sites before I was instantly smitten when I saw Keno's photo. As to the boys themselves, like any dogs they have their idiosyncrasies and lovable traits and I'm sure most dog owners anthropomorphise about their animals, I certainly do.

6.8.2.1 *Alfie*

When you return to the house at any time, after going to friends, to a restaurant or shopping, Alfie will bring you a present in the form of shoes. Similarly if you are talking to someone on Facetime, Skype or Zoom he thinks they are coming to the house so he will pick up and run around with a shoe in his mouth, consequently one tends to find them scattered around the house in odd places which causes problems when you are trying to go out or in a hurry. When it comes to his resources though, beds, toys etc. he is not aggressive/possessive over them.

He is quite high maintenance even for a collie and is constantly on the move and rarely settles for any length of time, unlike Keno who will spend most of the day laying down or asleep, apart from the occasional burst of energy or playfulness. Possibly because he wears his ears '*up*' he is extremely sensitive to loud/high pitched noises and hates the blender, the hoover etc. He will chase after balls or sticks all day, long after it is good for him these days and has now unfortunately got to the age where he pays for his enthusiasm in the evenings when it is sometimes a

The Move

struggle for him to get up. When out on a walk he is rarely bothered by meeting other dogs nor does he see it as a threat if other dogs bark at him but like all canines he seems to have a genetic hatred of felines and squirrels and will attempt to chase them at the drop of a hat. Still for all his quirks and idiosyncrasies he is devoted to his mistress and extremely loyal. If Joanne has been in bed with a migraine he can sense something is wrong and will jump up next to her and rarely leave her side all day. He is also very brave despite any disparity in size, like a couple of years ago when Joanne was in the garden with him one Sunday afternoon, she had apparently heard some weird noises and he suddenly flew off into the woods barking, growling and *'making a hell of a racket'*. In the next instant a wild boar came crashing through the undergrowth on the far side of the *étang*, down onto the decking in front of the summerhouse, across and down the banking and out the back of the garden chased by Alfie, who just doesn't tolerate intruders in his garden. Bear in mind that these usually tusked animals can vary between 60 to 100kg depending on whether they are male or female, whereas our collie is just 24kg.

6.8.2.2   Keno

After seeing him advertised and having spoken with them at length Keno was delivered to us by the charity in question and in reality he looked more Labrador than his pictures. He arrived with just a lead and collar and his only belongings were a transparent folder with his Pet Passport and a few training treats. But he bounded enthusiastically out of the car, introduced himself to Alfie and immediately settled under the table while we had lunch. He seemed so content and we looked at him and wondered what sort of life he had had both with his previous owners and on the streets, and what circumstances what prompted his appearance in a Dog Pound, although he had no collar, name disc and wasn't chipped when he was found, perhaps it's not the French way? Whether he had just wandered off and couldn't find his way back home, had been mistreated and left of his own volition or had been abandoned for whatever reason we didn't know. We decided to retain the name the charity had given him as we felt he had had enough disruption in his young life. After a week or so we realised that Keno had probably not been on the streets for too long as he was obviously house-trained and had probably lived in a single-storey house or even an apartment as he seemed unsure of the stairs at first. It was also apparent that he had had previous exposure to young children as he was quite unperturbed by them, although despite his size he couldn't eat a whole one!

The boy is a great companion and he loves affection but doesn't seek it. He is also quite a character, he likes to perform Quality Control functions on any shopping that one comes back with and generally has his nose stuck deep into the bag even as you are coming through the front door. Although we were quite taken aback and stopped finding it so cute when his head emerged out of a shopping bag one day scoffing a croissant he had managed to get out of its container. He also has a thing for being outside like most French dogs who seem to live there in all weathers, and he has a penchant for eating blackberries off any bush that he passes either on our drive or when we are out on a walk. He loves sunbathing and can often be seen either on the drive or on the unsheltered part of the veranda on his

The Move

back with legs akimbo on the hottest of days, and when it is colder he loves his creature comforts like laying in front of the log fire or just snuggling into his/Alfies bed!

While in the garden can the boy dig? His feet are like shovels and within a minute, two at the most he is a foot down and is usually in the hole with his head and up to his elbows after whatever poor mammal made a noise within his earshot. What is unknown is whether he has always been like this or it's a result of being on the streets. Not only does he like to dig holes but he also has a thing about hedgehogs *hérisson*. Clearly Madame Tiggiwinkle hasn't warned her offspring about the inquisitive white canine that likes to use them as his personal playthings. Whereas Alfie either runs around them or stares at them whilst barking furiously, Keno paws them in an attempt I guess to get them to unroll. What he would do then is anybody's guess, but when that fails he simply picks them up in his mouth and runs around with them which I didn't think was possible. So we find it strange that they keep re-appearing in the garden and need to keep a weather eye out for them at all times.

Unlike Alfie he is effectively Bombproof and totally nonplussed at the sound of passing Motorbikes, Thunder, Tractors or even the occasional low flying French Airforce jets screaming overhead when practicing their low-level flying, either when indoors or out on a walk. Despite his exterior demeanour, indoors Keno is quite unperturbed by pretty much everything and takes it all in his stride. The only time he was phased was on one occasion when the smoke alarm heralded the arrival of some toast but at least that sound is potentially life threatening so good on him. But as you can tell I have a real soft spot for him. Still someone else's loss………..

6.8.3 Rescuing a dog

Just a plea from me, if you are thinking of rescuing/adopting a dog, don't think of getting one from say Rumania which seems to be a trend in recent years. Although what happens there is truly shocking, there are many beautiful souls here in France just looking for their forever home. Though this is not something you should undertake lightly, remember that a Dog is most definitely for Life, not just for Christmas, Lockdown or to satisfy the latest whim of you or your family! You need to be committed to this course of action and not give up at the first hurdle. Go into your adoption/rescue with your eyes and your mind wide open. Again remove your rose-tinted spectacles. The animal will be in a dog pound *fourrière* or charity premises for a reason, but some for no fault of their own e.g. if their owner dies, so you should be prepared to work through any behavioural issues that may arise with integrating them into their new home rather than assume everything will be 'hunky dory' from Day 1. In fact most of our friends here have rescue dogs and think the world of them, in fact Alfie is the only the second non-rescue dog around out of the 20 others we know!

You need to invest in your rescue, not just with any adoption fee or in the cost of bedding, food, toys, vaccinations etc. but with your time so as to build a strong relationship with them and to let them know they are loved and cared for. You are training them, possibly for the first time on their lives, so you need to be patient.

The Move

6.8.4 Language

Do not necessarily assume that your new family member will understand English, you may need to acquire some basic French commands when you start your new journey together. However when it comes to food or being taken out for a walk I can reassure you that they cotton on very quickly, not only that, once you have established the ground rules your new arrival will soon fall in with the rhythm of the household. I'd like to think to a very small degree that both our dogs are now bilingual! You may find this odd but consider if your dog got out/escaped, there is every chance that the people that find him will not speak English, so it can only help in my view.

6.8.5 History and Behaviour

With a puppy you can mould their behaviour from day 1 but with the best will in the world charities or dog foster carers can't explain every facet of a dog's history and why s/he has ended up in their care, and as I said they will likely be in a dog pound/up for adoption for a reason. We are not sure what happened to Keno in his young life before he arrived with us although he did possibly break his tail at one point. We know because of his reaction in certain circumstances he was probably hit although he bears no obvious scars from this. (I don't believe in hitting dogs and he is hugged and walked every day to reassure him he is loved and secure) and his life must be better than being on the streets. We have found out he does not like water or at least the hosepipe. He has swam in our lake a couple of times and he doesn't mind being out in the rain but when the hosepipe comes out he is nowhere to be seen and whereas Alfie will happily play in the water jet it seems like it is Keno's worst nightmare. Some of this may well have been from his month in the dog pound where we know the kennels (and possibly the dogs themselves) are hosed down every day.

He may look like *'butter wouldn't melt'*, and to this end I struggle with every house guest we have as they tell us he is adorable and want to take him home with them. But don't be fooled, he still has something about his time on the streets in him such that when he leaves the gates on the drive he most definitely has his *'game face'* on as it seems his time there honed all his instincts to a razor sharpness. So I learnt very early on in our relationship not to be out with him when it is approaching twilight, his usually acute senses heighten still further and his behaviour noticeably changes, he reacts to the slightest sound or movement. There may be various *'hidden'* behavioural traits that you *'inherit'* with your dog that only become apparent over time as with Keno. You need to be patient and work through them together and if you can involve any existing dogs then you reduce the chances of jealousy creeping in. In hindsight we realise that we should have looked for a female dog to introduce to Alfie, it may have been less troublesome than a newly neutered young buck, but we wouldn't change him for the world and despite his aggressive tendencies in some situations he is above all,*'my boy'*.

6.8.6 Dog Integration

Once you've taken a decision to rescue/adopt a dog you need to make sure s/he integrates with your existing dogs if you have any. In which case you don't want their noses put out of joint or you will store up problems for the future, particularly as you are introducing a new dog into your existing dog(s) territory.

The Move

6.8.6.1   First Challenge

The charity that had Keno had arrangements with various Dog Pound's in their vicinity and once we had agreed that we would adopt/rescue him the initial challenge was how to collect him. I say this as he, and the dog pound he came from, was virtually 200km and almost 3-hours drive away. The charity were really good about it and gave us 3 choices.

1. Drive over with Alfie and meet on neutral territory and make sure they got on;
2. Meet halfway for the same purpose; or
3. Have them bring him to us.

For me it was a no brainer, the latter was the obvious choice but for practical rather than selfish reasons. No matter how well they seemed to get on at first to then have two big unfamiliar dogs spend a minimum of an hour and a half with each other in the confines of a boot, well compact SUV boot, was potentially asking for trouble. What I didn't want was for us to be driving along and for it to kick off in the back. Trying to find a safe place to pull over and stop, and then potentially getting one of them out without them or me getting hurt in the process or them running off would be a difficult task so I erred on the side of caution.

6.8.6.2   First Meeting

Also In hindsight what we should have done was meet down in our village rather than at our house, and then walked them both back home. From a territorial perspective when you first bring your rescue home it is probably best to keep it and your existing dog(s) on leads for 2-3 days. You might wonder why, but despite things seeming to be OK as any dog owner knows they live in the moment and their temperament(s) can go from apparent indifference to DefCon1 within milliseconds as they try to establish their own boundaries and pack order. Rather than escalate out of control things will generally go back to normal again in the same timeframe as their mindset changes back, but if something does happen and it either starts to get bloody or you feel like you need to intervene to restore normality to the situation you don't want your hands anywhere near their flashing teeth if you have to separate them. Therefore pulling them away from each other from a distance is much easier and safer. If they start to fight another way to stop them, albeit somewhat more difficult to execute, is to grab their back legs and pick them up (but that needs two of you). After a week or so they will all realise that the other one(s) aren't going anywhere and possibly change attitude accordingly. There will still be flashpoints but let them know what is and isn't acceptable. Keno who is half as heavy again than Alfie thought he could come in to our house and takeover, consequently we had numerous problems because he used to try and metaphorically throw his weight around, possibly because after being released from the pound and before he came to us he had been fostered for 3 weeks in a house with 3 Malamutes and he was used to playing rough, but in the end Alfie reasserted himself as pack leader (as would happen naturally in the wild) and we have had minimal trouble since, although there is the occasional flare up but they resolve it themselves quite quickly. Keno now even defers to Alfie when going through a doorway together, getting treats or going out on a lead etc.

6.8.6.3   First Impressions

Soon after you meet your rescue for the first time you will quickly start to understand what makes them tick. Whether they are aggressive, bored, destructive, energetic, a fussy eater, highly strung, nervous etc. Their behaviour will depend on how they were previously

The Move

treated, e.g. some poor creatures spend their lives chained/tied up so it will take time to establish a level of mutual trust and may initially dictate if they are affectionate or apprehensive towards you. Some will be happy in their own skin and won't need lots of stimulation in their life whereas others will need constant reassurance. After a while you will establish whether they like to chase balls or sticks? Alfie will run all day if it means he has something to chase, but then again he is a bundle of nervous energy, whereas Keno couldn't care less and will laze around most of the time but he is happy to play '*tug*' and will even seek it out and bring it to you when he is saying '*I want to go out and play now*'. If you develop a pre-exercise/walk routine they will get used to the signs and be ready to step outside with you. On other occasions if they get a plaything, stick, toy or tug or show signs of wanting to go outside, respond to it rather than staying caught up in your life/laptop/tablet/work. They are choosing to do this of their own free will, so don't disappoint them. They ask for very little and walking or playing will give you both joy, so try to take advantage of their energetic moments and enhance the bond you have with them.

6.8.6.4   *First Setback*

We found on our first outside walk with him that Keno has, what we now know through the help of a '*Dog Whisperer*', as Nervous Aggression, when he tried to pull me through a barbed wire fence to get at a small herd of cows!!! This condition also manifests itself when he sees other dogs particularly of the small or handbag variety and he reacts by jumping with a high-pitched squeal and by trying to run towards them, or kangarooing around on the end of the lead if I try and restrain him. I now know that when he kicks off in this way it is because his basic instincts have taken over and it takes a few seconds for his '*red mist*' to clear, and I try and remember this on the occasions he's turned on me when I have stopped him doing what he wants in this regard. I don't think it is something he can necessarily control as fear is an emotion, an instinctive reaction not a specific behaviour, and it needs to be trained out of him. We don't know exactly what caused it, probably from not being socialised as a puppy and it is not a simple thing to work through for a dog of his size. Five years on he doesn't mind people approaching us out on a walk now, although he will occasionally need reminding that it's ok for them to do so. Consequently I use a bright yellow lead with '*Nerveux*' written on it so it is obvious to anyone we meet (if they can be bothered to look at the lead) that he may react. However he will now generally walk pass fields of cows, horses, sheep etc. with an interest but not aggression but if they start to trot/run that seems to trigger his behaviour. He is still not comfortable around other dogs, seemingly developing black eyes because his pupils dilate massively when confronted with them. It is not helped by his apparently exceptional memory, or perhaps sense of smell, as to which properties have dogs when we are walking past. Not all French households have fenced/gated gardens, consequently any dogs they have tend to roam free and this can be quite disturbing when one (or more) of them run out on you when passing. I have just worked out various strategies to enable him to go on walks without him getting too stressed (or me getting bitten). His aggression has not been without its problems and I speak as someone who has had various bites and 5 stitches as a result of one but it is so rewarding to see how your dog's behaviour changes over the course of time due to the way you treat and train them, the satisfaction you get from that is beyond measure as you just want to enrich their lives. I write this not to '*big myself up*' as some kind of elite dog trainer, because clearly I am not, but to highlight that you can't be sure of what you get with a

The Move

rescue dog. You just need to make a commitment to their well-being and make their forever home. But this behaviour doesn't lend itself to him being kennelled so if we want a break a friend comes in.

6.8.6.5 First Weeks

Knowing how protective animals can be over their food it is probably a good idea to either feed them separately or if in the same room then at least have some physical separation between them to avoid un-necessary confrontations. Perhaps his time on the streets induced a behavioural change in Keno's eating habits as even now not only does he eat very quickly but if left to his own devices would return two or three times after each meal to assiduously ensure that any hint of food is removed from every square millimetre of his metal bowl. That said at least these days you can give him a dog biscuit or treat without fear of losing any fingers in the process. Something more subtle that you need to be aware of is your new rescue making moves straight out of the dog domination playbook. We thought it somewhat endearing when Keno would go to Alfie's bowl after feeding and make sure it was absolutely licked clean. Equally he would tend to lay in doorways keeping us in sight whilst we were doing chores and he would also lay down on our feet either under the table if we were eating or in the evening if we were watching TV. All of these are strict **No No's** as these were his subtle way of saying *'I'm in charge and can do what I want'*. In the three instances I have described remove all food bowls straight after mealtimes, make him get up and move so you can walk from room to room rather than step over him, and remove your feet from under him that way ensures his attempts at dominancy fail.

6.8.7 Endnotes

It bemuses me out on a walk as despite being completely different dogs (in size and temperament) you would never think so by looking at their shadows when out on a walk. Those of Joanne and I are clearly dissimilar whereas they appear to be identical wolves loping along at our side. We have since discovered that having two long haired dogs and mainly wooden floors is problematic. Although they are brushed frequently we and despite vacuuming regularly there are always seemingly endless *'tumbleweeds'* of black and white dog hair around on occasions! We are just thankful that those rooms don't have carpet.

We believe that Alfie is not entirely border collie, he is too big for the average male sheepdog, (given that we have had two previously) and we think he has some German Shepherd in his background. So like Keno they are strictly mongrels, but that tag is rarely used these days, probably politically incorrect? However I do enjoy mischief making with anyone who tells me that they have a Cockapoo, Labradoodle, Sprocker or the like and that they've paid a small fortune for it by saying *'mongrels were never that expensive when I was a boy'*. As for Keno, Joanne sent a picture of him to a friend on her phone, the next day as is the way in this joined up technological world it displayed pictures of what could have been Keno's brother. However the pictures were of an Akbash, or Turkish livestock guarding dog, not a Berger Blanc Suisse. If so I am not sure how such a breed made it to France but that may explain why unlike Alfie he walks around the boundaries of the drive and dog garden every morning when he goes out as though it's in his genes to do so. I was intrigued and wanted to find out more so thought about getting his DNA tested to definitively confirm it one way or the other but unfortunately it seems the two major players in the dog DNA market do not have any reference samples of that breed from Turkey.

Settling In

7. Settling In

There are various steps you can take to settle into both retirement (if that is what you are doing) and/or your new way of life and I attempt to list out some of them below, with what I deem the important ones first.

7.1 Retirement Itself

7.1.1 Change of Scene

There are lots of resources available that help one transition from a working life to retirement and I won't seek to replicate those here. What I will say is that every time I go back to the UK to visit family or friends I cannot imagine having retired in the UK.

Why? Probably the same routine, other than physically going to work, you are travelling the same streets, going to the same shops, seeing the same people and doing many of the same things as you previously did. It just wouldn't seem any different to me. Having a complete change of scenery and lifestyle certainly has helped me adjust to retirement far easier than I imagined, although some 30 years of consultancy with numerous different clients in different parts of the country/countries helped set me up for that. Certain habits are hard to break and I still list out tasks for the week in MoSCoW fashion, only I don't beat myself up if they are not done, there is always tomorrow; and I don't usually watch TV before the evening, unless it is the weekend and sport is involved.

Despite the change of scene and far less stress I still feel somewhat *'guilty'* if for example I spend the morning reading and not doing jobs, there is a little voice inside my head, or perhaps it's Joanne's(!) that nags away saying I should be doing something so I guess I haven't got retirement completely cracked yet. So I still make a *'to do'* list and employ the principles of time management. I thought I would be bored retiring here which is why we originally thought about having a business to run but far from it, our social life is far better here than it was in the UK, principally because every day is a weekend and you are not just tied to Fridays/Saturdays for entertaining, so why not Monday night? Lunchtimes come into play too, far more than they ever did because a lot of your new friends will be in the same position as you and you are not inconveniencing anyone.

On the subject of change of scene, within the first few months of arriving here we had been told of an assorted cast of local characters rejoicing in such exotic soubriquets as the Assassin, Barnsley Tony, Earring Alan, Irish Dave and Tattooed Tony, and we thought that we had become unwitting extra's in a Godfather movie sequel. However on eventually meeting them we realised that was not the case and breathed sighs of relief.

7.1.2 Projects

One limiting factor on the physical work you plan to do, and one not so pleasant consequence of ageing, is that virtually irrespective of how fit you think you are or how often you visit the gym, your strength will decrease as you get older. This is known as Sarcopenia or age-related muscle loss. Scientific studies have shown that one loses some 8% of muscle mass in each decade after our forties and this will impact on what you can achieve and/or how long it will take. Also the speed at which one's body heals bruises, cuts and scratches slows considerably too. So if refurbishment isn't your forte, don't pick a *'project'* that is too big or complicated because after a while you will lose energy and

Settling In

enthusiasm for the amount of work, particularly as the 80-20 rule will kick in, i.e. 80% of the work will take 20% of the time but 20% of the work will take 80% of the time. However you are likely to pick up a new range of skills e.g. I'd never mixed concrete or put up fencing before and having worked primarily in an office actually quite enjoy the outdoor tasks I now do, yes I've made mistakes but you do learn from them

To a degree the timing of your work is dictated by the weather and other factors so you must stay flexible. e.g. you may be actively filling gabion cages to act as a retaining wall or to surround a swimming pool but if in the meantime the grass has got to a certain height it will demand you stopping and it being cut else it will take an absolute age when you've finished, or you may have to stop what you are doing and deal with a newly discovered influx of rodents in the house or barn.

But now you are working because you want to not because you need to and that introduces a totally different mindset although these days I do seem to have swapped a suit for a T-Shirt and set of work trousers. I certainly have a lot of projects to do keeping up with Joanne's wishlist courtesy of her new best friend, Pinterest!

I believe that you can help yourself by having a number of (non House related) projects to look forward to. In my case that has been picking up and continuing my genealogy research again after 20 years (particularly now after the recent release of the 1921 UK Census), looking forward to digitising my extensive album collection. Yes I know there are multiple streaming services available these days and you may be thinking *'why bother'* but for me there is something about playing a vinyl disc, especially the old singles, not least the memories from playing them during my 4 years as a part-time DJ when I left college. Editing and putting finishing touches to various videos, slowly sorting out cataloguing and tagging my digital photos which have expanded exponentially and are stored haphazardly, and becoming proficient in Photoshop. Once I have finished all these and should I ever get sufficient inspiration I would like to write a (fiction) book but still have worries as to whether I will be able to develop a strong enough plot and have enough twists and turns to sustain a reader's interest over 2-300 pages

A new project since arriving is to edit/catalogue the photos and video's of the animals in our garden captured by our newly acquired Trail/Wildlife Camera. Ok so these are all interior and PC centric projects but they could equally be exterior, depending on one's available budget, e.g. going to the major tourist attractions in the area (where you will have the advantage of being able to visit out of season when it is less crowded), trying out new restaurants, photography, cycling (which is extremely popular in France), getting involved in something in your commune etc.

If you are retiring here and don't have ties like a business, dogs (thanks Keno), elderly relatives etc. then why not become a tourist in your own country? There are many fascinating opportunities to explore the length and breadth of La Belle France. Depending on your appetite, expertise or fitness levels, these might range from the athletic such as:
- Putting your climbing skills to the test in the Rhone-Alpes;
- Surfing the Atlantic breakers off the SW coast;
- Exploring Europe's highest sand-dunes, also on the SW coast;
- Canoeing/kayaking along the various native rivers; or

Settling In

- Rambling in the Alps, Massif Central or Pyrenees.

to the more leisurely or dare I say leisurely pursuits such as:
- Searching for lost chateaux in Burgundy or the Loire Valley;
- Checking out/sampling the different Champagne Marques around Reims and Epernay;
- Sampling different wines from various *caves* across the country;
- Tracking down and sampling all of the native cheeses (more than 300 of them);
- Visiting all of the 2 and/or 3 Star Michelin Restaurants;
- Deciding to visit all the French UNESCO World Heritage Sites (some 45 of them).
- Boating along the Canal du Midi;
- Touring the Normandy beaches or battlefields of Picardie;
- Exploring the many bastide towns in the South West; or
- Astronomically taking advantage of the relative lack of light pollution to enjoy stargazing in the crystal clear skies.

7.1.3 Recreational or Sporting Pursuits

Get involved in clubs or societies, ideally those that are not just expat focused. My longer-term projects aside I co-run a monthly lunch club (mainly for expats but with a sprinkling of French and Dutch as well) which generally meets on the last Wednesday of each month, depending on the restaurant. So there are always reconnaissance visits to look forward to, arrangements to make (in French), email invitations to draft and having *Menu du Jour/Menu Ouvriers* somewhere. More recently I have picked up the co-running of a bi-monthly charitable quiz for MSF although that was scuppered by the pandemic during 2020 and 2021.

In 2018 I discovered Indoor Short Tennis which I go to weekly, more for a different circle of people in a different location than the exercise. Also that year a friend persuaded me to go along to a weekly bowls club with him, nothing too serious and as I never did anything like this in England so the game was somewhat alien to start with but after a couple of weeks I got the hang of it. But it is just as much about getting involved with a different circle of people (including some French couples) and socialising for a couple of hours a week as it is for the '*sport*'. Unexpectedly for me a number of this new circle were heavily into rugby too which was a real bonus, and when it comes to actual sport however I go and actively watch Brive (where I have a season ticket) in the Top 14 and in 2019 the Brive crowd/supporters were voted the best public in France. The atmosphere is certainly very loud. Also watching the local rugby team gives me great enjoyment too.

You could join in with the locals and play a friendly game of *pétanque* on the local *piste* (pitch), note to the uninitiated, the *boules* are what you throw and you aim them at the *cochonnet* (the name of which means piglet or the small target ball); but it is taken very seriously by our French friends, and the tape measure is frequently in evidence. It can be played on any type of ground but preferably on a hard/gravel surface. The local dirt terrain features some embedded hard stones which can make one's boule shoot off to the side like an exaggerated leg/off break if it has the misfortune of hitting one. Though don't try and explain the difference in cricket deliveries or your new found friends eyes may glaze over. Whatever the pursuit, joining a club or perhaps even a Choir is a good way to meet new

Settling In

people in your area and you may find that the shared passion or competitiveness quickly leads to your being invited to use '*Tu*' to address them, even amongst the older residents.

7.1.4 Endnote

On a final note one should not underestimate the change in dynamics from just being with your husband/partner/wife on a 24 hour, 7-day a week basis. Something which apart from holidays very few of us experience before retirement. It helps if you both have a strong sense of humour and it will require a period of adjustment from you both but I can assure you it is well worth it.

7.2 The Maire (See also section 9.67 below)

It is always advised in various moving-in guides that, if nothing else then out of politeness, one should go to say hello *Bonjour* to the local *Maire* after you have arrived in your new house. I would strongly endorse this move as you never know when you may require their services for one thing and another and to just turn up because you want things from them may not sit well. That said it took us 5 attempts to see our *Maire,* so again, persevere. We first went along the week after we settled in but his secretary said he was on holiday. Time then intervened and we returned to the UK in the interim to collect Alfie amongst other things but I did email him with some questions though in advance of our meeting, nothing complicated just things we should be aware of with regard to BBQ's, Bonfires, Painting Shutters etc.

The second time we thought about meeting him the morning ran away with us and we drove down at around 1145 only to be met by a large funeral procession coming up the road from the church which is opposite the *Mairie*. Out of politeness and respect I stopped the car and switched off the engine to let them past, then it occurred to us that he may be in the cortege walking after the coffin and we didn't know what he looked like as his picture was not on the commune website, so we curtailed that visit. Attempt 3 on the following Friday saw us arrive at the *Mairie* only to be told he was very busy! We went back the following morning but he wasn't working that day. I think that they then felt sorry for us as they said to come mid-morning on the Monday. Attempt 5 was partially successful. Yes we met him and introduced ourselves but an administration hitch meant that when I mentioned the questions I had sent him he disappeared and we heard raised voices outside as it appeared he had not been given a copy. He apologised profusely, answered a couple of questions immediately and made an appointment for Wednesday the next week when he said he would have all the answers. He was true to his word although he had to telephone me personally when he needed to defer the appointment to the Thursday whereupon to his credit he did answer all our outstanding questions.

Since then he has had far more interaction with us than any local official in the UK ever did. Coming to see us the day after a big storm to check whether we had power and whether we had lost any trees or fences. He makes a point of coming over and shaking hands if we see him when we are out and about or attend a commune function, it's lovely. Also he was most apologetic and came in person to say that he could not come to our '*One Year On Moving in Party*'.

Hereafter the sections are in Alphabetical Order.

Settling In

7.3 Armistice & VE Day

Both of these events are public holidays in France and local communities place great store in the ceremonies that take place around the commune war memorial. Why? Because the ordinary people in France and the UK each had a very different experience of the war. It was particularly raw here in the Limousin, which initially suffered under the Vichy regime and then saw several atrocities committed by retreating Nazi forces, so respect them. In our village with regard to the Armistice it is preceded by a procession from the Cemetery to the memorial. On both occasions though the *Maire* gives a small speech and usually part of it involves children from the local school. Specially erected loudspeakers then play *Le Marseillaise* and everyone is then invited to retire to the *Salle de Fêtes/Salle Polyvalente* to partake in a *Vin d'honneur* at a small wine reception. Depending on your target location in France, Resistance memorial events are another good way to be seen in the community. Be visible in your new surroundings, participate in these events and become known to your new neighbours, one day some of them will become your friends.

7.4 Chasse (See also section 9.55 below)

Whether one condones it or not the local hunt *Le Chasse* is part of weekly life in rural France, indeed, after Football and Fishing, Hunting is the 3rd most popular leisure activity here. When I say hunt I am not talking about scarlet clad riders on large horses, more men on foot in high-visibility jackets accompanied by dogs and carrying shotguns. There are strict seasons (usually all in the Autumn-Winter) for the hunting of different types of animal, boar *sanglier*, deer *chevreuil*, foxes *reynards* etc. and the hunters *Chasseurs* actively pursue them most weekends in season.

The thought of the *Chasse* hunting across our land with, at the time, one dog, and the possibility of Grandchildren out playing was too much so when we moved in one of the questions we asked the *Maire* was the contact details for the President of the local *Chasse*. I wrote to him explaining same and asking them not to come anywhere near our property. I also put up signs, purchased at the local DIY store saying *Chasse Interdite* (Hunting Forbidden) around the boundary in places suggested by the *Maire*. Although we had seen and heard them from time to time we didn't have too much of a problem although we generally didn't venture into the garden on weekend mornings; there have been too many shooting accidents reported for that to feel comfortable. Consequently it was something of a surprise when sitting in our kitchen one sunny September Saturday two *Chasseurs*, one with a shotgun, appeared out of the trees on the boundary at the bottom of the garden and started to walk around the *Etang* and into our woods. By the time I had got my boots on to go down there 2 dogs had appeared as well. Now our dogs are fiercely territorial but I didn't dare let them out with me for fear of what might happen. When I caught up with the men I told them in no uncertain terms it was private property and they had to leave, which they reluctantly did.

Cutting a long story short I confirmed the name of the then current President of the *Chasse* from the *Mairie*, wrote a complaint to him and copied the *Maire* and the local *Gendarmerie* Commandant. When I didn't get a response the *Maire* got involved and directed the *Chasse* President to respond. I then had a visit from their secretary who spoke perfect English, albeit with an American accent, and I explained what happened. It appeared the *Chasseurs*

Settling In

had lied and said they only went into our garden after their dogs! He was candid and said that if historically people had hunted on certain areas of land they would tend to ignore any new signs that then appeared. However in their Meeting Room he said there was a large map of the commune that showed all the *Parcelles* within it (See section 4.3 above for more information), he asked me to write to him personally with details of the relevant *Parcelle* numbers for our property and he would ensure their map was marked accordingly. On a point of clarification he said that *Les Chasseurs* should not hunt on our land but if they had shot something elsewhere which subsequently came into it they were allowed to follow '*to finish it*'. Enough said!

The law states that *Chasseurs* are not allowed to venture within 150m of a house with a loaded weapon, however, as my French teacher said to me '*there is the law and there is everyday France*'.

7.5 Emergency Phone Numbers

When moving to a new environment it is very important to know how to get help should you need it. Programme these numbers into your house phone and your mobiles and make sure that your children know them too, and in their case make sure they learn their new address as you never know when they might need it.

In the first instance call

17	Police and *Gendarmerie*
18	All other emergencies You will connect to the fire brigade (*Sapeurs Pompiers*) they will also deal with small scale medical emergencies and should be your first port of call (if necessary they will contact *SAMU*)
114	Emergency Calls (Hearing Assisted or if you cannot talk you can communicate by text)
15	SAMU (*Le service d'aide médicale urgente*) If you have an urgent medical emergency
116 117	Out of hours Doctors

Other useful numbers

112	Universal European Emergency Services number works from all phones including mobiles
116 000	Report missing child
119	Report Child Abuse
196	Coastguard,
3237	Outside hours GP and pharmacy information

In addition:

09 726 750 dd	Gas & electricity emergencies + your department number (e.g. 19 for *Corrèze*)
01 46 21 46 46	English speaking SOS helpline

Settling In

7.5.1 Domestic Abuse

I hope that none of my readers will have occasion to need this but if you are being abused call 17 or 112 (or send a Text Message to 114) to request urgent assistance from the Police or *Gendarmerie*.

If you are being abused it is also possible for women to call 3919 (free and anonymous 24 hours a day, 7 days a week) to obtain important information.

7.5.2 Gas & Electricity

If you are unfortunate to experience a power cut then don't call EDF, you need to ring Enedis who manage the electricity distribution network in France. Contact your local area technicians on
09 72 67 50 XX (where XX is the number of your department).

Then turn off any electrical items to avoid a power surge when power is restored; and keep an eye on your freezers but don't open them.

If you smell gas or have a gas leak immediately turn off your gas and call GRDF on 08 00 47 33 33

Both these phone numbers are free to call and available 24/7.

7.6 Health

It is good practice to go along to your local *Maison de Santé* or the separate surgeries if one doesn't exist and register with a Doctor & Dentist (although Dentists don't seem to offer check-ups like in the UK, when I registered they were expecting me to make an appointment until I explained that I didn't have an immediate problem). See Annex C for details of how to locate a local Doctor and book an appointment.

7.7 Integration

Whether you are physically starting a new business or not, in business consultancy terms by moving here you will have implemented some New Ways of Working and will have different processes to adopt in your everyday life. You will have cutover to a new system, the old system is no more, so understand it will take a bit of time to bed in and adjust.

7.7.1 Clubs

A good source of contacts, clubs or information about your new area is the Internet. Key 'expats in <name of your *Département*>' into your preferred search engine and a host of contact information will be displayed which you can then follow up on.

7.7.2 Dog Walking

Obviously if you have a dog(s) it may be you want to walk them regularly to help with their claws or just to get to know your new neighbourhood? Being out and about you will start to see some regular faces, be they fellow residents or the local farmers and they will get to know you too and this is an ideal way of integrating into your new community. After a while you may start to have a (limited) conversation with them, it all depends on how good your French is and/or how confident you are.

When out and about once you get to the edge of your local town or village then pavements are likely to be few and far between so if you want to continue you have no option but to

Settling In

walk in the road. If you do so remember the country code and walk facing the oncoming traffic, and it is a good idea to keep your dog on your inside and at heel *au pied*. That way you have a good chance of seeing oncoming traffic and them seeing you before meeting. Obviously if it is overcast/misty or drizzly then wearing a High-Visibility Jacket is a sensible idea, equally it is sensible not to go out when it is foggy, however you are dressed! If your dog is excitable/nervous then get them to stop when you see/hear something approaching, if necessary shorten the lead and/or get them to sit until the vehicle is behind you.

I would not recommend this is on a flexi-lead as although they are fine for giving your pals freedom they are utterly useless if you have to recall them in a hurry should the need arise.

You will find that dog's which are used to town life will revel in the sights, sounds and smells of the countryside and will take every opportunity to dwell and pick up various signals left at gates and on fence posts, telegraph poles and walls, after all dogs have a sophisticated communication system based around Pmail. It might be boring for you but don't deprive them of this opportunity to understand and interpret the happenings in their new neighbourhood, it adds to their enjoyment of the walk. Oh and please, when out with your dog(s) don't adopt a *'When in Rome'* (or more probably Paris)……. type attitude, please pick up after them! Not only is this being socially responsible but it also enables you to monitor the ongoing health and well-being of your four legged friend(s).

7.7.3 Events

As well as Armistice and VE Day there are lots of local events in your commune that you will see advertised, be they Dances, Meals, Rambles or Quizzes. Join in and be visible rather than aloof. A local village, only 5 miles away is famous for its annual raspberry festival held at the beginning of July and it is included in the Guinness Book of Records for the largest raspberry tart made in place within the world.

7.7.4 Shopping

Use your local commerce where you can. I appreciate it is all too easy to pop to the Supermarket for your weekly shop but try and spend something in your local Bar, *Boucherie, Boulangerie, Pharmacie* or Restaurant. Yes you will find Baguettes, Croissants, *Pain au Chocolats* & *Pain au Raisins* much cheaper to buy at the supermarket but they will not be a patch on the size or taste of those from the local bakery, not if our *boulangerie* is anything to go by. So many French villages have lost their commerce as people have moved away and trade has slowed down to such an extent that it is uneconomic to remain open, just like a lot of towns and villages in the UK, but unless you want to live in one of those ghost towns give them some of your business on a regular basis.

Settling In

7.7.5 Traps

Here I am not writing about catching animals, although that may be a concern depending on where you live and what animals you keep, e.g. chickens *poulets*, goats *chèvres* or sheep *mouton*. (We had a particular problem with Coypu *ragondin* which necessitated actual traps, see section 9.25) no, this is about the everyday traps to avoid if you want a successful integration into your new life.

7.7.5.1 English Language

Obviously when one moves to a new environment it gives comfort to be able to have some degree of normality and so it is easier to make English friends (although see my caveat below) and speak English all the time when you see them. This is reassuring but does not help learning your new language and, in many cases, detracts from it. Try to limit your English exposure and tune into local radio in the car and the kitchen and watch French Television shows if you are able. Quiz programmes are generally easy to follow even if you don't know all the answers.

7.7.5.2 Food

Yes it is relatively easy to obtain most types of English food. There are travelling '*tuck shops*' and most supermarkets have an International section but they come at a price. If that is a price you are prepared to pay then so be it but surely one of the delights of moving to France is to sample the different types of cuisines and delicacies. To have a 3, 4 or 5 course *Menu du Jour* with accompanying Wine and Coffee and not pay through the nose so to do. There are also approximately 300 varieties of cheese to work your way through. If you ask a foreign national to name an English dish they will invariably say '*Fish and Chips*' yet in naming a French dish you easily get into double figures. Try some of them out!

7.7.5.3 Friends

Each to their own of course but we made a conscious decision before we arrived that we would not go out of our way to make friends with people just because they were English. Our view was if it was unlikely we would befriend them in England then why would we in France? Better to try and expand one's horizons and meet and get to know the French, Belgian or Dutch nationals that live locally.

7.7.5.4 Translation

Making word for word translations into English doesn't work in every instance and can greatly confuse you. Unfortunately, there is no real substitute for learning French idioms, phrases and sayings and then introducing them into your everyday conversation with your neighbours or local shopkeepers.

7.7.6 Other

Get to know your local postman/postlady *facteur/factrice* as they are a great source of local knowledge and can help you immensely with many local queries.

From our perspective we felt right at home here straightaway. Having driven back to the UK to collect Alfie some 2 and a bit weeks after moving in we immediately felt '*stifled*' there and couldn't wait to be back in our new home. Each to their own, it may take you longer to feel comfortable in your new surroundings depending on the type of person you are and to a degree who you meet after you arrive & what you get involved with.

Settling In

7.8   Internet Access

The internet and access to it are very much an integral part of everyday life and as part of moving in you will probably want to include internet access along with obtaining a telephone service. Nationally the current administration has some grand ambitions for all houses to be able to access *'very fast broadband'* Très Haut Débit (30Mbps or more) by 2025, (delayed from 2022 by Covid) and they want 80% of this to be supplied through fibre optic connections.

Whereas it seems that all *Départements* are planning to just service the major cities, towns and possibly large villages, the *Corrèze* has announced that it intends to deliver Très Haut Débit to **every household** in every commune by 2022. An unexpected bonus for us as we were completely unaware of this prior to moving. (See also 12.9).

7.9   Loyalty Cards

Most of the supermarkets here have their own loyalty cards *cartes de fidélité* although rather than collect points (think Clubcard or Nectar) their rewards are generally in cash which you redeem against shopping. Some give discounts on fresh fruit and veg' once you have shopped so many times in a month and generally they all run *'Promo's'* on certain goods, so when you buy them it puts so much money back on your card. You sometimes pay a little more for the product but get the excess refunded on your card so in that way they can act like a savings scheme if you want them to. Their schemes aren't always as comprehensive as in the UK in that you can collect across other stores in the chain but only redeem in *the one* where you opened the account, although you can spend any accumulated amount at any time.

Note There have been some recent advances in this area. On 1st July 2020 our local supermarket started to show the *fidélité* points accrued in other stores of the same chain, previously if you shopped somewhere other than your *'home'* store it was blank. Then in September 2020 we found out, via mailshot, that you could use your accumulated points in any nationwide store.

By and large these cards are very good value in that you can easily accumulate low three figure sums throughout the year to offset against your Christmas shop say or to acquire an otherwise costly domestic product. Most schemes are based on the calendar year but there is one supermarket that just rolls it over. Check at your local store.

In addition you may find that at different times of the year certain chains also have wider promotions, giving stickers/vouchers for say every 10€ spent in store for which you can obtain a branded product once you have collected so many. These seem great value as since we have been here we have acquired Geneviève Lethu porcelain kitchenware, Masterchef ovenware/roasting dishes, Picnic Glasses, Pyrex Dishes with covers, Villeroy & Boch Knives, and Wooden Chopping Boards as an added bonus by doing just that; but we declined collecting towels and dressing gowns as they were too expensive. However should you be looking to furnish a *Gite*(s) then this is a way of reducing the cost.

Another indication of how relatively *'backward'* things were when we arrived. In one supermarket if you picked up a reduced item from their display when you got to the checkout the assistant would not scan it but peel off the reduced sticker and stick it onto a

Settling In

separate sheet which accumulated all such items that went through her till. She would then ring up the price before scanning the next item.

One word of warning, show your card to the cashier when they are scanning your goods for rewards to be reconciled to your account. Unlike the UK showing it afterwards or even taking your receipt and card to Customer Services after you have paid will not get your points/rewards allocated, their systems are just not setup for it.

I have also subscribed to a couple of DIY Store loyalty schemes but in five years or more despite spending four figure sums there I have never received anything other than an invite to a promotional evening with limited items, so would not recommend rushing to obtain one of these.

7.10 Opening Hours

In the rural parts of France and indeed some towns do not be surprised to see that local commerce sometimes shuts all day on a Monday. In addition it is highly likely that many shops will close for a couple of hours at some point between 12.00pm and 3.00pm each day for lunch. You will also find that many local garages close on Saturday afternoons.

7.11 Petrol Stations

In the UK we are used to seeing service stations with major supermarkets as well as along the highway (and indeed some more rural roads too). Invariably they will all have a shop of some kind associated with them where you can stock up on supplies for the journey or even do the day's shopping if you need to. Here in France however it is somewhat different.

Yes some of the large supermarkets have an associated Petrol Station (where one generally pays at a kiosk rather than in a shop) but *'Pay at the Pump'* is uncommon, usually reserved for out of hours service and restricted to one or two pumps. Incidentally the pumps themselves don't seem to supply plastic gloves so bring a number of them out from the UK with you if you are worried about petrol smells on your hands and subsequently transferring them to your car

What you will also find different is that again you may be used to stations having Air and Water supplies, some free some payable. Again in France this is a rarity so it is best to have at least a foot pump in the boot of the car or alternatively one of those *'plug in'* compressors that work off the 12v socket on the dashboard just in case.

7.12 Public Holidays

It is often commented that France has far more Public/Bank Holidays than the UK, and indeed it does with 11 in all *Départements* with an additional 2 in Alsace and Moselle (one of which is Boxing Day which is not a holiday in other *départements* in France). However there are two distinct differences with the UK as regards Pubic Holidays in that:
a. It is not uncommon for the date to fall midweek, in which case the holiday will take place then, rather than the next Monday. (If it is a Tuesday/Thursday French working families will often make a long weekend of it *Faire Un Pont* by utilising the Monday/Friday to have a 4 day break; and

Settling In

b. If the date falls on a weekend then unlike the UK the Monday will not automatically become a Bank Holiday.

See Annex D for details of holidays in 2022-2024.

7.13 Septic Tank

If you are planning to move to a large City or Town then this topic may not be overly useful to you but if you are moving to a small village somewhere in rural France or indeed to the countryside itself then it is likely that you will not be connected to mains sewage and that your flushable household waste is accumulated on site in a Septic Tank *Fosse Septique*.

I suspect that the majority of readers will not have encountered one of these before, it being a concrete or more likely plastic chamber sited underground through which said waste passes fed by gravity. Basically the waste is then treated anaerobically (i.e. without air), the solids sink to the bottom and reduce in size and the liquid ultimately drains out through a runoff into the soil. Even if you don't know the location of this runoff you can usually work out where it is by the lushness of the plant or grass growth in a certain area around the house. The *fosse* will have various inspection points set into the ground and if the last of these is completely dry it is an indication of a healthy *fosse*.

7.13.1 Legalities

It is estimated that up to 80% of homes in rural areas rely on a Fosse and it is the commune's responsibility to ensure they don't become health or environmental hazards and enforce the strict regulations that apply. Most do this through *SPANC (Service Public d'Assainissement Non Collectif)*, a national body (See Annex C).

Legally each system needs to be checked every 10 years but if you are selling your house you are required to have your *Fosse* emptied before the sale.

7.13.2 Problems

For those of you new to having your house use a Septic Tank, be aware that you sometimes get a foul smelling sewer type odour when it rains, this may be because:

- If it is cold, it may cause a downdraft as such from your vent stack which disappears as the temperature warms up or it may vary during the day due to wind direction
- Frequently when it rains, atmospheric pressure changes and air becomes heavier meaning that the methane gases that are in the tank don't flow through the vent as they would normally do. Instead, they remain lower to the ground and this causes a foul smell, like the rotten eggs you will remember from school chemistry lessons.
- The vent system in the tank may have become blocked. This can happen if there has been work done on your house or in the garden adjacent to it and if the vents aren't working then the sewage gases can't escape from the wastewater.

For the unknowledgeable or for your visitors it is important to note that only material produced by the human body should enter your septic tank. That means no Baby Wipes, Cotton Buds, Cotton Wool, Feminine Hygiene products, Kitchen Roll or Tissues should be flushed down the toilet. You will find *fosse* tolerant toilet paper and other *fosse* compatible products e.g. bleach at your local supermarket. Don't make the mistake that we did initially in flushing tissues and kitchen roll '*down the loo*' as you will overpower the *fosse* and find that your house becomes full of nasty smells. Consequently when decorating you

Settling In

need to take care of your fosse so do not think about flushing unused descaler, paint stripper, wallpaper paste, white spirit etc down the toilet. They could seriously disrupt the smooth operation of the fosse, maybe find a place on your drive to dispose of them? Should you think that your *fosse* is not working properly don't despair, there are relatively cheap *fosse* cleaners or re-energiser/additive products that are available from supermarkets or specialist companies.

7.13.3 SPANC

If you are building or converting a property and have decided to install a septic tank there are a considerable number of rules and regulations concerning its' siting so be sure to take professional advice before going ahead with the installation.

In our 3rd year of residence we received a letter from SPANC saying our system was going to be inspected and an appointment was duly made. Such an inspection covers numerous aspects of the functioning of your system, e.g:

- The location of your tank and any relevant grease trap and the nature of the soil around it;
- The condition of your tank and the pipes running to it;
- The different access points to it and its ventilation system;
- The volume of material in the tank;
- The sludge and scum levels in it;
- The tank's filtration system; and
- Your tank's location in respect of any water courses in the vicinity.

If your system is unlucky enough to fail the inspection for any reason don't panic! You are given a year to get any necessary remedial work done to meet the required standard and the local office will provide you with recommendations and/or advice if necessary.

Unfortunately our appointment was then delayed by 4 months due to the national confinement relating to the coronavirus outbreak. When it was completed we were advised to get our system drained and to change the filter. Interestingly we were also advised by the specialist carrying it out to empty it every 2 years which wasn't my understanding, however the technicians who subsequently did the work said that as there were only 2 people in the property it only needed to be done every 4 or 5 years!.

Note that any emptying of your Fosse must be carried out by approved sanitation professionals. Ours turned up in a truck that was roughly the size of a UK Dustcart and it took them about an hour to drain and clean our 3000 litre tank.

Now if like me you may think that there will be a hidden cost to draining your fosse, and that is because in so doing you remove all of the active bacteria that it contains thereby rendering your fosse temporarily unusable. But I am pleased to say this is not the case. Why? Because it transpires that the vehicle that comes to do the work has various compartments. When it starts work the water from your fosse is pumped out and stored in the first compartment of the truck, mud and grease is then sucked into the second compartment, your septic tank and its pipe

Settling In

network are then cleaned, at high pressure, with clean water contained in the third compartment of the truck. Then to finish the work the water that was pumped into the truck's first compartment at the start of the operation is reinjected into your septic tank, thereby preserving the bacteria essential for the good functioning of it. What is more, during the draining process a small amount of sludge is retained at the bottom of the tank to allow the bacteria to continue their work in digesting the contents.

After emptying and cleaning your septic tank it then needs to be refilled with clean water which we undertook by taking stored water from one of our water storage tanks using a submersible pump which was far cheaper than using a hosepipe from the outside tap. The elapsed time period aside, how do you know when to drain your tank? Well all you need to do is to remove the lid and put a stick in the tank. If the sludge level reaches 50% of the volume of the tank, it means that it is necessary to empty it.

7.14 Television

A lot of people moving to France will have concerns that they will not be able to use their UK Televisions or they miss out on their favourite TV shows (as by reputation French TV is awful). As in the UK TV reception through an aerial can be problematic depending on where you settle. An English-French couple we are friends with had a holiday home here for some years before moving back here permanently. As such they had never really bothered with TV, when they arrived they found reception was poor so went to a TV installation company and asked their advice, and they said 'Move'!

7.14.1 Setup

The good news is that if your television is rated for 230 Volts it will work in France albeit with a different plug. I don't have any personal experience but I believe that older Freeview boxes will likely not work here although you can purchase newer equipment in most supermarkets and use it to pick up the French equivalent TNT (*La télévision numérique terrestre*) channels.

If you have a satellite dish it is possible to align it to the Astra Satellite and pick up the Sky TV you may be familiar with, even though they don't have a licence to broadcast in France. The rule of thumb here is that the further south in the country you are the bigger the dish you need. Geographically speaking we are located around 45°N and our 80cm dish works just fine. One thing you will find in newspapers & magazines, particularly those directed towards an expat audience is adverts for TV installers. Similarly you will find a number of companies who will supply you with a full Sky package of your choosing.

7.14.2 Sports, well Rugby Union

If you are a sports fan like I am and follow the oval ball game then you will find that there are other ways to watch:
- The French channel FR2 streams all French National Team matches, along with those in the Champions/Heineken Cup.
- The French subscription channel Canal+ shows French Top 14 rugby
- Eurosport shows matches in Pro D2 – second tier French rugby.

Settling In

You can pick up FR2 by streaming the games from their website whereas you can subscribe to Eurosport player or Canal+ for a preferred period of time and view matches this way in full HD on your computer.

7.15 Wiring & Electricity

This is something you rely on everyday but don't really notice unless the toaster trips the circuit breaker or a storm causes a power-cut, but there are some idiosyncrasies about wiring in French houses, so understand the necessary cable sizes, and how to safely install electrical sockets in your bathroom.

A great source of reference, if your French is up to it, can be found on: https://particuliers.promotelec.com/

It is a not for profit site that tells you pretty much everything you need to know about making electrical improvements in your new home.

7.15.1 Electricity Supply

When you buy your French property you are able to stipulate the kilowattage of electricity supply you require, in other words the power rating for your meter (*puissance de compteur*). This is usually set at one of the following levels: 6kw, 9kw, 12kw or 15kw and your standing charges will reflect this, these levels being the amount of power that your household will draw from the National Grid. There are plenty of online resources out there to help you calculate what you need, or you can start by continuing the level of the previous occupants.

Clearly if you are renovating a property you will want to ensure you install excess capacity to avoid having to use extension cables which are both unsightly and a trip hazard.

7.15.2 Wiring

As you may know the wiring system in UK houses is significantly different to those in France. The former is based on a ring main i.e. a circular system with sockets effectively chained together whereas the latter uses a radial or star system with the Fuse Board *Tableau* at the centre and circuits emanating from separate fuses within it. Thus any budding '*DIYers*' amongst you need to take particular care to understand what you are working with before rushing into putting extra sockets in. If you have any doubts it is best to consult a qualified electrician.

A good idea one you have moved in is to figure out which lights and sockets are on which circuits so you can label the main fuse box/consumer unit accordingly (ideally in French and English). This is best done on a trial and error basis but make sure you are not doing any washing or recording a favourite TV programme at the time as you may get some unexpected results. After we moved in and because my French was better than Joanne's I took a picture of the *tableau* to print and then annotated it in English for her in case there was an electrical problem and I wasn't in.

If you are renovating anywhere be conscious that in France there is a legal obligation for domestic hot water production to be set between 55°-60°C so as to avoid health risks, in particular below 55°C, there is a risk of legionella developing. Above 60°C you run the risk of burns although this can be minimised by installing thermostatic mixing valves.

Traditions

8. Traditions

Doubtless as you are settling into your new life you will encounter various of the many traditions that exist in France. If you have young children you will be pleased to know that some of the customs we are used to in the UK are the same in France, albeit they may have a different name.

- Father Christmas has a direct equivalent– *Pere Noel*,
  and in some parts of the country children leave wooden clogs under the tree for Santa to place gifts in;
- *La Petite Souris*
  puts coins under pillows and takes the place of the Tooth Fairy; and
- *Les Cloches de Pâques*
  is what brings Easter Eggs in place of the Easter Bunny
  (and this has its origins in the Catholic nature of the country).

France has certain other traditions that you will get used to living here:

8.1   Candlemas/La Chandeleur

On the 2nd February, 40 days after Christmas Eve and thus the last feast of the Christmas cycle the French celebrate Candlemas by eating crepes and packing away their nativity scenes. The religious significance stems from the Dark Ages and lighting a candle *chandelle* to worship baby Jesus. Latterly it was believed to stem from using up wheat before the new harvest and with a crepe looking like the sun it also symbolised the start of lighter, longer Spring days. Traditionally the first crepe should be placed in a wardrobe to guarantee a bountiful harvest later in the year.

8.2   Ceremonie des Voeux

As part of political engagement with the community, in January each year our *Maire* (but it happens in lots of other local communes too), along with his municipal council presents his 'wishes' to the local population. He successively lists the main achievements, decisions and actions carried out in the previous year and then discusses the main projects for the coming year. In recent years either a *départemental député* or the President of the Departmental Council attends and explains some regional intentions too. After which the hospitality flows!

8.3   Christmas Calendars

In the run up to Christmas do not be surprised to receive visits from your local dustmen *éboueurs*, firemen *pompiers* or postman *facteur/factrice*. They may not be overly concerned about how you plan to spend the festive season because It is Christmas tip time, but rather than blatantly drop by and just expect you to give them a tip they will bring along a calendar that they hope you will buy, and received wisdom is that 10€ is a more than generous donation, it is a goodwill gesture not an obligation after all. If you do not recognise the face at the door/gate or you are in any doubt then ask to see their business card *carte professionnelle* which should show the official logo of the organisation they purport to work for.

Traditions

8.4 Markets

These have been popular since the 1990's and many towns and villages abound with Christmas markets, sometimes lasting the whole of December, setting up wooden chalets in the town/city centre to house vendors of Christmas themed products and of course Santa.

8.5 Couronnes des Roi's/Galettes des Roi's

These puff pastry/frangipane cakes or sometimes brioches are circular in nature, filled with almond paste and covered with sugar or candied fruit and are sold in *Boulangeries* and Supermarkets during December and January, although the tradition formally starts on January 6th – Epiphany or the 12th day of Christmas, when the 3 kings travelled to Bethlehem and visited baby Jesus in the stable.

The cakes have a little plastic or occasionally glass figurine called a *'fève'* hidden in them and are generally sold in a box along with a gold coloured cardboard crown. Traditionally the figurine would be a baby Jesus but nowadays can be anything. Tradition is that whoever gets the slice with the figurine inside is made King/Queen for the day and wears the crown.

Older still is the tradition that the cake is cut into slices according to how many people are eating it plus one. This extra slice is called - '*la part du Bon Dieu*' (God's piece) or '*la part de la Vierge*' (the Virgin Mary's piece) – which is given to the poor. So that the slices are served randomly sometimes the youngest child will be asked to sit under the table and call out the names of the other diners. That way whomever gets the *fève* is not predetermined.

8.6 Fete des Meres

As if celebrating 4 (usually) bank holidays in May isn't enough Mother's Day in France occurs on the last Sunday of that month (although it is moved to the first Sunday of June if it falls on the same day as Whit Sunday/Pentecost*. Here the tradition dates from 1806 when Napoleon announced a special day to recognise mothers of large families.
*Pentecost is celebrated on the 50th day (seventh Sunday) from Easter Sunday

8.7 Fete des Voisins

The more recent tradition of Neighbours day that (in 2020) took place on the last Friday on May has its origins in both Paris and Toulouse, and aims to allow neighbours to meet in a friendly open way to maybe share a drink or a meal and to try and foster a sense of belonging to one's community/neighbourhood.

8.8 National Day

National Day, formerly Bastille Day on the 14th July is a public holiday, when a military parade sweeps down the Champs-Elysees in Paris during the morning and many towns and villages organise a large fireworks display for the evening and many are the recipients of travelling fairs.

For many the 14th July is the most important day in the cultural calendar. Locally, after an alfresco communal dinner in the main square people migrate up to the racecourse and stand and watch some 15 minutes or more of fireworks over the chateau set to a soundtrack of classical, pop or modern music before sampling the delights of the various fairground rides that are setup on the chateau car park.

Traditions

8.9 Reveillon

During December in the build up to Christmas you will hear the word *Réveillon* quite a lot. The name derives from the word *réveil* (which means waking), the term is believed to originate from the 18th Century when the nobles held night long parties. Nowadays it is usually because participation in it involves staying awake until midnight and beyond.

The term crops up in two senses; *Réveillon* on its own generally refers to Christmas Eve whereas *Réveillon du Saint-Sylvestre* is what we would call New Year's Eve.

8.9.1 Christmas Eve

For French people Christmas is very much a time for family and *Réveillon* is the name of a long and luxurious dinner with prolific amounts of food that starts late on Christmas Eve, possibly after going to Christmas Mass at church. It is luxurious in the sense that starters will generally include some or all of, lobster, oysters, smoked salmon or seafood which will likely be accompanied by foie gras on blini's or toast, all washed down with champagne or a high quality wine. Like in the UK the main course/*plat* is roast turkey with chestnut stuffing although it is not uncommon for this to be swapped for deer, goose, pheasant, or perhaps even wild boar depending on the family budget. After which the diners usually drink a *trou normand* or liqueur sorbet to (kind of) cleanse the palette. The very French Dessert which follows may consist of a Yule log, known as a *Bûche de Noël*, a cake wrapped into the shape of a Yule Log and iced with chocolate but these days many supermarkets will sell a variety of ice-cream *Bûches* which are not as heavy on the digestive system. However dessert lovers should maybe consider moving to Provence where a tradition of thirteen desserts is followed. The 13 represent Christ and the 12 apostles at the Last Supper and as part of the tradition the table is dressed with 3 cloths and 3 candles representing the Father, Son and Holy Spirit. The contents vary regionally but are essentially a collection of biscuits, bread, fruits, nuts, and pastries.

Depending on one's family, presents are either given after midnight on Christmas Eve, albeit before dessert, or on Christmas morning and to this end every family member traditionally puts a pair of shoes or slippers under the Christmas tree, so that Santa knows where to put everyone's presents!

Locally some seafood vendors setup their stalls in the local Chateau car park and the delicatessen does a brisk trade on Christmas Eve morning.

8.9.2 New Year's Eve

However, the *Réveillon du Saint-Sylvestre* (although it is sometimes called *Réveillon du Nouvel An)* is generally celebrated with one's friends, either in a party form or by going to some kind of cabaret in a hotel or restaurant or indeed watching same on television. There is no specific main course although smoked salmon and/or oysters will again likely feature. Champagne is usually served at midnight when the balloons, confetti and party streamers make an appearance.

Some towns and cities celebrate with fireworks at midnight and as is common with many major capital cities the New Year's Eve fireworks in Paris are shown on National Television.

Traditions

French people will usually wish *bonne année* (Happy New Year) to anyone they haven't seen since the past year through to at least mid-February however, it is not common to say it before it is the New Year.

8.10 Saints Days

In the UK we are used to celebrating the Saints of the four home countries but in France it is a little different. Originating with the Catholic Church literally every day is a (different) Saints Day with some days associated with more than one. Historically children were named after the Saint on whose day they were born although nowadays the name may be given as the middle/second name. Although my French teacher told me of a student he once had from an immigrant family called Fet Nat! It stemmed from that family having a small diary that of course named each Saints Day but they did not realise that due to space constraints it was merely an abbreviation for *Fete Nationale*.

8.11 Toussaint

All Saints' Day *Fete de la Toussaint* is a traditional day and public holiday in France that occurs every 1st November, and stems from a catholic tradition of honouring the dead. It officially starts at sundown on All Hallow's Eve or Halloween. People traditionally spend the day visiting the graves of their family, attending church services, dining together or enjoying the short holiday break with their family.

In honouring the dead family graves are visited, cleaned, weeds are removed and the ground around the tomb stones and crypts is often tidied up too. Fresh flowers, usually chrysanthemums of varying colours, are placed on the grave, because in France chrysanthemums are firmly associated with death as they are considered a symbol of immortality, due to the plant's ability to survive winter frosts and our local cemetery is a riot of colour at this time.

Note. The following day, the 2nd November is All Souls' Day also known as *le Jour des Morts* when religious people pray for the souls of the deceased

8.12 Weddings

Weddings in France are different to those in the UK and whereas couples can choose to have a religious ceremony that is for spiritual purposes only. To become legally married in France the ceremony <u>must</u> be carried out by the *Maire* at the *Mairie*. The ceremony is a public event so the doors of the room in the *Mairie* must stay open so that anyone who opposes the union can enter.

Based on what we observed when we were invited to a wedding in our village I can say it is definitely <u>not</u> all about the Bride but more about the two families coming together. The Groom collects the bride from her/their home on their way to the ceremony and on their way children stretch white ribbons across the road which the bride must cut as she passes, proving that she can overcome any obstacles married life might throw at her. The bride is assisted during the day by a *Demoiselle d'honneur* and the two families provided the *témoins* – witnesses. Because the public room in our *Mairie* is quite small the *Maire* had suggested he repeat the ceremony in the gardens afterwards for the benefit of all the guests who could not physically observe the ceremony, and at the end of which guests threw rose petals over the happy couple. We then joined a procession of over 30 cars who

Traditions

drove through the village to the chateau honking their car horns along the way. The reception was held on the Chateau terrace where an entertainer thrilled the children and canapes were eaten and copious amounts of champagne were drunk by the adults during the *Vin D'honneur* – Wine reception. Other traditions will be determined by the couple or the region of the country.

8.13 Writing to Father Christmas

If you have young children then you'll be pleased to know that they can still experience the joy of sending their Christmas list to Father Christmas *Père Noel* now they are living here. Annually, from mid-November until a week before Christmas Day, children have the opportunity to send their wishes to him at his personal address, in Libourne near to Bordeaux. They simply need to write '*Father Christmas*' on the envelope (or that can be embellished with Lapland, North Pole or Santa's Workshop as your family tradition dictates) and put their full name and address on the back, and **no stamp is necessary**.

The service itself is managed by *La Poste* but was created by the French Government back in the early 60's when life was somewhat simpler. It is extremely popular and in 2020 almost 1¼ million letters were received (from France and Worldwide) and processed and that part of the magic of Christmas is that Santa and his elves aim to send a personalised reply to every child who sends a letter.

These days though Santa and his helpers are technologically aware and children can send their letter by email directly from the pere-noel website.
https://pere-noel.laposte.fr/

This site also contains a counter so your little ones will know '*how many sleeps*' to go before the big day! But if you are going to be thorough make sure you sweep your chimney first so that he doesn't get soot on his suit ☐. (See section 9.24)

Still, if you want it, the formal address of the *Père Noel* secretariat is:
Pere Noel
33 500 Libourne
France

Everyday Living, an A to Z

9. Everyday Living, an A to Z

Once you have settled into your life in France you can start to appreciate the different aspects of living that drew you here in the first place. Be open minded, just accept that things are different to what you are used to. By way of example I've seen dogs (admittedly small-medium ones) in Boulangeries, Cooperatives, DIY Stores and Supermarkets. (See also section 12.4). There are so many different aspects to this section that I will not attempt to prioritise them as everyone will have their own sequence, I'll merely list them in alphabetical order for you to read through or dip into as required.

9.1 Abbreviations

To start this section I will highlight some common, almost everyday abbreviations you are likely to encounter here in France and should become familiar with as you settle in, and these can be found in Annex B.

9.2 Aires

As a Motorway driver in the UK you will be used to seeing Service Stations at various points on your journey where you can refuel yourself or your car but in France as well as the large *Aires de service* there are also many off-road parking/rest areas *Aires de repos* along the way where a driver can simply stop for a break. Government regulations demand that these are placed at a maximum of 20 km intervals, and distances to upcoming *Aires* together with pictograms of the features available can be found along the roadside; where fuel is available the costs are also displayed. As such not all have any kind of shop but most have a toilet block and many will have picnic tables that are free to use.

French motorways are operated by *APPR, Sanef* or *Vinci* and you can search for resting places on their websites (See Annex C) the latter also has a smartphone App that can be used although route planners or your SatNav may well display these too.

9.3 Alcohol Licences

Anyone whose business (plan) involves selling alcohol, for example a bar/restaurant, whether on the premises or for take away purposes needs to obtain a licence and as you might expect there are different types of licence available. However obtaining one is not cheap and can cost up to 20,000€ or so but the good news is that if you are buying an existing bar or restaurant they are generally sold as a going concern and will already have a licence so ensure this is included in the terms of purchase and that there will be no problems transferring it into your name or include it as a condition suspensive (See section 4.9.4).

Different Types of Licence
- Licence II (or *petite* licence) – allows the sale of fermented alcoholic drinks, e.g. beer, wine, cider and fruit-based drinks containing up to 3% alcohol by volume;
- Licence III (or licence *restreinte*) – this is the same as Licence II plus wine-based liqueurs and fruit-based liqueurs up to 18% alcohol by volume; or
- Licence IV (or *grande* licence) – this is the same as Licence III plus rum and distilled alcoholic drinks.

Everyday Living, an A to Z

Within each category, there are separate bar and restaurant licences but if a restaurant wants to serve drinks throughout the day or to customers who don't buy food, then it must obtain a restaurant-bar licence IV.

n.b. If you are thinking of installing a vending machine for sales out of hours be aware that this is not allowed whereas sales of non-alcoholic drinks on the other hand are.

If you need to apply for a licence then you do so at your *Mairie*, or if you are moving your premises to a different area then at the local *Préfecture*. Anybody who sells alcohol must undertake a basic training course covering issues such as the dangers of over-consumption, and the laws against selling alcohol to minors. To obtain the license, you must both hold an operating license which you get after specific training and is valid for 10 years, and make a prior declaration.

This declaration is mandatory for restaurants and premises selling alcohol, either on-site or for take-away purposes, and must be made at least 15 days before any:
- Opening of a new establishment; or
- Transfer caused by change of owner/manager.

If you are setting up either a bar or restaurant from scratch the *Maire* will arrange a *commission de sécurité* visit. This is an inspection of your intended premises by representatives from the fire, police and general council (*sapeurs pompiers, gendarmes, conseil général*) to see if you need to carry out any specific work in relation to provision of fire alarms, fire escapes etc. and you will also get a separate visit from *the Service des Vétérinaires* – because the service is concerned with enforcing food safety controls and hygiene and covers a wide spectrum of activities and control over the entire food chain, '*from farm to fork*' and are like Public/Environmental Health in the UK. As you might expect, any of these authorities has the capacity to shut you down if you don't conform to the relevant regulations.

n.b. If you want to hold live music performances or even play recorded music then again you will need a separate licence.

You can find assistance with the steps to take and obtain any necessary forms on the CERFA site (See Annex C).

9.4 Aoutat

If past years are anything to go by this small red mite (also known as Red Mullet or Harvest Mite) whose larvae bite causes itchiness seems most prevalent during July to early September. Found in forests and meadows, or meadow type gardens the mite feeds on tissues under the skin of mammals although luckily we have never been affected. It is a scourge for our poor Border Collie in the summer months as we think that he suffers most because of his long hair (whereas Keno who has shorter Labrador type hair seems immune). The effect on Alfie is a reddening of the skin between the pads of his paws, and it affects his face on his jowls and his snout back from his nose, and he also suffers a thinning of the hair around his eyes, possibly caused by rubbing his face with his paws. We could restrict him to road walking only for almost three months but that would be extreme. You can reduce the

Everyday Living, an A to Z

impact of this mite by clipping the fur on their feet and trying to keep it short or as we did last year get a spray from the Vet which ameliorates the symptoms quite spectacularly.

9.5   Apero's

Being invited for *Apéro's* by your neighbours is potentially either a sign of acceptance into your new environment or one of their curiosity. *L' Apéro* is an abbreviation of *l'apéritif* and is essentially pre-dinner drinks with some finger food, as such it can be equated to a cocktail party but it is very informal. It might just be some drinks and some olives and it doesn't last a specific time but it usually takes place sometime between 6 and 9pm for anywhere from 30 minutes to 3 hours or so and there is no obligation for it to lead on to Dinner. Because it is so relatively short in duration it works better for people/friends who live locally.

It is customary to bring something that is easy to eat and doesn't need to be cooked but don't take this to mean a few cans and some peanuts.

9.6   Apple Orchards

As a boy I had visions of an orchards *vergers* in my mind's eye formed from reading books by Enid Blyton and Richmal Crompton and they included huge randomly spaced trees that you could easily climb or build a tree house in. That is far from the case. Any notions I had about orchards before I came to France were dispelled when I moved here. The local orchards weren't full of mature trees bursting with apples but instead consisted of serried rows of dwarf trees a tractor's width apart with the trees in each row planted perhaps 2-3 feet away from its' neighbour and the trees themselves only 10-12 feet high and topped with an irrigation system and netting that is rolled out to protect them from hailstorms. The reason being that smaller trees don't put as much energy into growing branches/wood and can concentrate on producing fruit. They can be easily pruned to let light in all down the tree so all the fruit colours at the same time. After 15-20 years they are dug up, the field left fallow for a season and then they are replaced.

9.6.1   Economics

I have already spoken of the number of orchards in the Western *Corrèze* and in 2020 we went on a visit organised by the local tourist board to a nearby orchard to hear about their work, what they do and how they do it etc. Living opposite two such orchards I knew how labour intensive running one was with regard to fertilising, pruning, thinning out and tying up at all hours and in all weathers, watering the trees as well as rolling out and back the covers to protect the crop from birds and hail *grêle* and managing the grass between the trees, let alone the logistics of actually picking them, and assumed that growing apples was a family thing. It obviously paid its way but I thought it generally a labour of love. However the outing was a real eye opener as regards profitability and I changed my opinion when I heard that this particular farm had some 13ha of orchards in which they generally harvested some 700 tonnes of mainly *Limousin AOP* golden delicious apples which thrive here because of the altitude, climate and soil, which is a shame as I only really like Granny Smiths! They are then marketed through one of the 3 large-scale regional fruit co-operatives in the *département*, that's 700,000 kilos' of apples a year – do you own mathematics!

Everyday Living, an A to Z

In fact the profitability is such that it is not uncommon to see new orchards being created each year or established orchards being extended and/or automatic watering systems being added.

Given the sums involved you can understand why, when the trees are in flower in early spring and a late frost is forecast, the farmers deploy certain tactics to protect their investment as sadly frost damage is not covered by any insurance. By turning on their irrigation overnight, water is sprayed onto the trees and the ice cubes that are created around the flowers protect them. A second approach is by using wind towers which attempt to suck air from higher layers and direct it back onto the orchards. These are supplemented by large drums *'candles'* of paraffin that are burnt to raise the temperature. Other farmers utilise rolls of straw which are laid out around the orchard and set alight then sprayed with water so they don't burn too quickly. The resultant smoke clouds linger above ground like a smoke screen and protect the apples – incidentally the same approach is adopted by vineyard owners.

9.6.2 Picking Process

Apple picking is labour intensive and doesn't lend itself to mechanisation like picking grapes in a vineyard and like the farmers the pickers work in all weathers regardless, be it cold, raining or windy. I am assured that it is hard graft, apple boxes are supplied by the co-operative and are $0.8m^3$ (i.e. 100*100*80cm) and pickers have to fill 4 a day and ensure that the produce is not bruised/damaged in any way. If the crop is ultimately intended for the fruit bowl then the pickers will likely wear a sizing ring on a belt and if the apple falls through it's too small to sell and it's discarded, if it is destined for pies then size is not as important. Any/all discards stay on the ground to rot and provide compost for the trees.

9.7 Appliance Instruction Books

You know the kind of thing, you buy a new Appliance (nothing obvious like a kettle, toaster or vacuum) but maybe a Microwave or Sandwich Maker or some such where not everything is obvious and you just want to check how it works rather than plug it in and start pressing buttons etc. Do not be surprised if you find that the multi-lingual instruction and guarantee books don't contain an English section. French, German, Spanish yes; Dutch, Italian or Portuguese maybe but not English. I bought a thick polythene hose for a submersible pump and among 10 languages I found Polish, Czech, Hungarian, Russian and Greek but not English, it just seems to be the way of things. Of course you may strike lucky but if not you will need to look on the internet or contact the manufacturer via their website to download a usable copy. However a well-known German supermarket chain has English language manuals available for all their products online.

Of course it depends on your fluency in French or your patience keying various sections into translation software but technical French is a world apart from the everyday. Our car manual was indecipherable in places but I was lucky to get an English version from our local dealer back in the UK which made life so much easier.

Everyday Living, an A to Z

9.8 Asian Hornets

9.8.1 General

These insects were accidentally introduced to France back in 2004 and since then have had a devastating effect on the resident bee populations. They nest in papery looking structures high up in trees and underneath the eaves in houses.

Hornet Queens generally come out of hibernation between February and April to found a colony which grows over the summer. It then becomes the most dangerous towards the end of the summer period when the heat and thunderstorms make them more nervous. They are also more numerous than at the beginning of spring since the colony has had time to develop. As a result, the nests also become larger and larger in order to accommodate all the individuals.

Hibernation usually starts from October to November. Once the frosts begin and the overnight temperatures start to drop the hornets begin to die off and only mated queens survive by finding temporary homes in tree bark or under logs etc. until the spring. As there is then no ongoing maintenance work the nest becomes more susceptible to hail, rain and winds. During winter the hornet colony is deserted and there is no point wasting time and money trying to destroy nests during this period. The bonus for householders is that Hornets do not re-inhabit old nests.

9.8.2 Attributes

The Asian Hornet (*frelon asiatique*) is about 25mm in length, mostly black with a yellowy/orange face, the last segment of their bodies is yellowy/orange and they have yellowish legs (at least at the ends). As such they are slightly smaller than European hornets but are considered to be far more aggressive and have been known to attack if anyone comes with a few metres of their nest but worryingly they can also sting without provocation. A single such hornet can sting multiple times and they have been known to fly up to 15 metres in pursuit of their victims.

If you come across a nest, be very careful! Back away slowly as if the hornets sense their nest is threatened they can aggressively attack you to neutralise that threat. Why is this a problem? It is because Asian Hornet stings contain a neurotoxin, which is defined as a poison that interferes with the functions of the nervous system. Whereas bees for example can only sting you once a Giant Hornet can sting you repeatedly and if stung it is likely you may need some kind of medical intervention. Consequently there have been some fatalities associated with Asian Hornet attacks, especially if the victims suffer an anaphylactic shock as a result of the sting or they are stung multiple times. If you spot their nest don't disturb it or the surrounding branches and switch off any electrical garden equipment you may be using as they can sense the electrical energy and it may provoke them. If practicable take pictures of the nest and then send/take them to your *Mairie* who should be able to help you arrange its destruction. **Do not attempt to climb the tree and do this yourself!**

9.8.3 Removal

All is not lost if you discover you have a colony of these pests around your property. The way their nests are destroyed depends on a number of factors such as accessibility of the nest, degree of slope of your site, scope of services of the company you employ and of course your budget. If you want a quick response key '*SOS Frelons dd*' (Dept No.) into a

Everyday Living, an A to Z

search engine to find the location of local services who will help deal with them. Amongst the options that can be considered for their destruction are:

9.8.3.1 *Cherrypicker*
This method allows direct access to the nest and is the most efficient, albeit potentially the most dangerous. The entrance to the nest is blocked with polyurethane foam and then insecticide in the form of a gas is injected directly into the nest. Once the colony is exterminated, it is enough to unhook the nest and destroy it.

9.8.3.2 *Paintball (Type) Gun*
Use of these modified guns allows extermination of nests of up to 30m high without the need for a ladder. The gun shoots insecticide balls that are both eco-friendly and biodegradable and can be fired directly into the hornet's nest from a relatively safe distance away from it. Between a dozen and twenty balls are usually sufficient to complete the job.

9.8.3.3 *Rigid Mast*
This method is effective for interventions up to 18m in height. At the end of the mast, there is a pistol equipped with a reservoir and a needle which allows access to the interior of the nest for injection of a powerful insecticide.

9.8.3.4 *Telescopic Pole*
Such a method offers several options depending on the model of pole such as a camera or a carbon rod. It is possible to reach nests about 16 meters high and spray insecticide into it.

9.8.3.5 *Telescopic Shears*
This method involves using telescopic shears to cut the nest and then dropping it into a bag. The bag that contains it is then itself covered by two other bags for more security and the whole must then be destroyed.

9.8.4 Personal Experience

We have had a couple of encounters with these critters. During the late summer of 2020 a mini-nest (about 25 x 25 x 15cm) appeared at head height amongst the roots of an old tree on the banking of the orchard opposite our front gates. I kept an eye on it whilst walking the dogs and it didn't appear to be getting any bigger. Then one afternoon I was doing some work in the front of our barn at the side of the house and was '*buzzed*' by a couple of them flying about. Now the previous week we had had to rush Keno to the vets when he was out on the veranda and jumped up to try and catch a wasp which promptly stung him above his eye and it swelled up like an egg and anti-histamine had no effect, so this was a big concern for me. He wouldn't know the difference between flies, hornets or wasps, to him they are all just an (possibly noisy) irritation that needs to be dealt with, so for me their possibly innocuous flypast effectively signed and sealed their death warrant.

Due to the small size and relative accessibility of the nest I had a plan! I did a couple of basic reconnaissance walks to check that activity did shut down late in the evening and then decided to deal with this late one Saturday night when all movement in the nest would have ceased and I assessed **there were minimal risks involved**. We were returning from a party and I pulled up a couple of metres away from it at an oblique angle alongside the banking in our car, switched off the lights and engine but kept the ignition on. Despite this I was wearing a thick jacket with hood, mask, protective goggles and work gloves – I think

Everyday Living, an A to Z

Joanne was secretly pleased I had changed and hadn't actually gone to the party dressed like this. I was using a projectile repellent spray that was good for up to 6m distance and I knew from using one on a wasp's nest earlier in the year that I had about 30 seconds worth of content available. I half opened the driver's window, she leant across me and directed a high intensity torch at their entrance hole and I unloaded a cloud of insecticide from half the can at it. It appeared to do the trick as in the following days there seemed to only be the odd one or two of them flying around. As it happened my pest control activities may have been a lifesaver? What I didn't know was on the Thursday morning one of the commune workmen would come out in their tractor to cut the grass on the banking and the verge and its cutting deck completely decimated the nest. On reflection, had I not dealt with it any hornets that made it out of the scene of destruction may have swarmed toward the driver's cab with fatal consequences. I say this as a farmer in the Charente *Département* was killed (Nov 20) when his tractor disturbed a nest hidden in a hedge and the hornets attacked him and he died of anaphylactic shock.

9.8.5 Almost But Not Quite

A second encounter was once autumn started in earnest (although it was late to arrive in 2020) and the deciduous trees started shedding their leaves. We thought we could see the emergence of a bird's nest in the cherry tree at the side of the house but as more leaves dropped, we realised that it was in fact a huge hornet's nest high up in the branches (I estimated about 15m) that hitherto had been hidden. In fact the hornets that buzzed Keno and I may have come from this nest that I didn't know about. As more leaves fell more of the nest became apparent. The nests themselves are amazing structures and I'd love to have had a time-lapse camera charting its construction over the months as one can only stare in wonder as to how it was both made and reached the size it did, let alone how it stays there in all weathers. There was no point in wondering how long it had been there or how we hadn't see the constant swarm of hornets flying to and from, it would have to go but there was no way I was going to deal with it. A visit to the *Mairie* furnished me with a list with the contact details of 4 companies in the area who specialised in hornet removal. I was in no rush to do so as the temperatures had started to drop and there were minimal signs of access and egress.

Then one morning one of the commune workmen dropped by with our new *Maire* who said he was meeting a specialist (who was on the list I had received) that Saturday morning down at the *Mairie* and that I should ring him

The Summer House is 2.4m to the apex

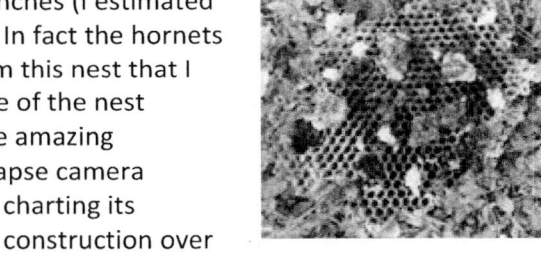

Everyday Living, an A to Z

and arrange for him to come up to the house afterwards. So I rang him, three times in fact, and ended up leaving a message. Saturday came but the specialist didn't. I went down to the *Mairie* just before it closed and they hadn't seen him, neither had he rung to postpone. He didn't contact me in the next couple of days either. I bemoaned French customer service and called another name from the list who was far more helpful and provided me with much better customer service. He explained that at this time of year with the frosts coming (by now it was early December) there would be no problem in leaving the nest be as the hornets would die off, the nest wouldn't be maintained and it would fall foul of the elements. What is more he didn't want to take my money for something that didn't need doing! (Luckily the man had an English wife so it was easy to understand his comments)!
Note He was spot on with those comments, within a week a chunk had fallen off one side of the nest and a large hole appeared on two sides as though a very thick arm had punched through the nest.

9.9   Baguettes

The name baguette is generally agreed to stem from 1920 and you may not think so but the humble baguette has exact specifications needing to be 55-65cm in length and weigh between 250-300g. In fact Paris holds an annual competition to determine the cities best baguette and the exotically named *National Observatoire du Pain* says that 10 billion of them are consumed each year. Traditional baguettes are protected by a 1992 law – *Décret Pain* that says that they can only comprise 4 ingredients, Wheat Flour, Salt, Water and Yeast, which is probably why if you don't eat them on the morning when you buy them they can harden up and become offensive weapons by the afternoon. That same law decrees they have to be made in the building where they are sold and the *Boulangerie* has to close one day a week. France has now nominated the baguette for UNESCO intangible cultural heritage status. The decision will be announced later in 2022.

Buying such bread straight from the *Boulangerie* is wonderful, but the *'French bread'* here is very much the downfall of many an expat who finds it so *'moreish'* that they put on weight during their first year here. I could happily sit and munch through a whole baguette for lunch if it wasn't for having to share it with Joanne.

9.10   Banking, Cheques & Cash etc.

I'll leave the choosing of a bank to host your account to you but just pass on this tip with regard to joint accounts. It was explained to us on setup but not all banks are the same. With a *compte indivis* you will see your chequebook in the name of *monsieur et madame* meaning that 2 signatures are required (and that in the unfortunate case of death of one of the account holders it will be frozen). However a *compte joint* whereby just a single signature is needed will show as *monsieur ou madame*.

9.10.1 Account Access

Once you have successfully setup your French Bank Account and have a bank card and chequebook don't be under the illusion that now you can access all your monies as and when you want – this just isn't the case here! There are upper limits set as standard for both cash withdrawals and payments. Typically an International debit card will allow you to access 450€ cash per 7 days and 2300€ per calendar month in payments.

Everyday Living, an A to Z

You can ask to increase these amounts, but may be charged for doing so, or upgrade your card/account.

9.10.2 Account Alerts

As with internet banking on accounts in the UK it is relatively easy to setup warning alerts on your account whereby you will receive an email or text message if your account balance falls below a certain threshold. However as you will find here these are not always as instant as you would like/need. Consequently I would suggest to start with setting a much higher value than you are used to until you become familiar with your bank and the way it operates.

9.10.3 Bank Charges

If you are worried about whether your Bank Charges are excessive there is a very useful government site that enables you to compare charges on both High St and Internet bank offerings across a range of criteria e.g. account fees, bank transfers, cash withdrawals, debit card costs and SMS alerts etc. (See Annex C).

9.10.4 Banking Ban

Operating your bank account here in France is a little different to the UK. As long as you have the relevant monies in your account you can write a cheque for any amount you wish. But the French system takes a very dim view of anyone writing a cheque that can't be honoured, and a bounced cheque can result in you being backlisted for up to 5 years by the Banque de France. A process known as *Interdit Bancaire*. This also applies if for example your account is systematically in the red or you exceed any authorised overdraft (as regards any overdraft it relates to consistently bad account management and abusing spending limits not just a problem being overdrawn for a few days).

Not only that, if a customer issues a bad cheque on a **Joint Account** then **both account holders can be banned from banking** on the same basis. The banking ban is a general one, and includes all personal accounts of an individual, even if they are opened with other banks, not just the bank declaring the banking ban.

If you have had account problems in the past then it is possible to nominate a single manager when you open the account so that if such an incident arises they will be the only one affected.

Interdit Bancaire results in a person(s) being **registered in the Central Cheque File** (*FCC-Fichier Central des Chèques*) of the Banque de France, a file all banks consult when a new customer wants to open an account with them. Being issued with a banking ban means the customer can no longer write cheques and so they must **immediately return all cheque books to those banks where they have accounts. Registration in this file will also affect one's ability to access credit as most banks are loathe to lend money to someone who has experienced such an incident.**

Although the **ban is issued for 5 years** it is possible to cancel it before the end of the legal period, by repaying the amount of the debt. When the payment incident is resolved, the bank concerned informs the Banque de France, who are responsible for cancelling the banking ban on the Central Cheque File.

Everyday Living, an A to Z

9.10.5 Cheques

In the UK cheques had 5 separate components. The date, the payee, the amount in writing and then in figures and the signature. French cheques have 6 elements as they somewhat perversely also include the name of the place where the cheque was written. Further, rather than write the payee first then the amount you are paying them, on French cheques it is the reverse; one writes the amount first (in French obviously) with the payee on the line below.

As well as being used to irritate the people behind them in the queue at the supermarket cheques are extremely handy when making deposits *cautions* for goods and avoid eating into bank/credit card limits. A hidden benefit is that some larger companies only seem to bank monthly - our fosse was emptied on the 3rd of the month but the cheque did not clear until the 30th and there is always a 2-3 week delay with our dentist too.

A cheque is a means of payment accepted by businesses for goods but it is not compulsory. A business can refuse to accept payment by cheque or only accept it above a certain minimum amount (10€ for example) or conversely up to a maximum amount e.g. 100€. Why? Simply because in France a cheque is not legal tender as such. Only money made up of Bank of France bank notes and metallic money (coins) is legal tender.

Nevertheless, any business who refuses or limits payment by cheque must display a notice of such a restriction either at the till or on the menu if it is a restaurant for example.

9.10.6 Low Cost Accounts
The following should not be construed as Financial Advice!

9.10.6.1 Compte Nickel
If you want a simple '*low risk*' bank account with the usual banking guarantees a '*Compte Nickel*' may be the answer. They were originally partly established to offer banking to people barred from other banks no questions are asked. Nowadays anyone over 18 who is a French resident (with a residency permit) or has an EU passport (this includes holiday home owners) can open such an account at a local *Tabac* (See section 9.114) at the cost of just 20€ for an annual membership fee. The account opening process is straightforward, requiring only ID (such as a passport) and a working mobile phone number.

You get access to internet banking, online statements and a Mastercard debit card – but no cheques, and can take out money at any banks' cash dispensers showing the Mastercard symbol or other *tabacs* offering *Compte-Nickels*. You cannot go overdrawn because payments are not accepted above your balance. There are 25,000 *tabacs* in France and those participating in the scheme are evenly spread across the country.

9.10.6.2 Mafrenchbank
Providing one already has a European bank account and is tax resident in France an alternative low cost account is available through *La Poste* and is called *Mafrenchbank* (www.Mafrenchbank.fr) which is *La Poste's* new mobile online banking service. The principal marketing thrust is to manage one's account in real-time and get categorisation of one's expenditure through your Smartphone. To open such an account one must supply:
- Basic personal information and reason for opening the account;
- Copy of a Passport;

Everyday Living, an A to Z

- Copy of secondary ID (Drivers licence or Tax Notice); and
- Copy of RIB (See section 9.95) from French Domiciled Bank;

all copies can be scanned and uploaded online.

Successful applicants will then receive:
- Visa Card; and
- The ability to make payments through SMS or Applepay.

For an extra 2 euros/month one can then insure one's card, cash and all purchases made.

9.10.7 Online Banking

We have become used to progressively more sophisticated online banking services over recent years, notably with the introduction of faster payments but things generally are much slower here in France.

9.10.7.1 Banking Limits

Again you will likely have been used to making all manner of payments online. Two things to be aware of here are that your account will likely have a payment limit that will be lower than you expect so don't just assume because you have the money in your account that you can make a 5-figure transfer to a garage to buy a car for example.

9.10.7.2 Online Account

The clearing system is different to what you might expect in England and in particular online banking always seems to be '*missing*' various debits when you look at your account as it takes longer for them to show up. This can be a source of great irritation when you look online and see your balance but then can't withdraw a lower level amount from the cash dispenser as what you can't see are the uncleared debits (and credits).

9.10.7.3 Setting up Direct Debits

Once you have setup a Bank Account it then becomes much easier to pay for things because you just show/give a copy of your RIB (*Relevé d'Identité Bancaire*) to the organisation/company in question. (See section 9.95)

9.10.7.4 Setting up Payees

For security reasons there are limits to the amount you can transfer to a third party online. When setting up payees etc some banks e.g. HSBC France require you to use a card reader, others like CA Britline allow setup without. Equally once you have setup a new payee do not expect to be able to pay them instantly. You will have to wait two days between adding a new beneficiary and making your first online payment to them.

9.10.8 Pin Codes

Once you have received your bank card in France unlike the UK one cannot change the PIN on the card, *the one* that is issued with the card when you receive it is *the one* you have to use.

9.10.9 Widespread Use of Chequebooks

Unlike the UK where they have been progressively phased out cheques are still in widespread use here in France where it is both illegal to write a cheque if there isn't sufficient money in the account to cover it and where if you do you will be likely blacklisted by your bank. Beware also the short queue in the supermarket, you may find that once everything is bagged up the customer then gets out a chequebook to pay and of course

Everyday Living, an A to Z

takes an age to sign it before the till takes an age to process it. Our local supermarket passes a cheque backwards and forwards through the till 10 times before the cashier shows it to the customer. Typically, customers do not write the whole cheque out, they just sign it and the till does the rest, albeit slower than writing one out manually. At least our Vet's does it all in a single pass.

9.11 Blood Doning

I have given blood since I was 18 and with everything I had heard about the nature of the French Healthcare System I thought I would be able to do the same once I'd moved. A couple of months after arriving I saw the banners advertising for donations in my local town. I went along and explained that I was a regular donor in the UK but they would not accept my donation. Seemingly if you have lived in the UK between 1980 and 1996 you cannot donate due to concerns arising from BSE! Perversely should you suffer a tragic accident your organs are acceptable to be donated! Consequently I have to try and fit in any continued donations during visits back to the UK, but that is not always possible with the NBTS appointment system that is in force.

9.12 Bonfires

You may think that you are perfectly at liberty to incinerate rubbish or garden waste at any time. You will be surprised as depending on your Commune you may find for example that lighting Bonfires is limited to between 1st October and 31st March. It may also be that you can only set these up in specific *Parcelles* depending on the number of them that your property consists of. As with all local matters you should check with your *Mairie* as to what is permissible, what isn't and where and when.

Practically don't just pile up cuttings etc. and hope they will burn as not all green foliage burns that well. In addition, piling up twigs/branches etc creates a latticework with lots of air gaps and fire doesn't take hold of that too well. Yes you can run your chainsaw through the assembled pile to condense it somewhat but it may not solve the problem. Do **not** make the mistake of throwing/putting petrol on it as not only does it endanger you or at the very least your eyebrows but any surface fuel on branches soon burns off and you are no further forward. Better to create an adjacent pile of kindling in a tepee shape, possibly with paper too, add some old offcuts of wood and get that going first, before then moving your pile of garden waste over once the fire is well established.

Not all communes allow the burning of Garden Waste, either for health reasons or for the potential nuisance it causes to neighbours as each *département* has its own regulations. The best way to find out what is applicable in your area is to ask at your local *Mairie* as the local *Préfet* has authority to derogate from the health regulations issued by central government which state that burning of household or other waste in the open-air is forbidden as the regulations give preference to composting or mulching of green waste. Practically though it is only banned in large urban populations or in a National Park/protected area.

9.13 Bug Bombs

Once you have found 'the one' you may find that it has stood empty for some weeks or months, and in some rarer cases years. This is not to say that there is necessarily anything

Everyday Living, an A to Z

wrong with it but as one of the basic tenets of French law is that one can't disinherit one's children it is common when parents die and there are multiple children they can't always decide what to do with the house. In such cases there can be disputes between some who might want to live in it and others who want to sell it. Consequently it may stand empty for some time before agreement is reached.

Accordingly there may be hygiene concerns before you move in. This is where Bug/Carpet Moth/Flea/Smoke bombs come into play depending on what one is trying to eradicate. One places the *'bomb'* on a heat resistant substance in the room/area in question, lights the fuse and then vacates the area having shut doors behind one. After the recommended period of time thoroughly ventilate the area in question and you should be good to go as the insecticidal smoke from the bombs will kill most insects quickly and efficiently. Some friends of ours used one in their house that had been vacant for a year and found it worked a treat.

9.14 Bus Shelters

Out in more rural locations most of the bus shelters that you are likely to see are actually for schoolchildren to use whilst waiting for their buses in the morning, so don't sit there expecting to see a bus arrive to take you to the local town unless you know one definitely stops there.

9.15 Cars

On our third viewing trip we drove our leased car over from England for the week and it suited us just fine. However it reinforced the idea that if we were going to be living here fulltime that we would need a left-hand drive car as it simply made more sense to us from a practical and safety perspective. Some of the local roads are quite narrow and driving *'on the right'* in a right-hand drive car definitely restricts your view as a driver and you are generally more reliant on your passenger, if you have one. Right hand drive models will also give the driver problems at Autoroute Toll Booths, Car Parks and Petrol Station Pay Kiosks. For us it was also a commitment worth making as we intended making France our home so why would we buy/bring a right hand drive model over?

Indeed there are women that Joanne knows (all of whom have right-hand drive cars) that do not like driving here and prefer to let their husbands do it as they do not feel safe nor confident. In which case the question has to be *'what will you do if anything happens to your husband'*?

Those issues aside if you are staying in France for longer than six months (in any twelve month period), then French law requires that your car is formally registered here in France and plated with a French registration number and naturally there will be a number of costs associated with this.

The UK's DVLA driving agency says that if a UK-registered car is taken out of the country for more than 12 months, it is deemed *'permanently exported'* and may not remain registered in the UK. In which case you should embark on getting a French registration for it. (See Annex C).

Everyday Living, an A to Z

9.15.1 How to register your British car/Caravan

If you want to bring your existing (UK) car with you or you intend to purchase a new car in the UK and import it to France, it is quite straightforward although there are various documents you will need to assemble and costs to take into account. In case of changes it is best to check the current requirements online, but in summary:

9.15.1.1 *Get your car EU/France ready*

- Request a Certificate of Conformity (an original **not** a photocopy) from the manufacturer's offices in France, as post Brexit, France no longer accepts British issued ones. (This certificate is their assurance that the car complies with current legislation.)
  n.b. This used to be free but now costs in the region of 130€;
- Ensure you have all the necessary documents;
- Change your headlights for driving on the right-hand side of the road. The Temporary stickers you may have used on holidays are not sufficient; and
- Ensure your speedometer can display km (otherwise you will have to change it for one that can).

The costs for these last two items could run into hundreds depending on the make and model of the car. Although if you bring it over separately to your move here it will be liable to both VAT and Customs duty.

9.15.1.2 *On Arrival*

You now have a month to register it.

- Contact your local customs office to obtain a 846 A certificate. (This is used in lieu of the tax certificate (*quitus fiscal*) that had to be provided by anyone importing a vehicle from within the EU);
- Arrange for a *Contrôle Technique* (if applicable) at a local/recommended garage, cost c65€.
  (Make sure you take the Certificate of Conformity, a proof of address (e.g. a utility bill), proof of identity (e.g. passport), and your blue V5C from your UK registration document).

9.15.1.3 *Subsequently*

- Apply online to register the car and obtain your Carte Grise *Certificat d'Immatriculation*. You have one month after your arrival to obtain this. There is a fee and various taxes to pay and the cost will depend on the make and model of your car, its emission rating, where you intend living and potentially a pollution tax too. It will likely cost upwards of c250€ but use the calculator in Annex C.
- Then once received obtain your French Number Plates from a local/recommended garage; and
- You can then also get the car insured.

9.15.2 Selling/buying a used car

Buying a second hand car can be highly problematic and in the UK you may be familiar with an HPI (Hire Purchase Investigation) check to satisfy yourself that the vehicle doesn't have outstanding finance nor has not been stolen, written off etc. A couple of years ago to reduce the number of potential frauds here the Ministry of the Interior introduced a free

Everyday Living, an A to Z

vehicle history website for both buyers (subject to conditions) and sellers called *'HistoVec'* (See Annex C).

On it one can find e.g. the date of first registration and the vehicle characteristics, its ownership history and whether it has been stolen or has credit claims upon it. Ultimately the intention is to display the odometer reading for each CT visit. The site can also provide a *certificat de non-gage*, confirming that the seller has unencumbered ownership of the vehicle and that they can freely dispose of it.

Currently the service is such that it is not directly available to buyers. For them to access the system, the seller must initially enter the vehicle details, however if the buyer knows the seller's email address they can request the history report via the website.

9.15.2.1 Process
This procedure can also be accomplished on your behalf by garages and showrooms, so the following is effectively for private sales.

When a person sells a car in France they have to notify the authorities within 15 days via what is known as the ANTS *(l'Agence Nationale des Titres Sécurisés)* website (See Annex C). You can setup an account on ANTS using your email address and creating a password. You get sent a link with your id which you click on to validate. Within your account you have different pages/'*spaces*' for Driver, ID or Vehicle. Within the latter there are various options relating to a vehicle but surprise surprise – you cannot access '*Buy or Receive a used vehicle*' because if you do you get a message saying that this tele-procedure isn't available online and you have to sign-in using France Connect (See section 9.45).

Step by Step
n.b. To accomplish this both Seller and Buyer need to have/create their own account on the *ANTS* website.

9.15.2.2 Not more than 14 days prior to the sale
The Seller needs to give the Buyer a *certificat de non gage*, an official document that states that there is no known reason why the vehicle can't be sold to a buyer, i.e. there are no encumbrances on it.

9.15.2.3 On the day of the sale
a) The Seller gives the buyer the *certificat d'immatriculation (carte gris)* after having drawn 2 diagonal lines across it and written either *Vendu – Sold* or *cédé* surrendered, on it and written the date and time of the sale and signed it; and

b) Both parties need to complete and sign the *certificat de cession d'un véhicule d'occasion* – (CERFA 15776) a 2-page document (one for each of the Seller & Buyer) and keep their respective pages, this needs to be completed irrespective of the value or age of the vehicle.

9.15.2.4 No more than 14 days after the sale
The seller completes an online declaration (about the sale) on the *ANTS* website, in return for which a *code de cession* is given to the Seller.

9.15.2.5 No more than 15 days after receipt of the code de cession
a) The Seller must give the code to the Buyer; and
b) The Buyer must then notify *ANTS* of this code.

Everyday Living, an A to Z

9.15.3 (Re-)Register a French Car

So after a period of time you decide you want to buy a French car, how do you go about registering it? (If you buy through a garage then there is a high likelihood that they will do everything for you).

If you buy the car privately then you will in all likelihood try to do it yourself so you will need to establish an *ANTS* account. Rest assured that if you do run into trouble with either logging onto the *ANTS* website or with France Connect (because you are not tax resident, don't have a Carte Vitale, or a French mobile number) that there are numerous registered garages that can do it for you. (See Annex C). In which case you will need to take with you:

- Your recent Proof of Address i.e. within the last 6 months, e.g. Electricity/Gas/Phone/Internet Bill;
- The car's previous Carte Grise with 2 lines striking it through and the words *Vendu Le* (d/m/y) and the signature of the previous owner;
- A *Contrôle Technique* certificate dated within the last 6 months, (but only if the car is more than 4 years old);
- Certificate of insurance (In the name of the new owner);
- A *code de cession* (this is a sale code that you should obtain from the previous owner – generated when they conduct an online formality for the sale of the car; and
- Copy of an ID document e.g. your passport.

9.16 Car Sharing

Carpooling *Covoiturage* is a mobility practice that is increasingly used in France. Its regulations are governed by the Ministry of Transport. You will find Carpooling parks common at the outskirts of many towns and at autoroute junctions where people taking advantage of carsharing opportunities can park their car. There are various carpooling sites setup where you can plan your journey & find potential sharers. (See Annex C).

9.17 Carte Vitale

On the 1st January 2016 France established a universal system of healthcare for anyone who lives or works here called *Protection Universelle Maladie* (known as *PUMA*). Once someone (including expats) has resided here for three consecutive months and who intends to reside here for more than 183 days each year in the future they can apply for their Carte Vitale which gives them access to the health services the state provides.

The main public health insurance fund provider in France is *Caisse Nationale de l'Assurance Maladie* (*CNAM*) which covers more than 90% of the population through some 101 local health insurance funds and is supervised through both the Social Security and Finance & Economy Ministries. On the other hand *Caisse Primaire d'Assurances Maladie* (*CPAM*) is the local *département* level of the national health insurance administration.

Receipt of a Carte Vitale is one of those milestone stages that new residents' in France look forward to as it reinforces one's sense of belonging. It signifies your acceptance into the French Healthcare system whereby the French Government covers approximately 70-80% of one's medical costs. If this is insufficient for your means you should consider buying

Everyday Living, an A to Z

some form of *'top-up'* insurance *mutuelle* (See section 9.75), which can cover most if not all of the outstanding amount.

9.17.1 Ways to obtain your Carte Vitale
So, how do you gain access to this system? Well you have to apply for the *Carte Vitale* and there are numerous ways to do this.

9.17.1.1 Call assurance maladie
Dial 3646 from your phone (incidentally this is not a free call) and the automated system will *'speak'* to you in French. You will need the *département* number that you live in and your Social Security Number to progress. The former is most important as the individual documentation requirements are different between offices.
Note It is possible to create an account on *Ameli* (French Social Security Website) and use this to make your application however I did not pursue this route as you need a Social Security Number and as a retired immigrant at the time I didn't have one not having filed a tax return.

9.17.1.2 Go to your nearest office
The easiest way to find out where is to access the *Ameli* website (See Annex C) and enter your *département* number. The office will be somewhere in your *préfecture*, and ask them what documents you need to provide? Once you have assembled them you can then deliver them in person. To be honest we went to our local office in the *Département* Capital (it was the best part of an hour away and I doubted whether any horseman would make it in a day) they gave us a checklist and I thought, this process is easy. It was only later on in our application we found they had given us incorrect information!

9.17.1.3 Send it by Post
When you understand what documentation is required you can package it all up and send it to the relevant *CPAM* office by post but I would suggest it is obligatory for you to send it by recorded delivery (*Recommandée avec accusé de réception*) (See section 9.87.2.1).

9.17.1.4 Use the Service Public Website
I would also suggest that by far the simplest method to kick off your application is to go to the Service Public website (See Annex C) then search for and download *Formulaire 736 – Demander l'ouverture des droits à l'assurance maladie* - Request the opening of health insurance rights. Assemble the necessary material and then either send it/take it to the office in question (Points 2 & 3 above).

Once the processing of your application starts if you have omitted anything from the application or they need further clarification or documentation then at some point afterwards you will get a letter, although it always seems to arrive 2-3 weeks after the date on it.

You then wait for the application to be processed. Until then, with any visit to the Doctor or Hospital, once you have paid you will be given a brown printed care sheet *feuille de soins* which details any prescription and charges made. You need to keep these whilst you are waiting for your Carte Vitale to arrive as any sheets dated from the date of your application for the Carte to its arrival can be retrospectively claimed for/sent to your local health authority for reimbursement (full or partial) to be made. (If you also have complementary health insurance, most main insurers are linked into the social system through which their share of the charge will also be reimbursed).

The final letter you receive will ask you to send a passport photo back to the central issuing office (in Rennes). Don't use any spares that you may have laying around, go to a photo booth and get a specific one taken as the rules for what constitutes an acceptable ID Photo in France are very strict, but the booths explain the requirements in great detail.

9.17.2 Final Steps

When your Carte Vitale does arrive you will then have a social security number. The card itself has an embedded microchip which contains your social security insurance details but will not include any personal medical information and it is not a means of payment! Once finally in receipt of your card you can then:
   1) Access Ameli.fr and setup your online account; and
   2) Make your *déclaration de choix du médecin traitant.*

This is the medical professional who you consult first about your health, they will also optimise any necessary follow-up. Probably the nearest one to you and the one you first registered with. There is a financial advantage to this as well in that your *CPAM* then reimburse you the full amount of the charge (i.e. 70% less 1€ of the consultation fee), however if you consult a different doctor then you only receive back 30% - although situations such as consulting a locum stand-in for your Doctor or seeing a different Doctor if you are on holiday (in France) or in Hospital for an emergency still qualify you for the full reimbursement. If you are in frequent need of a Doctor's services or you judge that 70% less 1€ is not adequate for your needs you will need to invest in Top Up Insurance, a *mutuelle*. (See section 9.75).

n.b. The percentage reimbursement you actually receive will depend on what further treatment you may undertake as each type of service has its own percentage but the public statement is that 70% is reimbursed for the majority of healthcare needs. For some serious conditions the percentage of state health cover is higher or even complete, i.e. 100%.

9.17.3 Thereafter

If you need to make a visit once you have your Carte Vitale the Doctor/Hospital will take the details from your card and you will still pay however any reimbursement due is usually sent directly into your bank account within a week. For hospital charges you are sent an invoice in the post some weeks later. That changed on 1st September 2021 from when you have to make an upfront payment to the hospital (See section 9.53).

9.17.4 Reality

Based on the time taken to process our application it is not a quick process. I don't what to discourage anyone and I don't know if we were the exceptions to the rule but after you have sent all your documents to your local office, you simply have to wait and …. wait some more. It took 3 months to get any response at all and we then went on a document merry-go-round among 4 different offices and yes we duplicated material that had already been sent before ending up at the office back in our *préfecture* where we first started. It was as though they couldn't possibly forward the material or, perish the thought, have a centrally accessible file, and every office seemed to want their own copy of documents, even things

Everyday Living, an A to Z

like birth certificates and passports. Although we applied at the same time, my card took 14 months to arrive and Joanne's 17 months.

In between times I had to call the DWP in the UK to confirm that I was not entitled to healthcare in the UK. This took some weeks and a follow up call during which I elicited that although their office was in Durham all mail was sent to Wolverhampton to be dispatched. Obviously some business consultant convinced them that was a sensible thing to do at some stage! When the letter came however we did get two versions, one in English and one in French which was both helpful and unexpected.

9.18 Cashback

A regular feature of everyday life in the UK, usually in supermarkets but many different shops will offer this if you ask, providing you are using a PIN entry to validate the transaction. In France however this is not an everyday occurrence and cashback is only offered in a very limited number of places and at the time of writing this means Supermarkets or Hypermarkets in the Casino chain.

9.19 CEDEX

French residential postal addresses will be laid out similarly to those in the UK however business addresses are liable to be different. The *Cedex (Courrier D'entreprise à Distribution EXceptionnelle)* method allows companies who pay a subscription to *La Poste* to receive priority mail processed in dedicated offices. The use of the Cedex facility means that companies on the periphery of large cities can benefit from the dedicated office(s) of that city.

In large urban areas there may be several *Cedex* offices, Paris for example has one in each *arrondissement* and it is identified by a two digit number after *Cedex*, in smaller areas without districts but which have several such offices they are just numbered 1, 2 etc. So for example the code for the French office that processes driving licence exchanges/requests is shown as:
44035 Nantes CEDEX 01 (Nantes is in department Loire-Atlantique, postal code 44).

The Cedex facility can also be used in conjunction with a P.O. Box (*Boite Postale*) Number e.g. BP 27 44040 Nantes CEDEX 01.

9.20 CERFA

As you browse through different government related websites or read about how to apply for something or another you will likely come across the abbreviation CERFA (*Centre d'Enregistrement et de Révision des Formulaires Administratifs*) and wonder what it is? Originally relating to the center itself who were responsible for editing and registering official forms nowadays the term relates to the administrative forms prepared and recorded by them which can be found on the Ministry of Interior website. What is more the template/layout of each of the forms is regulated by government decree. They are all referred to in a standard fashion by a 5-digit number followed by a star (*) and a two-digit number indicating its version (if different ones exist). For example the annual tax return has a standard number but is modified each year as the system evolves, just as in the UK. Consequently when completing such a form you need to ensure that you use the latest version of it.

Everyday Living, an A to Z

9.21 Chain Link

I only got involved with looking for this because the chaotic storm of 4 July 2018 blew a tree into my lake *Etang* and as I had no idea of its weight figured that I would need the help of some chains to attach to my winch in order to drag it out.

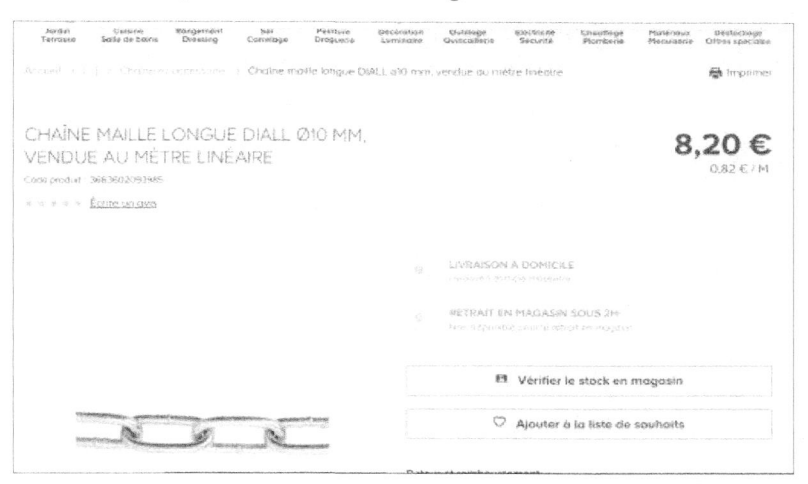

A word of warning, I found a suitable (to my mind) length of 10mm diameter chain at a reasonable price. I called in to purchase it on the way back from going to the airport so hadn't made a special journey. I then found that it would cost 10 times what I expected!

The reason? On the website in question it listed it with a price of 8,20€ but also 0,82/m. My mistake as in this instance the '/m' is not per metre but per *maillon* which translates to link!

I thought that I might get away with 4-5 metres but disturbingly the store could not tell me the breaking strain of the chain and I was uneasy about overpaying for something that might not be suitable. Luckily I found some rope in my local Farmers Co-operative with a breaking strain of 4 tonnes, which was more than man enough for the job and would match the capabilities of my 4-ton winch and at a far cheaper price.

9.22 Chickens

9.22.1 Introduction

In times gone by almost everyone had chickens to supply eggs for the family but progressive industrialisation and urbanisation steadily reduced this an option for most. However a lot of people's dream of moving to the wide open spaces of rural France is to have chickens running around the garden and to benefit from high quality fresh eggs every day, it was certainly Joanne's aspiration at one point but after careful consideration she decided against it. However we are not averse to accepting those offered by our neighbour from time to time!

Now I don't own any rose-tinted glasses – my photochromic ones turn brown in sunlight, so if you don't acquire/'*inherit*' any with the house purchase then you should at least consider the following before getting all '*Good Life*'.

Everyday Living, an A to Z

9.22.2 Acquisition

For the uninitiated, Hens don't need a Cock in order to lay eggs. Without one the eggs are infertile, so there is no danger of them growing into young chickens. If you do have a cock be sure to collect the egg's daily and keep them in a cool place before using them, that way you can be sure they won't develop.

One can buy point of lay pullets *(pondeuse)* for between 10-15€ each from the local markets but you can also buy smaller chicks which are cheaper, you just have to wait longer for them to start laying eggs. Often you have to book them one week and wait until the next market to collect.

n.b. The *cou nu* (naked neck) chickens you will see around are boiling hens not layers and you will only get a few eggs from them.

When your newly purchased birds arrive at their new home they need to be kept shut in for 3 - 4 days wherever you want them to come back to every evening before you release them to the outside world.

9.22.3 Housing

Then once they are acquired, if you don't already have them you need to build/buy a chicken coop (*Poullaillier*) although an old disused shed is great, and an enclosed run to keep the aforementioned poultry in along with safe nesting boxes and perches and this will be your main expense. n.b. Plastic boxes can work well too but check how hot they get inside.

You don't need a vast array of special equipment just a container to remove waste bedding roughly once a week (great for the compost heap), a hard brush, food and water dispensers, disinfectant for the feeders and the coop.

If you are building a run you should put chicken wire down on the floor and ensure it is secured to the sides to save foxes or pine martens digging under the fence to get at your chickens. Also consider putting it on the in/outsides of the coop itself as I know of someone who lost his chickens to a pine marten initially eating and then breaking through the wooden structure from outside to get to the flock.

9.22.4 Feeding

Free range hens need a bowlful of wheat every morning (inexpensive from most bricolages, Co-ops, etc) oyster shell and grit to peck at and they like dried mealworms, you can always add in some corn as a treat, along with fresh water and hay or straw for the nesting boxes which you should change on a weekly basis. But be sure to keep your bedding and chicken food out of reach from mice and rats as they love it. You can safely feed your Chickens cheese rind, fruit and vegetable scraps, melon and pepper seeds etc. (but be careful though, especially not avocado or onions) and in this respect they are not expensive to maintain. They also eat snails and slug eggs, although they are not so keen on the slugs themselves. What not to feed them is easily found online.

Then just pop in each day and collect your bounty and say thank you.

9.22.5 Personalities

Friends who have them tell me the birds have very distinctive personalities and characteristics and maintain strict pecking orders (sorry, it had to be said). The dictionary

Everyday Living, an A to Z

definition of which is:

the basic pattern of social organisation within a flock of poultry in which each bird pecks another lower in the scale without fear of retaliation and submits to pecking by one of higher rank.

They are very companionable and curious creatures, they are also very sociable and enjoy hanging out and interacting with you and are happy to listen to you chat away about all and sundry, so are very therapeutic to have around. If you start digging in the garden then provided your chickens are completely free range (which give far and away the best eggs) it is likely that all the chickens will immediately appear as they want to get involved in everything you are doing and keep you company as long as you work in the garden. The downside to that is that you need to safeguard any seedlings you are planting as they are otherwise immediately scratched up, you will also need to ensure that your dog(s) is cool with the feathered guys running around their garden.

Because of this one of the downsides with free range chickens is their wayward decisions to start laying their eggs other than in designated nesting boxes which potentially means hours spent hunting for their current favoured egg laying spot.

9.22.6 Safety

Thereafter they need to be securely locked up before dark each night which means you have to find a reliable friend/neighbour to do this if you need to be out. If you decide to go away this friend/neighbour will need to drop by a couple of times each day to check on their wellbeing which is not usually a problem as they get free eggs in return. In this respect unfortunately Chickens are as much a tie as Cats and Dogs but at least your furry friends can be boarded in a Cattery/Kennels should you decide a break is on order and go on holiday.

Also you will need to clean and periodically disinfect the coop - especially if it's wooden as your girls could get red mites, which tend to hide in the dark corners of the coop during the day and come out to gorge on the blood of your girls at night. You also need to ensure their general well-being as there are a number of diseases that even free-range birds are susceptible to. Again look online for details.

9.22.7 Conclusion

Also be aware, that Chickens only lay for a couple of years whereupon you either have to despatch (and presumably eat them – which is why it would be best not to name them) or look after them (possibly for another 3-4 years) feeding and treating them until they naturally expire. It is not cheap having your own free-range chickens.

That said, it's hard to go back to shop bought eggs, knowing that yours are both truly organic and that your girls are well cared for, happy, and producing eggs with the most wonderful golden orange coloured, and in a lot of instances, double yokes.

9.23   Churches

9.23.1 Church Bells

Irrespective of possibly marking of the hours, funerals and weddings you will find your village church bells will automatically ring out at certain times every day, a legacy from a far more religious time when the church bells sounded a call to prayers at:

    7.00 – for Matins

Everyday Living, an A to Z

    12.00 – for Midday Prayer
    19.00 – for Vespers/evening prayer

and the bells were meant to be heard by everyone in the village, although nowadays it seems that the midday bells trigger a rush to the local restaurants by workmen keen to make a start on their *Menu Ouvriers* and shops start to close for business too.

There are some amusing stories around about the ringing of church bells in villages. In one locality apparently some Parisians had hired a nearby *Gite* and after a few days petitioned the *Maire* to ask his technical team to get the bell ringing delayed as it was waking them up. Needless to say the *Maire* politely declined saying that he didn't have a technical team but amusingly mentioning that he could not do anything about the cockerels crowing either as it was the countryside after all. (See also 9.101).

9.23.2 Proximity to a Church

If your *'One'* is situated close to a church you will not just have the ringing of the bells to contend with. There are various constraints on what you can and cannot do to your property if it is visible from the Church. This varies from place to place so it is best to make enquiries at the *Mairie* before you set your heart on doing something.

9.23.3 Proximity to a Chateau

Equally the houses and business premises on the main road past the chateau in town are subject to various restrictions imposed by *Bâtiments de France* (part of the Ministry of Culture). For example as an owner:

- No Velux windows can be installed in the roof;
- The roof tiles have to be (expensive) Ardoise slate;
- The colour of the external doors/shutters cannot be changed; and
- The colour of the external walls cannot be changed.

9.24 Cleaning Chimneys

If you have a woodburning stove(s) in your house it is usually a condition of your house insurance that these are swept annually. It's your decision of course as in some areas finding a *ramoneur* is as rare as finding hen's teeth but if you were unfortunate enough to have a chimney fire or some kind of fire with the stove identified as the cause then you can bet your life that your insurance company will ask you for a copy of the latest certificate. So my view is it is better to be safe than sorry.

Regulations for chimney sweeping can vary from *Département* to *Département* and even commune to commune but are typically based on the number of *cordes* of wood you burn annually. Check the *Départemental* Health Regulations to be sure.

9.25 Coypu

Depending on the location and physical features in or around *'the one'* you may well encounter these rodents during your time here. I knew there were some Coypu *Ragondin* in an *étang* beyond our village but did not exactly put down the welcome mat when I saw one swimming in our *étang* a couple of years after we moved in. I was going to happily go out and buy a gun to get rid of it but thought I had better check with our *Mairie* first. I went down there one Monday morning to ask what I could do about them, after a hasty phone

Everyday Living, an A to Z

call to the President of the local Chasse I was told I could not shoot it but I could trap it……………….. then I could shoot it! Welcome to France!

I guess this is because they are concerned that shooting it from a distance may wound it and they are concerned about causing it distress. However not being a country boy I didn't feel comfortable about shooting it whilst it was in a cage by my feet but I had no qualms about trapping it. A cage was duly purchased and loaded with cut up apple, carrot, and pear which I had read they were apparently partial to and I added some kiwi fruit for good measure. Sure enough after a few days one appeared in the cage and I duly relocated it some miles distant. It must have been solitary as nothing else appeared over the next 2-3 weeks and nothing showed up on my trail camera/camera trap, having moved that to overlook the *étang*. But since then I have at different times trapped and relocated a further 3, and without going into too much detail I'll just say that Keno helped remove 2 on another occasion!

Why am I not keen on them? Well they can dig tunnels in the sides of rivers or lakes up to 10 metres or so in length and some 20cm in diameter (roughly body width) with generally submerged entrances which make them really difficult to spot, consequently this activity serves to undermine the banks. So I blame them for the loss of the trees into the lake. They have enormous appetites and can eat copious amounts of vegetation, consuming about 25% of their body weight daily. As a result any aquatic vegetation is often completely removed from an area. In appearance these animals resemble a large rat or beaver (but with a rat-like tail). They can reach almost 60cm in length (excluding their tail) and weigh some 6kg or so, although more extreme examples can reach more than 15kg and have a 45cm tail. They have pronounced top incisors, about 4-5cm in length and webbed feet. They are also prolific breeders, with a gestation period of just 130 days they can give birth to as many as 12 youngsters at a time who can all start to eat the local vegetation within hours of being born. With the adults capable of reproducing up to 3 times a year, that is a lot of Coypu, particularly as they have no natural predators. So once they are established in an area they are very difficult to dislodge and I certainly didn't want a colony at the end of my garden.

When I mentioned this to my French teacher he just laughed and showed me '*YouTube*' videos about preparing Coypu to eat, apparently dating from WW2 when there wasn't much meat around in the countryside and people resorted to any means to add some protein to their diet!

9.26   CU

So you are on a viewing trip driving around and see a site for sale with wonderful views or that you believe will be perfect for you to build your dream house in France. If you are lucky it will be advertised with a '*CU*' *certificat d'urbanisme* if not you will need to obtain one as part of drawing up your plans and it could be likened to Outline Planning permission in the UK.

The certificate itself consists of 2 parts:
Form A is the Information Certificate (*certificat d'information générale*) which explains the general planning rules associated with the land, any limitations on the right of ownership; and

Everyday Living, an A to Z

Form B is the Operational Certificate (*certificat opérationnel*) that tells you about any services that are provided etc and describes the feasibility of the project

It is valid for a period of 18 months from the date of issue and you apply for one online through the Ministry of Urban Planning. As ever you can find the information you need on the Service Public site – item N19808 and on form 13410 on the CERFA site (See Annex C for details of both).

The form explains which additional documents must be provided and the overall file of information must be sent or taken to the *Mairie* of the commune where the land is located. 2 copies are required together with an additional copy if the land is in the protected perimeter of an historical monument and another 2 copies if it is in a National Park.

Further, if you find a house/barn that looks ripe for conversion to what you aspire to you have to understand that an important difference in France compared with the UK is that Planning applies to any existing building and not the land. Consequently if you find for example a barn that you want to convert to your new house then you will first need to apply for change of use, as you will not be renovating an existing building (the barn) but changing its use from an agricultural building to a residential property.

Although you might have a CU you will still need to get all the relevant facilities/utilities connected. If arranging these doesn't appeal then you could always consider buying a *lotissement* (See section 9.66).

9.27 Customer Service

In the UK we have been spoiled, '*the Customer is King*' after all. Although Brits somewhat reluctantly step forward when it comes to making complaints about poor service or overcharging we now expect our complaints to be dealt with quickly and professionally. I do now suggest that you leave some of these pre-conceptions behind. Organisations here do not seem to have many CRM systems in place as such. The fact that you have complained or even enquired about a product or service, by email, in person, or through a website doesn't always mean you will get a speedy or indeed satisfactory response here. It may even to all intents and purposes be ignored. I have to say that the failure of companies, government departments and other organisations to confirm applications or receipt of documents etc. is endemic. If you chase them to ask if they've received what you've sent, you are more than likely to continue to receive no reply! This isn't universal but it's very common. Certainly attitudes such as described here are more likely attributable to the more southerly *départements* but maybe not so much up north. Irrespective, **do not lose your cool.** It all ties in with a slower pace of life and a different mindset. Re-adjust your expectations, downwards!

9.28 Déchetteries

Recycling has improved a lot in France over recent years but one area that has not caught on is that of recycling food waste. Although you may be well attuned to putting leftovers, tea bags and vegetable peelings etc into a food caddy which is then collected weekly/fortnightly the waste management companies here haven't advanced that far yet, it just goes in your dustbin with the rest of the household rubbish *ordures ménagères*. So it is likely you will become familiar with the local dump or council tip as it is in the UK and the

Everyday Living, an A to Z

same exists in France where they are known as *déchetteries* (See Annex C for information on locations etc).

They are just as organised as you have come to expect in the UK, with separate containers for some or all of Garden Waste, General Rubbish *déchet*, Glass, Hard Core, Metal, Oil, Paper, Plastic, Polystyrene, Wood etc. together with specific areas for old appliances and paint tins. If your load is predominantly garden waste you will find pitchforks and shovels available to help you disgorge it. Generally they are only staffed by a single person who zealously maintains the cleanliness and order of their site as one would do in one's own workplace; so if you make a mess transferring rubbish from your car or trailer into the bin expect to clean it up, or you will be asked to do so. Equally do not expect them to give you a helping hand, it is not always forthcoming and until you become familiar with the specific personnel, and vice versa, you will likely be asked which commune you have come from as they expect you to be a local and you will be subjected to numerous questions if the *département* plate on your car does not correspond to the local area.

Their usual opening times are 0900-1200 and 1400 to 1800 and they are not open on Sundays/Bank Holidays, although do check first. Like a lot of French workers their lunch time is sacrosanct. Before now we have arrived at a local *déchetterie* at 1145 and had to wait 10 minutes or so for a lorry to exchange an empty container for a full one only to then be told that we had to leave (before we unloaded) as it was closing at lunchtime.

9.29 Death

As a part of life, death is a traumatic and painful occasion for everyone associated with the deceased, and certainly not anything you are thinking about when you move here. During this painful time probably the last thing you will want to do is trawl the internet for information but the Service Public website (See Annex C).
Item F1444 sets out what you need to do to obtain a Death Certificate; Item F16507 explains how and who to inform after the event; and
Item F1621 explains your rights if you are in a PACs relationship.

9.29.1 In the event of a death
However trying to remove the emotion from the event, in factual terms the following need to take place in the event of a death of a spouse, family member, partner or friend in France.

9.29.1.1 At Home
The first thing to do is to contact the fire brigade (*sapeurs-pompiers*) (Tel: 18) or call your local doctor, or (Tel: 112 or 15.) A doctor will then certify the death and issue a medical certificate of death (*certificat de décès*).

9.29.1.2 In Hospital
It is highly probable the local town hall will deal with the registration of the death. You will still have to give the personal details of the deceased person, such as passport copy, social security card and health insurance details. However if the death is in a hospital and the hospital doesn't declare the death, they will give you a form to take to your *Mairie*. The deceased person will be kept in the hospital mortuary and you can then arrange a transfer

Everyday Living, an A to Z

to your chosen undertaker or your home. This must take place within 24 hours (or 48 hours if the body is embalmed).

If the doctor who certifies the death is satisfied that no suspicious circumstances exist and the death was due to natural causes then no further inquiries are held.

9.29.1.3 Unnatural Death
If the death is violent, suspicious or a suicide you must contact the local police (Tel: 17 or 112). If the death occurs in a public place or if foul play is suspected an inquiry is held. In such cases the responsibility for issuing the death certificate and burial permit lies with the Public Prosecutor (*Procureur de la République*) at the local high court (*Tribunal de Grande Instance*).

9.29.2 How to register a death in France
The death must be registered at the local town hall (*Mairie*) in the locality in which it occurred within 24 hours (excluding weekends or public holidays). A relative or formally appointed representative usually registers the death.

When reporting a death you need to take a number of documents with you:
- Proof of identity of the person declaring the death;
- Passport, marriage or birth certificate of the deceased; and
- Medical certificate of death issued by the doctor or police.

Once reported, a certified copy of the entry - a death certificate (*acte de décès*) is usually issued immediately if all necessary details are available. Numerous copies of the death certificate are provided; and these can be used when notifying authorities and service providers of the death. No fee is charged for the medical certificate or for the registration of death.

The *acte de décès* gives details on where and when death took place but not the cause. Once the death is registered, the town hall issues a burial permit (*permis d'inhumer*) indicating the time and date of death. Burial may not take place in the 24 hours following the death.

9.29.3 Choices after death
Contact an undertaker to take over and manage the arrangements for burial/cremation or repatriation of the body (It is obligatory for an undertaker to provide a detailed breakdown of costs and any optional extras).

Thereafter it will be necessary to approach a *Notaire* and obtain an **'Act of recognition'** (*acte de notoriété héréditaire*). This is a document which provides proof of heirship and is needed by the surviving partner or immediate heir to close bank accounts, change ownership on the Carte Grise vehicle registration documents and so on.

9.29.3.1 Cremation
If you want your loved one cremated it has to be authorised by the *Maire* of the locality in which they died. Approval is given if the deceased has stated it in their Will or perhaps in a letter written by them, or if the surviving spouse or partner requests it. You will need to provide a medical certificate stating that cremation will not pose a medical/legal problem. The coffin must be closed in the presence of a police officer, which involves a small fee. The

Everyday Living, an A to Z

cremation usually takes place in the crematorium closest to the place of death, although if the deceased or their family has requested it take place in a different location that will be honoured. After the actual cremation, the ashes are placed in an urn provided by survivors of the deceased.

The Cremation must take place at least 24 hours but not more than six days after death.

9.29.3.2 *Ashes*

After the cremation, the crematoria can store the ashes for up to one year if necessary. By law the crematorium has to place ashes in an urn that displays both the name of the deceased and the location of the crematorium. If the ashes are not claimed during the year, they are scattered in the town where the death took place in a space provided for this purpose. The ashes must not be divided but are conserved in the urn and then can be:

- Scattered in a designated area at a cemetery
  most cemeteries and crematoria have a Garden of Remembrance available for the scattering of ashes;
- Scattered publicly
  One is not allowed to scatter ashes on a public pathway, road or river (which is considered to be a public 'path'). Approval is needed by the *Mairie* and the name of the deceased and the date the ashes were dispersed will be recorded by them; or
- Sealed in a tomb or monument in a cemetery, buried or placed in a structure known as a columbarium. This is a building (sometimes with walls with separate niches within it) room or specific wall used to store urns containing ashes of people who have been cremated.

One cannot keep the ashes in one's home or scatter them in a private garden however the ashes can be kept in a memorial on private property. If you want/need to take the ashes outside of the country you will need this to be sanctioned by the *Préfet* of the *département* before the Cremation takes place. You may also require the help of the relevant local embassy or consulate. The crematorium will provide you with additional information about transport if required.

9.29.4 Burial

There is a general misbelief that it costs less for someone to be cremated than it does to be buried as recent studies have shown that the average cost is actually some 4-5% higher than that for burial.

You are entitled to be buried in the commune in which you live, and this is authorised by the *Maire*. It must take place from 24 hours to six days (excluding Sundays and public holidays) following the death. The departmental *Préfet* may issue a waiver if there is a problem meeting the burial deadline. A burial may be arranged by a funeral parlour or the immediate family of the deceased. Documents required are:

- Burial licence; and
- Burial certificate issued by the commune in which the death occurred.

if the deceased wishes to be buried in a different place, you will need to ask permission (of the relevant *Maire*, but this may not always be given. In France, burial (*inhumation*) without a coffin is prohibited!

Everyday Living, an A to Z

9.29.4.1 Burial Plots

As ever in France there are differences in the allocation of plots depending on one's Commune. The plot is generally allocated on a temporary basis, although this can vary between 10 and 50 years, or in perpetuity as determined by the *conseil municipal* who also decide on the rates applicable. (Our commune lists them in the Municipal Bulletin we receive each year). However if the actual cost is a problem a plot may be made available at a reduced cost. Within three months of the burial, the grave site must be covered by a concrete slab. Thereafter a decorative tomb stone may be erected and in France graves must be cared for and maintained by family members.

9.29.4.2 Burial on private ground

Burial may take place on private property with the permission of the *Préfet* of your department although certain conditions apply, numerous documents must be produced and the private burial must have been requested by the deceased (in their will).

9.29.5 In the days that follow:

Once the initial steps regarding registration and choice of undertaker and type of burial/cremation have been taken thereafter you will want to consider notifying where relevant the deceased's:

- **Bank** to close/transfer their account);
- **CPAM health insurance office** to return their *Carte Vitale*. To seek reimbursement of any death benefits and final medical expenses;
- **Employer**;
- **Life Insurance Company** to stop future premiums and claim on the policy;
- **Mutuelle Provider** to stop future premiums;
- **Other Insurance Companies** to stop future premiums; and
- **Pensions** authorities.

Please note that if the deceased was in a PACS relationship, this must be dissolved by the court (*Greffier du tribunal d'instance*).

9.29.6 Other Legalities:

The law states that within five months of a death, you must inform your *Notaire* and any Inheritance tax due must also be paid within seven months, if not, hefty fines will begin to apply.

Incidentally, under French law when a relative dies the heirs have three options.

9.29.6.1 Acceptance

They receive their share of any inheritance and then pay their share of any debts up to the limit of their share in the estate (e.g. 3 successors each pay ⅓ of the debt).

n.b. If the debts were unknown at the time of acceptance and payment would damage one's personal assets then it is possible to appeal.

9.29.6.2 Acceptance of Net Assets

A complex option meaning that any heirs don't pay debts in excess of the deceased's property value, and thus personal assets are protected from any creditors. This requires an estate inventory to be made within 2 months of the death. At any time in this step it is possible to stop and elect for the first option.

Everyday Living, an A to Z

9.29.6.3 *Renunciation*

This means the heirs receive no property and pay no debts. They have four months to exercise this option.

9.30   Defenseur des droits

This position is constitutionally independent of the state and looks to defend persons whose rights are not respected and allow equality for all in access to rights, as such it can examine whether Government Legislation is fair and equitable and rule accordingly.

9.31   Depot(s) de Pain

On average, France has some 35,000 bakeries and indeed it used to be the case that that every town was required by law to have a *boulangerie* (bakery). However, if a town or village is too remote, a *dépôt de pain* is allowed, where bread is made off-site and delivered fresh daily. As the name implies, a *dépôt de pain* is a place where bread is deposited & sold by a third party, this could be a local bar, hotel, restaurant, *tabac* etc.

Another alternative is whereby some *Boulangeries* will come to a nearby village in a van maybe a couple of times a week tooting their horn as they drive down the street and park up before selling their wares. Indeed it is not unusual to see bread dropped into bags hung from gate posts or windows if people are at work. If you are a fan of the baguette then you would do well to check out the potential *Boulangeries/Dépôts de Pain* in your search area. In the same vein it is not unusual to see stand-alone 24/7 Baguette dispensers such as these in larger/more popular towns and not adjacent to/just outside a Boulangerie either, campsites or industrial areas are prime candidates. In our town there is one next to the Lavage and Car Wash. The bread is kept refrigerated and then warmed up before it is dispensed.

9.32   DIY Stores

Think practically. Depending on your plans for *'the one'* how close is the nearest DIY Store and is it likely to stock everything you need? Is it a few minutes in the car or up to half an hour or more away? Do you have the sort of car that will enable you to make and transport large purchases? If it is not very big and you don't have a trailer (See section 10.14) then you are looking at paying for a delivery each time, and delivery in France is not cheap and would need to be factored into your budget for the work.

Don't be surprised when going into your local *brico* if as well as displays of Bolts, Nails, Nuts, Screws etc. you see relatively small plastic bags of differing sizes next to them. Because here it is not uncommon to buy an assortment of the same according to either weight or size of bag, irrespective of content. Although I noticed on a recent trip back to the UK that some DIY stores are now selling screws in such bags.

Everyday Living, an A to Z

9.33 DMP

Within the health framework in France one has the ability to create a digital health record in which all of your allergies, medications, test results, treatments, etc are held as well as details of any hospital visits you make or consultations you receive. Called a *Dossier Médicale Partage* (Shared Health Record) it allows you to share the relevant information with any health practitioner who treats or needs to treat you and allows for co-ordination and continuity of your care. You control access to it, and apart from yourself only specific health practitioners can view it, e.g. a consultant, doctor, nurse or pharmacist. In an emergency, at a hospital for example you can give verbal consent for the treating physician to access your file, and like with every other access their actions will be recorded too. You can look at it at any time and it holds a complete record of every access – date, time, identity and occupation of every accessor and what they did.

You can create the account free of charge via your local *CPAM*, and it is also available as an 'App'.

9.34 Drainage & Guttering

In the UK you find that PVC has taken over when it comes to Drainpipes and Guttering. Something you will get used to with your properties here is that the materials you will be working with, brackets, guttering, pipes etc will very likely be made from Zinc/Metal, principally due to the warping effect of the heat experienced during summer. This has a downside in that with PVC all of the connectors, joints etc. will have a snug fit when pushed together. With Zinc/Metal it is not quite so clear-cut. For example one end of a drainpipe will have a slightly larger diameter than the other as will the bends, so you will be doing a lot of *'offering up'* etc. when putting a run together. You will also find that once you have worked out what goes where as part of the assembly process you will likely need a mastic type glue to seal the joints and stop it leaking once in place.

9.35 Driving

9.35.1 Distances

Road maps generally indicate the distance from Paris and *'Point Zéro'* the reference point for distances along the roads is measured from the square in front of the Notre Dame Cathedral. Tradition has it that tourists who stand on *Point Zéro* will one day return to the city. In other cities distances are measured from the *Mairie*.

9.35.2 Driving Licences

Here in France, a driving license is granted for life and without medical examination unlike in the UK where one needs to renew it on reaching 70 years of age and every three years thereafter.

Post Transition there was quite a delay to France and the UK signing a reciprocal agreement over Driving Licences which caused much anxiety in those expats (mainly in rural communities) whose licences or Photocards had expired, as the only way to renew them was to sit a French Driving Test. Eventually a new deal came into effect on the 28th June 2021.

Should you ever lose/mislay your licence a replacement ordered through ANTS will cost you 25€.

Everyday Living, an A to Z

9.35.3 Driving Tests

Should you or a loved one take a Driving Test here in France, like in the UK they are 2-part, theory and practical but after the latter they will need to wait a minimum 3 days for the result (introduced to avoid unhappy candidates attacking their examiners)! Should they be successful the licence granted will be *Un Permis Probatoire* and it will come with 6 points. Two more will be added for each of the first 3 years providing no offences are committed. Young drivers must observe lower speed limits and are subject to lower alcohol limits.

9.35.4 Legal Alcohol Limit

Unfortunately some people still decide to drink and drive. In England and Wales, the legal alcohol limit for drivers is 80 milligrammes of alcohol per 100 ml of blood, 35 microgrammes per 100 ml of breath or 107 milligrammes per 100ml of urine. Be aware that in France (as in Scotland and most European countries) things are more stringent and the limit is less here, 50 milligrammes per 100 millilitres of blood.

Also in France, drivers caught drunk-driving can decide whether to have their licence suspended or for an ignition breathalyser to be installed in their car, at their expense, which will prevent it being started if the driver has a level of alcohol in their system above 20 milligrammes per 100 millilitres of blood. Such a device has to remain in their car for a minimum of 5 years.

9.35.5 Legal Requirements

The principal difference here is that French law the *Code de la route* states that you have to have your driving licence, your original insurance documents and your car registration papers (*carte grise*) with you in your car at all times. The *Gendarmerie* are not keen on photocopies!

Also required at all times and another legal requirement in France is to carry High-Visibility vests for all occupants in case of a breakdown or you have to leave the vehicle in an emergency. Consequently any such vest needs to be in the car, say the glove compartment or door pocket rather than in the boot so that it is readily accessible and can be put on before getting out of the car. We have ones for the dogs too, just in case. One good way of carrying them is to wrap them around the seats so they are visible when you are driving around, particularly as when you first arrive you will likely have a UK vehicle which even if you re-register it here to obtain French Number Plates will still be Right Hand Drive and as such will be more apparent to the local *Gendarmerie* who may be more inclined to stop you to check you are fully equipped.

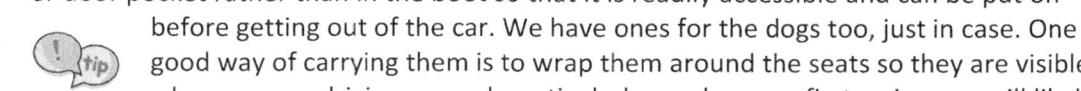

Whilst driving, if for example you get a bad puncture or one of your tyres wears out and you are looking to replace it then you need to be aware that in France to remain legal the two tyres on a single axle have to be the same brand and type, mixing and matching is not permitted. You are also legally bound to carry a red triangle in your vehicle in case of breakdown.

Also if you are driving with a SatNav you need to update your '*preferences*' to ensure that you de-select the display of (fixed) speed cameras as this is illegal too. Fines are quite punitive and can involve confiscation of your vehicle. However these sites are well

Everyday Living, an A to Z

9.35.6 Motorcycles

It's never been my thing but if you are a motorcyclist as of Feb 1st 2021 you are not allowed to weave in and out of other traffic on the road, you have to stay in lane. A new law sees offenders risk a 135€ fine and three points being deducted from their driving licence

9.35.7 No Claims Discount

Your No Claims Discount is different here too, and can be shown on any paperwork you receive for example as 0,68 so how does this work in practice?

In the UK once you have built up say 4 or 5 years claim free driving you will likely have a No Claims Discount of 60-65% or so and even further years of blame free driving will not increase this figure, although you can also pay a slightly higher premium to protect this bonus figure. Be aware though that not all companies put the actual number of years you have accumulated on any No Claims Certificate so even if you have say 10 years blame free driving the certificate may only show 4/5 years.

Now as you will expect the French do it somewhat differently. Here you need 13 years of claim free driving to reach the maximum discount of 50%, or 0,5 as it is displayed on quotations. Any driver who has never been insured starts with a bonus level of 1,00 then for every year you don't have an accident (where you are to blame) that figure is multiplied by 0,95 until after 13 years it reaches 0.5.

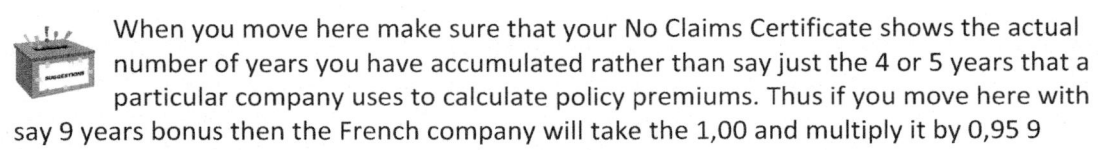

When you move here make sure that your No Claims Certificate shows the actual number of years you have accumulated rather than say just the 4 or 5 years that a particular company uses to calculate policy premiums. Thus if you move here with say 9 years bonus then the French company will take the 1,00 and multiply it by 0,95 9 times to arrive at a figure of 0,63 i.e. a bonus of 37%.

It is further complicated if you do unfortunately have an accident where you are to blame. For subsequent years the rate that you have achieved hitherto is then multiplied by 1,25 (although some companies will use 1,125 if they say both drivers were at fault). The bottom line is that making your first responsible claim doesn't mean you necessarily lose your bonus like as in the UK.

The other downside is that in France one cannot protect one's bonus, but if you have been at the maximum level for more than 3 years some companies will let you keep that bonus after your first responsible accident. As always with anything to do with insurance, it pays to shop around and look at the small print. Don't pay for features you don't need.

9.35.8 Number Plates

In the UK we are all familiar with the Vehicle registration plate *plaque d'immatriculation* format and, apart from personalised registrations, know how to tell the age of the car from its plate. That doesn't apply here and neither it would seem is there an interest in or market for personalised plates. The French don't seem to be into materialism as much as people are in the UK.

The number plates in France are set out with 7 alphanumeric characters vis:
2 letters, 3 numbers, 2 letters
this identification is allocated to the car and doesn't change, even when the car is sold.

Everyday Living, an A to Z

n.b. The right hand side of the plate sometimes contains a regional logo with the relevant *département* number below it.

> Consequently you can still keep the kids amused when out on a long journey by seeing who can spot the most *départemental* numbers on the various registration plates you pass.

Prior to 2009 the numbering system followed a different convention with registration numbers in the format of:

nnn aaa dd or
nnnn aa dd

`1233 DC 33`

where nnn/nnnn was a 3 or 4 digit number;
aa/aaa was a 2 or 3 letter group; and
dd indicated the *département* the car was registered in.

Exceptionally cars from Corsica were identified with a *département* of 2A or 2B (South or North) and those from the overseas territories had a 3-digit *département* number between 971 & 978.

> Vehicle owners must re-register their vehicle if they relocate permanently to another *département*.

9.35.9 Penalty Points

As in the UK any driving penalties in France are based on a points system. However the major difference is that here a driver normally starts with 12 points on their licence. Then depending on the seriousness of any offence between one and six points are deducted each time. There is a website that will explain the points lost for different offences (See Annex C).

9.35.10 Red Number Plates

Sometimes when you are driving around you will see the odd car with Red Number Plates. These plates have the letters and numbers in white and the right hand band of the plate displays what is actually an expiry date. There is a common misconception that these Red Number Plates are displayed on diplomatic cars but this is not the case. They are in fact temporary or '*Transit Temporaire*' plates which will generally be found on new cars that are going to be exported and on which TVA has not been paid, hence the expiry date on the plate.

n.b. Vehicles purchased in the free trade zones of *Gex* and *Savoie* (to the North and South of Geneva respectively) also carry red plates, but with the regional code.

9.35.11 Speed Limits

Driving in France these days can be a challenge. It is not just driving on the right hand side of the road that poses difficulties to those of us from the UK with left leaning tendencies (although I must say that having a left hand drive car makes the process of driving on the right immeasurably easier), but it is knowing what speed to drive at?

On motorways it is straightforward, the limit is 130kph or 110kph when it is raining (or over certain bridges) and under normal road conditions it is also illegal to drive less than 80kph in the fast lane. On dual carriageway's it is 110kph and 100kph when wet. But thereafter it is a whole lot more complicated. The reason being, in July 2018 the national limit on non dual carriageway roads (those without a central divider) outside of towns went down from

Everyday Living, an A to Z

90kph to 80kph in an attempt to reduce road casualties. However not all *départements* either agreed with this change nor had the wherewithal to change the road signs over, meaning that although the signs still showed 90kph the limit was actually 80kph. So far so complicated but it has got a whole lot worse. A year on M Phillippe (the then French Prime Minister) announced that Departmental councils could reinstate the former 90kph limit if they wished! However in France only some 10,000 kilometres of road are managed centrally and this proposed revision gives discretion to the approximately 380,000 kilometres of departmental roads leaving the 80km/h to continue to apply on national roads. Early indications were that although a majority of *départements* reverted to the former 90kph limit it was not unanimous, so speeds will vary from *département* to *département* and you can't necessarily rely on the signage.

As of December 2021 some 37 (mainly rural) *départements* had raised the speed limit back to 90kph. But only on their/local roads where the limit could conceivably be higher than the national limit. So confusion reigns. The message from all this is drive at a sensible speed, do not assume the limit is 90kph just because other motorists are travelling at that speed.

Note if visibility drops to below 50m then a limit of 50kph applies to **all** roads.

9.35.12 Speed Camera's

During the *Gilets Jaune*' protests and civil unrest that swept the country at the end of 2018 and early 2019 many ground sited speed camera's (some estimates say 80% of them) were destroyed/burnt out but these are slowly being replaced by Tower Radar's - more high-tech devices capable of monitoring the speeds of increased numbers of individual vehicles and various other potential transgressions e.g. drivers using mobile phones, not wearing seat belts or without insurance. It is therefore incumbent on me to point out that in France it is illegal to have a radar based speed camera detector in your car (even if it is not in use). There is an official government map showing the location of fixed speed camera's (See Annex C). To make things more difficult for motorists the Tower speed cameras have '*plug in*' electrics which can be shared among similar units. So the driver will not know whether a Tower is '*live*' or not!

signposted.

Be aware that it is not just Radar Towers/Speed traps that check your speed. There are a reported 400 or so unmarked radar cars driven by the Police, *Gendarmes* or privately contracted firms on behalf of the government to take into consideration throughout the majority of the country and these will operate 24/7.

9.35.13 Speeding Tickets

Brexit means that British drivers will now escape most speeding fines in the EU as *the EU Cross-Border Enforcement Directive* no longer applies and arrangements for sharing details of drivers caught by speed cameras has stopped. Equally the British authorities will not be able to send out fines to visiting European motorists who transgress. Being stopped by the Police/*Gendarmerie* is a different matter as they have the power to enforce on the spot fines or even confiscate your vehicle until the fine is paid!

The generally reduced speed limits in towns and villages actually apply from the start of the town/village sign – the rectangle with the place name in – even if there are no physical

Everyday Living, an A to Z

speed limit signs there. They are in force until you pass the rectangular sign with the place name crossed out.

In France, anyone caught travelling at more than 25km/hr above the speed limit can have their licence confiscated on the spot. Don't assume that any speeding tickets will wing their way to you immediately. A friend of ours got one 7 months after the incident. So long in fact that although he remembered the (long) trip they were making at the time he didn't have a clue as to which one of the four of them was driving at the time in the place it was issued.

9.35.14   Tyres

Sourced through your local garage, tyres tend to be a very expensive commodity in France, not only that but it is very hard for you to actually get a quote for just tyre fitting, garages always want to give you an all-inclusive price. If you need some the sensible approach seems to be to buy them on the internet where you will find them much cheaper and many of these national operators have links with local garages where you can not only have the tyres fitted but delivered to as well.

9.35.15   Use of Car Horns

We have all met those impatient drivers who sound their car horn in traffic jams or when things aren't going their way and if you are one of them be wary because France views the use of a car horn in a town centre quite differently to that of the UK. Yes you can warn another driver or pedestrian of some imminent danger but indiscriminate use of one's car horn can lead to a fine of 35€, increasing to 150€ if you don't pay within 45 days. Outside of town centres and built-up areas one can use one's horn if safety is involved, e.g. someone pulling out, an oncoming car on your side of the road or on blind corners where you might want to let potential oncoming vehicles know you are coming. Other than that you need to exercise restraint. This law was restated by the Supreme Court of Appeal a couple of years ago after a case involving someone who had used their horn in a built up area when there was no danger to their vehicle was escalated to them.

Ironically the same law is supposed to apply to anyone using their car horn to celebrate a wedding or winning a sporting match but I note that neither the court nor the local *gendarmerie* seemed too bothered on 15th July 2018 after France won the Football World Cup as our locals' celebrations continued long and late! Equally many wedding celebrations seem to include long and loud playing of car horns, but hey, I am just telling you what the letter of the law says.

9.35.16   Other

While you are out and about if you see a round white sign on the back of a car with a Red "A" on it, it stands for *apprenti*, meaning that the driver is newly qualified and has had his or her licence for less than 3 years.

Driving on Autoroutes at night in drizzle, fog, mist or rain can be quite tricky as the edges of the fast lane next to the central reservation and the slow lane next to the hard shoulder only have rumble strips in the white lining and do not have cats eyes that we are accustomed to in the UK, and neither are they used to separate individual lanes.

Everyday Living, an A to Z

⚠️ As a woman don't be surprised if you apply for a French Driving Licence and find it is issued in your maiden name! Yes this is likely to cause you problems if you need to rent a car as typically your passport and credit card will be in your '*borrowed*' i.e. married name.

9.35.16.1 Mountain Departments

If you are thinking of moving to one of the '*Mountain*' *Départements* (which practically effects some 4 dozen mountain communes) then as from the 1st November and until 31st March each year under the *Loi Montagne* it will be necessary to use Winter Tyres (on all 4 wheels) on any routes prescribed by the *préfecture*. On some routes it will also be mandatory to fit snow chains or snow socks to the driving wheels (as well as using Winter Tyres) and this will limit your speed to 50kph. Failure to comply will result in a fine and could result in your car being taken off the road. The aims being to improve safety and reduce risks of travelling on icy/snowy roads by making sure that all vehicles are suitably equipped and is applicable to any vehicle (commercial, private or public) with four or more wheels, even if you are only passing through.

Panneau B58: Entrée de zone d'obligation d'équipements en période hivernale

Panneau B59: Sortie de zone d'obligation d'équipements en période hivernale

9.36 Dustbins

If '*the one*' is in a commune that has more than 500 inhabitants you should find that your household rubbish *Ordures Ménagères* is collected on a weekly basis. Below that number of residents collection is not obligatory but is organised by the *Mairie*. If you are lucky then your dustbin will be provided by the commune otherwise the *Mairie* can request you purchase bins of specific size and colour. Irrespective, the *Mairie* will advise of the times that the bin can be put outside your property for collection. Beware, putting/leaving it there outside this time period can result in you being fined!

Some communes also provide households with a separate yellow lidded bin in which you can put packaging, paper and plastic out for collection along with the household rubbish. In addition, a lot of villages & towns have communal containers for recycling glass, packaging, paper and plastic. Containers for old/unwanted clothes are usually found in Supermarket Car Parks or you can take them to your local community tip *Déchetterie*, but as with all local matters the *Mairie* can advise. Anything electrical or bulky will also need to be taken to the *Déchetterie*.

Although use of the *Déchetterie* is free communes charge for their waste collection services through the *Taxe Foncière*. This may be itemised separately under an entry for TEOM *Taxe d'Enlèvement des Ordures Ménagères* but it is optional as some communes just aggregate it into their general budget.

It may not be common everywhere but our bin has what appears to be an RFID chip fitted so the waste management company can monitor your usage of collections – indeed our vendors told us there was an annual limit beyond which one was charged, although I have not verified this.

Everyday Living, an A to Z

9.37 Etiquette

9.37.1 Official

As you will find when you initiate correspondence with the Health System as well as any Wedding Certificate they will also likely request a Birth Certificate in your wife's maiden name. Thereafter it is not unusual to receive official correspondence in the form of M <Married name> *et* Mme <Maiden Name> or your wife to just receive letters in her maiden name. The Tax Office also refer to your wife by her maiden name on their correspondence and on your tax return as well.

9.37.2 Public

Despite their reputation as being rude the French people are actually very polite. People that you don't know, even groups of teenagers say hello *bonjour* to you as you meet them/are walking down the street and it is only courteous to reply in the same manner. Similarly when you enter a shop it is expected that you will say hello to the person serving so if they are not in front of you look around and direct your *bonjour madame/monsieur* to them, also say goodbye *au revoir* when you leave. Handshakes (pre-covid) are not uncommon, either for the first time of meeting or seeing someone on a more regular basis. If there are mixed sexes present then *bonjour messieurs dames* or just *messieurs dames* will suffice when you enter, similarly if you meet a couple when you are out.

It seems that *Bonjour* can be replaced by *Bonsoir* around 5pm although many older people will only ever say *Bonjour*, no matter what the time. Unlike in the UK Good Afternoon *Bonne Après-Midi* seems reserved for farewells rather than greetings.

If/when you meet someone you already know, albeit informally, it is customary to shake hands with them (assuming you are male).

9.37.3 Kisses

Friends and family also kiss (*la bise ou bisous*) when greeting each other and this extends to the male members too. The number of kisses range from two to even four depending on which part of the country you are in. By kisses I am just talking a light brush on the cheek whilst usually making a kiss sound rather than a real smacker! One falls into this approach quite quickly with the friends one makes but I have to say amongst our new circle of friends none of the (English) guys do it to each other!

9.37.4 Second Person Form

One area that can cause both confusion and offence in France is when one uses 'you' in the second person singular form. English has one construct whether it is singular or plural, French however uses *Tu* and *Vous* respectively. The singular form is used with friends, people you know really well, or children. Use *Vous* when you meet someone for the first time or confusingly if you are talking to two friends, a husband and wife perhaps.

If you use '*Tu*' in the wrong context it can be seen as disrespectful unless one has been invited to use it! A restaurant not too far from us even sacked a waiter because he was over familiar with its clientele, in other words he kept '*tutoying*' diners. It is therefore useful to know the verbs *tutoyer* – to speak with *tu* and *vouvoyer* – to speak with *vous*. There is even an expression that covers it would you believe, *on peut se tutoyer?* which means can we use *tu* with each other? (When we speak).

Everyday Living, an A to Z

9.37.5 Other

Note however, once you have moved in it is unlikely that there will be a constant stream of neighbours beating a path to your door to introduce themselves as it doesn't seem to be the French way, but you'll meet them in time. In fact you are more likely to receive visits from local Brits, particularly if you buy from one as the word will get out there are *'new ones in town'*. Some of these visits will be friendly in nature whereas others you sense are purely for them to promote their business.

9.38 Euro Notes

Banknote denominations across Europe are far higher than in the UK and there are 7 different value notes. 5€, 10€, 20€, 50€, 100€, 200€ and 500€ although the 500€ note is being phased out.

50€ notes are commonplace here and not treated with the suspicion that someone offering a £50 note in the UK is. I recently stood behind someone in a *Brico* who casually pulled out 3 such notes for 126€ purchase. The checkout woman just put them straight in the till without a second glance and that is not an unusual reaction to receiving one. The 50€ notes are also offered in ATM's unlike the UK. A second illustration of their attitude to large notes was when I was standing behind a builder in a DIY store who was buying some coving and 6 lots of mastic and he whipped out a 200€ note. The cashier didn't bat an eyelid neither did she give it any extra scrutiny - swipe it with a marker pen, put it under a UV light or even hold it up to the light. She just put it in the till and gave him the 120€ or so change!

9.39 Euromillions

If you are fond of a flutter then prize winning EuroMillions tickets bought in France must be claimed within 60 days rather than the 180 in the UK, and if you play using the 'Lucky Dip' feature, here you need to ask for a *flash*.

9.40 Eye tests

See Section 9.79 for more information.

9.41 Farmer's Cooperative

Something that you may not initially consider as they are not particularly widespread in the UK is the nearest Farmers' Cooperative *coopérative d'agriculteurs* (or sometimes just *agricole*) as a source of DIY products. Yes they can be agricultural in outlook but they will stock a wide range of e.g. Clothing, Electrical Items, Fencing, Paint, Plumbing Materials etc. and they are not as expensive as you might think and it could be that it is a lot closer to you than your nearest DIY store.

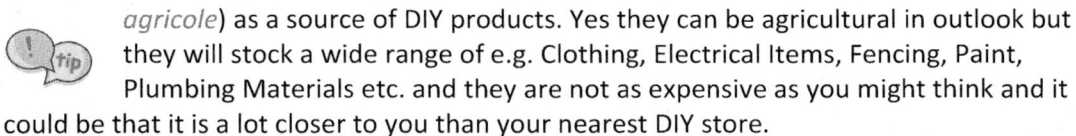

9.42 Fencing

Rigid wire/metal fence panels in Green, Grey or white are very common hereabouts and they have wide price differentials too. If you are budget conscious shop around by all means but don't assume that they are all (mounted) the same. Yes you have to concrete the posts into the ground but the fixing mechanism between post and panel differs depending on where you buy it, you can't mix and match. We bought as many panels as were in stock from a large DIY chain and got the balance from the *Brico* half of a local Hypermarket. Only

Everyday Living, an A to Z

when coming to use them did I find that they are totally incompatible so the Hypermarket stock had to be returned and we had to wait for the DIY store to be resupplied.

It is said that rescued dogs love freedom and are always trying to escape their boundaries. Keno is no exception. The metal fences I've put up do deter him but it is far too expensive to erect them around our entire boundary so there are other fences which are effectively just rolls of wire that have been unwound and staked into the ground every couple of metres or so. When he is on a scent he has a habit of putting his nose under these, lifting upwards and squeezing underneath to *'explore'* the land beyond. In these instances I have found that binding/wiring old decking planks to the bottom of the fence stop this behaviour as it is nigh on impossible for him to lift them up and get his body under them.

9.43 Film Classifications

If you decide to go out to the cinema in France, unless you are a fluent speaker, you will probably look for the initials VO *Version Originale* after the film title as it signifies that the film is in its original language (and this doesn't have to mean just English) although it may well have had French sub-titles added. Note the VF *version française* can mean that the version has been dubbed in French.

In terms of film classification it is otherwise similar to the UK, vis:
U (Tous publics) valid for all audiences.
12 (Interdit aux moins de 12 ans) forbidden in cinemas for under 12
16 (Interdit aux moins de 16 ans) or forbidden in cinemas for under 16.
18 (Interdit aux moins de 18 ans) forbidden in cinemas for under 18.
On Television there is also a **10** classification – unsuitable for children under 10.

9.44 Fishing Lakes

Angling is an extremely popular pastime in the UK and I know many fishermen would love to acquire a property with a lake with a view to setting up a fishing business here in France, but it is not as straightforward as you might expect. It is a complicated area but in summary:

9.44.1 Registration and Permits

Lakes in France must be registered with the Department of Agriculture (usually through one's *préfecture*) and fall into 2 different fishing categories (*catégorie piscicole*) each of which has different permit requirements and seasons:
1. Category 1 (*première catégorie*):
   These are mainly trout waters, and those with fish of the salmonidea group (salmon, trout, freshwater whitefish) requiring protection;
2. Category 2 (*seconde catégorie*):
   Covers all other rivers, canals and lakes.

Each year the seasons for the different categories change and to further complicate things they also differ depending on where you are in the country. You should be able to get the relevant information from your *Mairie* or failing that the National Fishing Federation (See Annex C).

If you want to come to France and fish then first off you need to get yourself a permit (*carte de pêche*) which contains your ID Photograph as it is illegal to try and fish without one. Fishing is managed at a regional level here and the sport is strictly policed, so it is important

Everyday Living, an A to Z

to get the correct type of permit as there are numerous types available.
e.g. Annual, Day or a 15-day *Carte Vacances* with different cards for youngsters too.

9.44.2 Potential Problems

I am told that there are three common mistakes people make when buying a lake in France, vis assuming:

1) That the rules don't apply to lakes if they are privately owned;
2) That the details will be covered by their *Notaire*; and
3) Everything is fine because it already operates as a fishing lake

(Make sure you have genuine and up to date documentation of both registration & category).

If you have to register a lake then ideally you want it to be recognised as Category 2 - Closed, and if there is no brook or stream running through the lake and/or there is no possibility of free movement of fish in and out of it then this should be straightforward. However even if you are told it is registered it may be subject to various restrictions such as *'fishing licences required'* or *'no night fishing'* and I would suggest that you don't want to discover this when the Water Police pay a visit and close the fishing down on the spot! Not to mention the heavy fines involved.

If you think that it could be possible to re-direct a stream so that you could become a *'closed'* lake you can't just do it as you have to formulate a project plan and submit a formal request and you could find this a costly process.

Two other problem areas arise when
1. Wanting to drain a lake (even partially) as you need to get permission (from the Department of Agriculture).
2. Restocking your lake as there are strict regulations around this (you will need to show receipts for and the provenance of your fish i.e. where you obtained them from, which will ideally be from an officially registered *pisciculture* business).

A couple I know with a lake unknowingly operated it on the fringes of legality as they believed what they had been told by the previous owner when they bought their property. When they came to have it formally inspected prior to putting their house on the market they were surprised to find that it would cost in the region of 40,000€ to rectify its deficiencies. So, *'caveat emptor'* again applies if you are considering a project with a lake.

9.45 France Connect

If you are accessing a Government website for the first time you will likely encounter a link to France Connect, a similar service to and like the *'GOV.UK Verify'* service in the UK. This is a government run service, with the motto *'Simplify access to your public services online'* that provides one with a mechanism to logon to various official websites. In principle the service guarantees a new potential users ID by accessing existing accounts for which their identity has already been verified to assure the new site of your identity. Currently, the system offers five identity providers:

- Ameli - The Health Insurance site;
- Impots.gouv.fr – The tax office site,

Everyday Living, an A to Z

- La Poste – Who can set you up with a Digital Identity;
- Mutualité Sociale Agricole - Providers of protection to agricultural workers; and
- Orange - Mobile Connect.

So once you are *'known'* to one of the above providers creating new government related accounts should be straightforward. This is all very well but if as in our case I setup the Online Tax and *Ameli* (Healthcare) accounts which effectively cover both of us. When Joanne tried to set up one on her own account it wasn't recognised. Consequently we tried to get an ID through France Connect for her to use when buying her car.

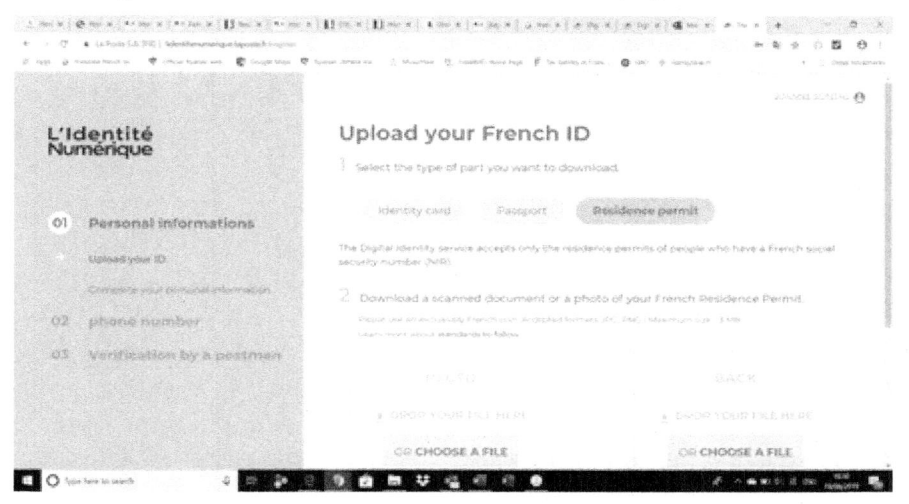

Note however that although *La Poste* allows one to create an account with them for general post related matters, to get a digital ID through them you need to be French, i.e. have an Identity Card, Passport or Residence Card. If you try and set it up using a UK driving licence or even a Carte Vitale it tells you that the system isn't available at the moment and to try again later!!!

9.46 France Services

Part of the Ministry of Territorial Cohesion, this very useful government service provides people with help, practical assistance and support with those various aspects of governmental administrative procedures that might be problematic for you, or in using a digital/online service through a multitude of *'one-stop'* shops nationwide. As of October 2021 there were >1750 local offices and the nationwide objective is for >2200 by end of 2022 such that everybody is within 30 minutes' drive of such an office.

It partners with other government departments e.g. the Ministries of Economy and Finance, the Interior, Justice, together with ANTS (Driving Licence & Vehicle Registration) CAF (Family Allowance) Health insurance, *La Poste*, Pension insurance, *Pôle emploi* (Jobcentre) RSA (DWP) and their trained agents will assist you with sorting out those day to day aspects of French life that you might otherwise have difficulty with.

9.47 Fuel Prices

There is a government run website (See Annex C) where one can check local fuel prices for your car. It is quite comprehensive as one enters

Everyday Living, an A to Z

- The type of fuel required;
- A place (Commune or Post Code);
- Type of supplier; and indeed
- The type of services offered.

to get a list of relevant stations displayed together with the price(s) and date and time the data was captured. What is also extremely handy is the fact that if you are making a trip somewhere you can obtain details of the prices on route.

9.48   Gas Supply

If you cook with gas or have gas fired heating you are probably used to gas just being there through the mains. Not so in rural France. In towns you are ok but elsewhere you may find your cooker uses propane gas (and you can obtain the cylinders from the local garage or supermarket, some of which have installed automatic dispensers so they are available 24/7) and the gas for your heating comes from a tank which is sited in your garden, either above or below ground. So far so good.

However should you wish to change gas suppliers because you find you can get it cheaper elsewhere you could be in for a nasty financial shock, as it seems that the tank is not actually yours but is owned by the Gas supply company. Not too bad if your tank is above ground but if it is buried below ground you can be charged upwards of 500€ for them to come and remove it. What is more your new company will then charge you some 100€ or more to install one of their tanks. When you factor these hidden charges into the cost of supply you may well find that your new deal is not as an attractive proposition as it first appeared.

9.49   Health & Safety

You will find that France has not been overtaken by the pervasive Health and Safety culture that has become commonplace in the UK, so you will find that there are not as many constraints. It is amusing/scary watching sometimes for example when you see two ladders up against the front of a house and a horizontal plank placed between them on the ladder stays for a tradesman/builder to attend the roof. Joanne is convinced that I have adopted this *laissez-faire* attitude to my work but I think that is just because she times her arrival at my worksite as I am tripping over a tool or extension lead that I had temporarily forgotten was there in my desire to complete the job.

Our house, which the previous owners had operated as a B&B, had a veranda at the rear, which because of the slope of the garden beyond had anywhere between a 6 to 10 foot drop along its length. However there were no railings or fence of any description along its edge – *Laissez faire* again springs to mind. Its absence did help both dogs on different occasions when they decided to go off the veranda to chase a feral cat but wouldn't help any guest who was a bit uncertain on their feet or indeed anyone if they had over imbibed. Needless to say we took a more conservative view when replacing the structure and had it done properly.

Everyday Living, an A to Z

9.50 Healthcare

One particularly good source of free information about health matters in France can be found here.

https://www.santepubliquefrance.fr/docs/livret-de-sante-bilingue-francais-anglais

This is an extremely useful and above all bilingual handbook, that is in excess of 200 pages, but explains your way around the health system here in France. The subject matter is laid out with French on the left and the translated English text on the right of each page, and is laid out in colour coded sections covering; Access to healthcare, Health, Useful Information and Abbreviations so as your confidence and knowledge of the language grows you can easily start to expand your vocabulary.

9.51 Holiday Absences

As in the UK if you are going away on holiday you can advise the Police/*Gendarmerie* to look out for your property during your absence (some forces will even include second homes). They will keep an eye on your property each day, including evenings and weekends. To arrange it download the appropriate form (Operation *Tranquillité Vacances*) Item R41033 from the Service Public website (See Annex C).

Complete the form and take it along with your proof of address to the police station/*gendarmerie*. For a copy of the form see Annex E.
n.b. You need to give at least 48-hours notice, or 5 days in Paris.

9.52 Home Visits

Do you have grown up children? Are they comfortable with you moving to France? Do you or they worry about your aging? If so then they may be reassured by a service recently offered by *La Poste*. The fall in the amount of mail caused by increased use of email and text messaging has resulted in excess capacity for them. As a result they have created a service *Veiller sur mes parents* (Watch over my parents) which can help. For currently less than 20€ a month the local postman/lady will pop in and have a brief chat with people up to 6 times a week whilst out on their rounds. It potentially overcomes loneliness and assures their well-being. The staff have been given special training and families provide a list of contacts locally who can help out in the event of problems arising. The relatives themselves are messaged through an '*App*' that gives updates about the family member and whether anything is needed.

9.53 Hospitals

So the worst happens and one of you needs a hospital or you think that when you see your doctor they may refer you to one. If you don't know where your nearest one is prior to your arrival in France then I suggest in the case of an accident that you will quickly be searching for it online or driving to the town where you have been told it is. Don't be confused by naming conventions as here in France the hospital name may have a number of abbreviations before it. e.g.

CH	*Centre Hospitalier*	Standard Hospital
CHR	*Centres Hospitaliers Régionaux*	Regional Hospital

Everyday Living, an A to Z

CHRU	Centres Hospitaliers Régionaux et Universitaire	Regional Hospital providing teaching & research in addition to normal care
CHU	Centres Hospitaliers Universitaire	Teaching Hospital

Once there and parked if you are looking for A&E type services then you need to look out for and follow signs for '*Urgences*'.

Note - Hospitals now make a fixed charge of 18€ for all attendees at A&E *Urgences* who aren't subsequently admitted. The charge is not reimbursable by the state but the majority of *mutuelles* will cover it. This doesn't apply to people with long-term health conditions or women who are 6 months pregnant or more.

9.54 House Numbers

If you walk down a French street you sometimes see the words '*Bis*' in the context of house numbers, e.g. 7bis. When it comes to addresses it means a second house/shop etc of the same number as another one. So a second No 7 in a particular street calls itself 7a in English and 7bis in French (pronounced *'sept biss'*) or 7½ in the USA.

Equally '*Ter*' means a third house/shop so a third 7 would be 7b in English and 7ter *'sept ter'* in France.

n.b. In other contexts, '*bis*' means '*encore*' and it's what concert audiences shout when they want one from a performer.

9.54.1 Number Allocation

As part of introducing fibre optic broadband, at least here in the *Corrèze*, all of the Communes have put up new roadsigns and allocated house numbers. A lengthy job when you consider that most of the house hereabouts are known by house names. So our house name in the address we used for 3½ years has been replaced by no. 36. The thing is there are only 2 other houses in our road, numbers 248 and 503. Bizarre I know but apparently the numbers are allocated in relation to the distance (in metres) the house is from a road junction. Although how you know which end to start counting from......?

9.55 Hunting

Hunting has a long history in France and it polarises public opinion as much as it does in the UK but I will leave the ethical & moral arguments aside for this section as it is a way of life for many people in rural France where it has long been a subsistence activity like fishing.

I mentioned its' popularity earlier and there are almost 1¼m registered hunters, principally male and more than 50% of whom are over 55 years of age, more than any other European country. There is a strong hunting lobby and President Macron is an open supporter of it and has halved the cost of national licence fees and allowed more flexibility on hunting dates and animal quotas to encourage more people to hunt.

9.55.1 Getting Licenced

If you want to hunt in France then you need to obtain a *permis de chasser* (either National or Departmental) and these are awarded by the ONCFS (*Office National de Chasse et de la Faune Sauvage*) or Departmental Hunting Federations. To get one you need to pass a two part examination, theory and practical, although such a *permis* is valid for life it is granted

Everyday Living, an A to Z

for a set time-period within a geographic area every year and it needs to be validated and renewed every year (in 2021 it cost 54€) before the start of the hunting season. To be validated one needs to supply details of one's insurance.

To take the exam an obligatory training course is required and candidates need to be at least 15 years old. One can't progress to the practical element until the theory has been passed. The theory includes questions based on knowledge of the following:
- **Wildlife** (recognition of game and protected species, biology and an animals' way of life);
- **Hunting** (vocabulary, different techniques, knowledge and use of hunting dogs);
- **Rules and laws** (concerning hunting policies and nature protection); **and**
- **Arms and munitions**, (their use and associated security rules).

To pass the theory examination a candidate needs to score more than 75% including correct answers to 2 questions on security. If successful, candidates have a further 18 months to pass the practical exam which has three parts:
- **Hunting simulation** (shooting with blanks);
- **Target Shooting** (of either black or red targets representing animals than can be hunted or animals or protected species that can't be hunted respectively); and
- **Moving Targets** (shooting thereof).

Anyone exhibiting any dangerous behaviours is automatically failed and again more than 75% is required to pass. Once the licence is awarded a prospective hunter must obtain insurance (*Assurance obligatoire de responsabilité civile*) known as RC, and is basically civil liability insurance. Proof of cover must be shown annually to have one's *permis* validated.

n.b. A 15 year old who passes the test can only hunt if they have a guardian with them; and
In 2019 the law changed to introduce obligatory refresher training every 10 years.

9.55.2 Starting and Stopping

In 2020, summer had officially finished although the still warm days were keeping the advance of autumn at bay but all across the land a certain number of blood-thirsty Frenchmen (and a very few women) had started salivating over the impending start of the hunting season.

The start and finish times of the season itself vary by *Département* but it approximately runs from September to February. See Annex C for further information. Legally some 90 different species of animal can be hunted but there are limits to the numbers within a species and these limits are either applied Nationally or Locally (as determined by the *Préfecture*) dependent on the species itself.

9.55.3 Practicalities

The French *Code de l'environnement which covers* ecology and rural life means that no one can hunt or has the right to hunt on other people's property without the consent of the owner. However, often hunting is carried out on land by default and the onus is on the landowners to take action to prevent it, on the grounds of moral objection. So, if you own land and want to stop the local hunters traipsing over it in pursuit of animals to kill you need to get a ban in place. How one accomplishes this depends on who has jurisdiction over hunting in one's area.

Everyday Living, an A to Z

7If it is under the auspices of a *société de chasse* which is a simple association or club you can get the hunt banned by sending a letter to the local *société* President and copying your mayor. (Maybe for good measure you copy the local *Gendarmerie* commandant too?)

On the other hand if the local hunt is managed by an organisation approved by the *préfecture*, called an ACCA (*association communale de chasse agrée*) the process is more complicated unless the land in question is within 150m of your house or it is completely fenced. In this instance it is best to seek advice from ASPAS or the LPO (See Annex C).

9.55.4 Safety Rules

Of continued nationwide concern is the number of hunting related accidents each year, 131 in 2019 alone and sadly with 7 fatalities according to the ONCFS. Of those 131 people involved, 22 were neither hunters nor involved in hunting, and neither was one of the fatalities. The ONCFS go on to state that most accidents are apparently linked to the hunters failing to observe basic safety rules. These are:

- When hunting the *Chasseurs* must wear some high visibility clothing (at least in almost 70 *Départements* although in the others it is merely recommended);
- To only shoot in a 120° Arc (i.e. the green/light grey area illustrated below) to their front at any time;
- To **NOT** shoot in the direction of roads, paths or public places;

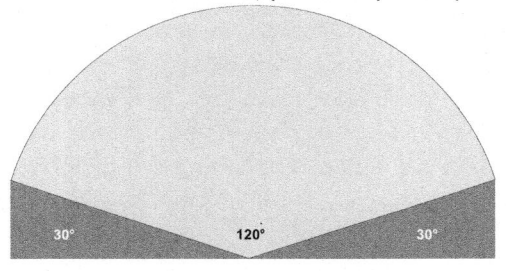

- To put out signs to warn the public when/where they are; and
- To NOT shoot within 150m of a house.

Practically boar are unlikely to attack you as their sense of smell is so acute they can smell you up to 500 metres away. They will avoid you because they are scared of humans (for good reason). But if you decide to take a weekend walk in the woods during hunting season I would also recommend:

- To stay on paths and do not cross into other areas;
- Wear bright coloured clothing;
- Do not let any dogs off lead;
- Put bright collars on your dogs and/or bells on their collars; and
- Checking with your *Mairie*, Commune Website or local hunt to see if they have any information as to where they intend hunting that day.

9.55.5 Accidents

9.55.5.1 2020/21 – Hunting Season

Despite these rules safety continues to be a huge concern, both to Hunters and Householders alike. Indeed during the official start of the hunting season in *Corrèze* in 2020 (on 13 Sep) a rifle bullet ended up in the stairwell of a house although fortunately nobody

Everyday Living, an A to Z

was injured. Needless to say a complaint was filed by the inhabitants and an investigation was setup to determine whether the bullet was fired directly or ended up there by ricochet.

The following weekend, a Dutch tourist who was a passenger in a car travelling down the A63 in Landes, South West France, was hospitalised after being airlifted from the scene because he was shot in shoulder through his car window. The local *gendarmerie* and prosecutors believe he was the victim of a hunting accident as the local hunt were out after wild boar. Luckily his wounds were not deemed life-threatening. In a third incident, a bullet had crossed the passenger compartment of a car which was then traveling on the D11 in the direction of Bidache-St Palais and the legal proceedings following the investigation revealed five breaches of security rules.

It was out of these concerns that I had occasion to meet with our local hunting society to understand their ways, I found it both enlightening and frightening in equal measure. You can read about it in Annex G.

On Wednesday 2nd December in the Lot in *Occitanie* a French man in his mid-twenties was chopping wood on his property, 100 metres from his house when he was shot dead by a stray bullet fired by a hunter on a wild boar hunt. A couple of days later the apparent shooter was charged with manslaughter. He faces between 3 and 5 years in prison.

9.55.5.2   *2021/22 – Hunting Season*

In October 2021 the French news channel (TF1) stated there have been 4000 hunting accidents in the last 20 years in France.

On the 28th October 2021 a 29-year-old man was shot in the chest while walking on a hiking path with his mother near a hunt in Haute-Savoie *Département*.

Two days later a 67-year-old man was rushed to hospital in a critical state after being hit by a ricocheting bullet while driving on a dual carriageway 15 kilometres south of Rennes. The 9.3mm bullet was fired by a hunter aiming at a deer in wooded countryside and fields alongside the RN137 but the bullet ricocheted off a stone causing it to change trajectory '*by 90 degrees*', crossing through the hedges alongside the road before hitting the poor driver. His uninjured passenger managed to steer the vehicle to the roadside and park before contacting the emergency services. The man sadly died later from his injuries.

The hunter who fired the shot was taken into police custody and subsequently charged with manslaughter.

5 local *Maires* then wrote to the *Préfet* asking that the authorities take '*all necessary measures to guarantee the public safety of their citizens*' and stating that this should include national discussions '*to define necessary legislation for public safety during hunts*', including requirements for hunters such as eye tests and new conditions for obtaining permits. They also called for restrictions on the organisation of hunts, such as greater distancing from populated areas and possible non-hunt days.

Coincidentally at the same time, a petition organised by the *Un Jour Un Chasseur* (One Day a Hunter collective) – created by the friends and associates of the *Lotois* man killed in December the previous year, and calling for two hunt-free days in France gained more than 100,000 signatures, meaning its proposals will now be debated in the *Sénat*. The petition

Everyday Living, an A to Z

demanded the implementation of the following measures and the in-depth modification of laws that clearly do not guarantee one's safety or well-being, i.e:
- a. Sunday and Wednesday without hunting;
- b. Stricter training and strengthening of safety rules;
- c. Control and monitoring of hunting weapons and risky behaviour;
- d. Criminal sanctions commensurate with the crimes committed; and
- e. Freedom of speech and recognition of the victims of hunting by the State.

Nevertheless, regulation of hunting activity in France is beset with problems. Not least of which is that some ¾ of its' forests and woodland (c 12m ha in total) is in the hands of approximately 3 million private owners. These private individuals are at liberty to grant hunting licenses to whomever they wish in exchange for controlling boars in particular (a female boar can gestate up to ten babies). Hence the many pieces of woodland that you encounter with *Défense d'Entrer* or *Chasse* signs on it.

Within forested areas boars are not a problem as they eat acorns, berries, earthworms, leaves, mushrooms, roots, snakes, twigs etc. They need water to drink and like elephants and hippo's they like to roll around in any available mud. However they threaten farmer's livelihood's because they can munch through their crops or damage them. Hence the reason why hunting is actively encouraged.

So if you like the look of a property and think it's '*the one*' but have concerns about hunting try and meet the owners in person if possible and ask them about hunting in the vicinity. Ask the agent to find out as well. Although hunting is permitted and part of the French way of life you'd like to think that a good agent should be upfront about the advantages and disadvantages of any property even if it means they might lose the sale. But one shouldn't ignore the bleeding obvious! Drive around looking for Chasse signs at the entrance to nearby woods/forests to consolidate your view of the house and area.

9.55.6 Weapon Control

Unrelated to this, the first half of 2022 will coincidentally see the introduction of a new registration system for guns, the intention being to simplify the application process for a firearms licence, crackdown on fraud and make it easier to track weapons. New purchasers along with all types of holders of existing weapons will need to setup an account and register on a new weapons computer system *système d'information sur les armes* (SIA) by 1st July. They then need to submit identification documents, and register the serial number of their weapon. SIA will then check applicants criminal records, police files, as well as any psychiatric history and highlight people trying to buy using fake or third party documents. Weapon sellers will then know whether they are legally able to sell a firearm to a given customer. Future checks and licence updates will then be made annually as opposed to just at the time of purchase.

The new system is set to speed up processing and remove the risk of document loss.

9.56 Inheritance

This does not constitute financial advice! Just be aware that there is no Inheritance Tax between spouses in France but it is not possible to disinherit one's children so they are all entitled to inherit a proportion of their parents' estate. However matters are further

Everyday Living, an A to Z

complicated with re-marriages particularly if Step-children are involved so proper estate planning is essential, you should employ the services of a professional.

9.57 Insurance

Cancelling French Insurance used to be quite complicated compared with the UK but the passing of the *Loi Hamon* in 2014, effective from the 1st January 2015 made things more straightforward as it served to strengthen consumer rights.

What used to happen was that in the first instance it was necessary to send your insurer notice of your intended cancellation by registered letter. Depending on the circumstances behind the cancellation you then found that the required notice period varied e.g. so if you wanted to change:

- At the anniversary date (*Date d'échéance*),
  you needed to give 2 months written notice before the actual policy renewal date;
- Because your premium or policy excess changed adversely
  then you had up to a month after receiving notice of same (but your policy, and thus your premiums, did not stop for a further month after receipt of the instruction); or
- Because you have sold your car,
  then you cancelled it on the day the car is sold because you simply sent them a copy of the *certificat de cession d'un véhicule d'occasion*, as without the appropriate paperwork it is illegal for the company to stop the insurance contract before its anniversary date.

As this 2-month rule was quite punitive since the start of 2015 you can cancel your car/house **but not health** insurance anytime you want providing you have held the policy for at least a year. Under the *Loi Hamon* one simply writes to the House Insurer and the policy is cancelled a month and 3 days after receipt. As for Car Insurance any new insurer can cancel your old policy, but you as an individual can't because Car Insurance is a legal obligation in France and, simply put, the government doesn't trust individuals in this respect.

n.b. If you decide to change to a new company because they have given you a more advantageous quote you need to be careful if they say that they will notify your existing company and you need to keep on top of things. I say this because a friend ended up paying 2 premiums (their old one and new one) for a short period of time as the new company weren't quite as diligent as they should have been.

If your house has shutters you need to make sure they are locked shut when you go out, particularly if you are away from the house for 24 hours or more as not doing so may invalidate your household insurance policy.

9.58 Ivy

Ivy *lierre* is quite copious in our commune both on the ground and on trees and the ivy in our garden is quite prolific as well. Although for me it is just a parasite and best left alongside holly at Christmas. When it establishes a stranglehold on a tree its additional weight combined with the larger profile it creates can act like a sail and lead to the tree's downfall in high winds and if it and the tree get covered in moss it can be really hard to spot. It grows quite vigorously and when I see it strangling the life out of a majestic oak tree

Everyday Living, an A to Z

I just want it gone and so I have made it my mission these past 5 winters to slowly excise it from all the trees in our garden if at all possible.

That is easier said than done as we are not talking a little snip with some secateurs, because our ivy can be as thick as your arm when you have been weight training, and generally needs both a chainsaw and crowbar to remove it. As well as any tools that you might choose to use for the job I would strongly recommend that you wear a hat and a mask, even eye protection if you have a sensitive disposition and possibly take an anti-histamine too to avoid any residual problems. Reason being is that long established ivy gives off fumes/dust that can cause respiratory problems or sore throats, been there, done that, read the book, got the T-Shirt! For this reason you should not burn it either once it's been removed but take it to the *déchetterie* instead.

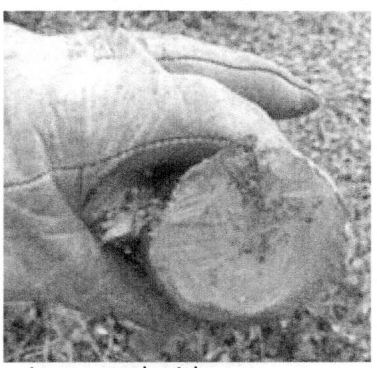

If you feel you have too much ivy on your trees where possible just cut a 12" section out near the root and it will slowly die off over the year. If you can't wait attach it to a rope and to your mower and pull it off in one. Pulling off Ivy when it is or has just rained is a good idea as it greatly reduces the amount of dust that is generated – although you can get much wetter doing it at this time.

When you have achieved your objective in removing the ivy you will find something definitely satisfying about passing said tree some six months on and seeing it totally rejuvenated with new unencumbered growth.

9.59   Junk Mail

A curse as in any country. If you want to opt out of receiving large volumes of unsolicited post write *Pas de Pub(licité)* on your postbox. Also adding *pas de démarchage* to your door/gate will let it be known that you do not want any canvassers to call.

9.60   La Rentrée

It seems that school children no sooner break up for the Summer Holidays (start of July) than adverts start appearing for *La Rentrée*. These days this French tradition not only refers to the return to school in September but also the return to the office/work after the summer break, as it still seems like all of France goes on holiday in August. It basically heralds the return of one's normal routines and social life.

Radio adverts work *La Rentrée* into their promotions at every opportunity and these continue through to the end of September. The written media gets in on the act too. Bookstores offer relevant Books and Stationery, DIY stores advertise for example storage solutions so one can stay organised. Supermarkets push Books, PC's, Stationery and even Wine! I have also seen Estate Agents introduce it to talk about being able to buy properties near schools. After a while the adverts seem as ubiquitous as those that are produced for 'Black Friday'.

Over and above that other retailers use it to announce promotion periods, for example various local opticians introduced it into their material in 2020.

Everyday Living, an A to Z

There is an argument that this somewhat celebratory approach to *La Rentrée* actually helps schoolchildren as much store is placed on their progression through the school and their growing up rather than seeing the end of the summer holidays as a bad thing.

9.61   Lavage/Laverie

This would be deemed an oddity in the UK as we have launderettes in towns but here it is possible to drive along and see a purpose-built housing usually containing a couple of washing machines (of differing capacities) and a tumble dryer either by the side of the road/in the vicinity of a supermarket. Often people deposit their washing/drying here, set the machines running (the wash cycles supply their own powder) and pop off to the shops before returning at the end of the cycle to collect and/or dry their loads.

This may be entirely specific to our area as there are often large transient communities associated with equestrian events or apple picking in the local orchards who can take advantage of these permanent features. However if one has large quilts or multiple dog beds, towels etc. these facilities are ideal for residents too.

9.62   Les Routiers

Travel down any main road here for long enough and you are sure to pass one of these establishments. Founded in the 1930's it was originally setup to provide information for professional truck drivers. It has since expanded its horizons and today it encompasses some 1,600 unassuming restaurants that belong to the *Chaîne des Relais Routiers* that nowadays caters for all types of road user. Offering simple hearty (non fast) food served at tables that are generally adorned with paper tablecloths and with just 2 or 3 choices per course at a modest price. But it is not just food, users get access to warm showers and safe parking facilities. *Les Routiers* publish an annual pocket guide to help drivers locate sites and companies frequently have accounts with them for their employees to lunch here whilst working.

9.63   Letterboxes

Many letterboxes in France are actually that, a physical box rather than a slit in the door. You will find that the standard French letterbox is 34 cm long * 26cm wide * 26cm high and are sold with locks that can be opened by the postman's master key. This is convenient as it means that parcels can be deposited in there if you are out. Equally you will find they have passkeys to the hallways of some apartment blocks where all resident letterboxes are situated.

Obviously this is not applicable in towns but in a lot of rural locations one's letterbox will likely be situated on the left-hand side of one's drive so that the postman *facteur* can deliver your mail without getting out of their van!

9.64   Linky Meters

As in the UK electrical generating companies are in the process of installing Smart meters to monitor a household's electrical consumption. The Smart/Linky meters themselves are actually installed by Enedis, the company responsible for managing the electricity distribution network in France, rather than the generating companies themselves. The

Everyday Living, an A to Z

advantages over a traditional meter are that the Linky measures actual consumption in real-time which should mean that one's bill is calculated as accurately as possible.

9.65 Loir

This is not to be confused with the longest river in France, what I am talking about here is the so called *'edible'* dormouse that resembles a small squirrel but is in fact a domestic pest. They may look cute but if you find them in or around your property you could be in for a whole heap of trouble. Some friends on the other side of our village were renovating an old cottage and experienced strange sounds coming from their roof at night. Investigation uncovered a couple of these creatures trying to eat their way through the plasterboard. They made that more difficult for them by judicious placement of chicken wire at floor level behind the plasterboard in the roof to restrict their access. However that wasn't the end of it as having been ejected from the roof they found that the *loir* shifted their attention to downstairs. Them turning the lights off and going up to bed sent an open invitation for the *loir* to come out of their nest and run around the lounge.

Over the next couple of months the couple persevered with different types of trap but to no avail. They also tried the ultra sticky pads you can buy to trap them but you then have to dispose of it and its live captive. As our friend is an ex-military man he told me it was natural for him to then think about using an air-rifle to despatch them. You may think this extreme but if I report that in 2020 he had killed 45 of them in that year alone you will realise that seeing one or two means you might well have a large colony to deal with. Luckily for them the incursions have now stopped.

With rodents you are rarely talking about 1 or 2, for example earlier in 2020 Joanne tidied the two rooms in the upstairs of our barn to make an office and therapy room. We saw evidence of mice in the office and since then I have trapped 19 of them and it can feel never ending.

9.66 Lotissements

Literally meaning a subdivision, you may come across these *Lotissements* whilst driving around. They are the equivalent to the various property development sites in England, although generally on a much smaller scale. They result from an enterprise acquiring a plot of land and subdividing them into *parcelles* on which they build pretty similar size houses. With smaller developments and in smaller communes the sales may be facilitated by the *Mairie* but on larger sites or in the *Grande Villes* it is the developer who sells them. The advantage for anybody buying a house on a *Lotissement* as opposed to an individual plot of land and developing it themselves is that with the *Lotissement* one will likely find that Electricity, Gas, Internet, Sewage (Possibly), Telephone and Water is generally already connected to the site if not the plot/property. One just has to take out a contract with the appropriate supplier, whereas with a DIY build you may find the cost of connectivity in some areas can be quite expensive. There is also likely to be a fire hydrant nearby for the pompiers to use should the need arise.

Generally speaking, an estate will have a particular set of rules and communal charges for lighting, maintenance of the septic tanks etc.

Everyday Living, an A to Z

9.67 Maire

There are more than 36,000 Communes in France each with an elected *Maire* who as the administrative head of the commune chairs the municipal council. They are elected for 6 year terms and are likely to be someone well-known and with standing in the community, someone prominent in business perhaps or a local personality. The *Maire* of our village is a business man and that of the local town a practicing physiotherapist.

The *Maire*, address them as *Monsieur/Madame Le/La Maire*, is in charge of the day to day running of the Commune with help from their deputies *adjoints* and the town/village council *conseil municipal*. Together they set the rate for and receive local taxes (*Fonciere & Habitation*), help with planning applications, hold registers of birth's, marriages and deaths and are responsible for nursery and primary schooling, roads, sport and culture in the commune. As well as their secretariat they are also a great source of local information as they have a wealth of knowledge about people, places, rules and regulations. Get to know them, they will be a great help to you.

Don't make the mistake of taking a bottle or two of whiskey (or some such) with you when you meet your *Maire* for the first time. Simply because he won't know you and he may misinterpret your intentions and report you to the *Gendarmerie* for attempted bribery!

9.68 Mairie

The workplace of your *Maire* (equivalent to the Town Hall) and They are also the first port of call if you find a stray dog.

An approach I used in my consultancy days was to get to know and be friendly with the receptionists, secretariat and security staff of any company I was contracted to – *'friends in low places'* as one of my non PC brethren used to say, but it would pay dividends during my assignment. This approach certainly holds true with the *Mairie* and its staff (and equally with any barman/server as you can never be sure when it might be useful). In my experience I would say it is definitely beneficial and pays multiple dividends to foster a good relationship with your local *Mairie*.

Maybe because of this approach our secretariat are extremely helpful and will readily give you copies of any paperwork you need to supply them with, including in A3 colour without hesitation, questioning, or charging like you would expect in the UK.

Note that in the smaller/quieter communes you may well find that the *Mairie* is only open in the mornings or the afternoons rather than all day.

9.69 Marianne

Much as the Cockerel is the national symbol of France and it is proudly displayed on the shirts of their Football & Rugby teams you won't find it on anything official, e.g. from your CPAM, on your DMP or from the Tax Office. Instead you will find *'Marianne'* on the envelope. *Marianne* originates from the days of the French Revolution as *'she'* symbolises the French

Everyday Living, an A to Z

Republic and as a *'Goddess'* of Liberty represents the values in the motto Liberty, Equality, Fraternity. As such a picture of Marianne receives a place of honour in the town halls and official buildings of the French Republic. The profile also appears on official government documents, stamps, and on French coins. There is also a famous sculpture - The Triumph of the Republic - in *Place de la Nation* in Paris and a statue of her in *Place de la République.*

9.70   Mediatheque

As its' name implies these media libraries provide information facilities on a variety of media for people to consult, view and possibly borrow for home consumption. In larger communes they are usually sited close to the *Mairie.*

9.71   Money Transfers

If you have attended any property shows or carried out any research at all about moving here then you should be aware that when it comes to buying a foreign property or making regular cost of living transfers it doesn't matter how helpful they are or what sort of relationship you have with them, do **not** use your bank for this service. Please use a Foreign Exchange broker as you will get a far far better rate.

Why? Some reasons being that it is not necessarily a bank's prime specialism, you won't necessarily get a dedicated resource/contact to use, brokers work with different margins and can usually provide far better rates and they won't charge you fees to make the transfer. Many of them offer live exchange rate feeds that you can look at on your smartphone or laptop. If you don't believe me then make a couple of calls on buying varying potential amounts and compare the results.

Be careful. FX Companies may advertise being commission free but offer relatively poor exchange rates. When making comparisons ask how many euro's your pounds will buy or vice versa once all charges have been taken? Thereafter look at the convenience of making transfers, how quickly you will receive your money and/or what transaction limits there are to see if it is suitable for you. It is vital that you understand both that exchange rates can move very quickly and how significant such movements can be in relation to your available funds. Most importantly how is your money safeguarded? All Money transfer bodies in the UK have to be FCA-registered.

9.71.1 Hedging

Something also to consider if you are concerned about exchange rates fluctuating due to political and stock market influences, or even if your purchase will not materialise for some months, is to secure today's rate in the future and take out a *'Forward Contract'*, which is also known as Hedging. The name comes from the traditional hedge surrounding a field, it just means putting a barrier round your potential losses. In currency terms that means fixing your exchange rate at a level that allows you to fulfil your plans, lest the exchange rate moves against you to such an extent that you can longer afford to fulfil them. In simple terms it is like a *'Buy now pay later'* deal where you guarantee your future buying rate for an upfront payment (usually c5% of the total) even if you don't have all of the necessary funds available at the time you take it out. That is certainly something that worked in our favour. I secured a 4-month forward purchase to buy our house, if I hadn't, by the time I actually needed the money the exchange rate had decreased 9.2% and so the house would have been more expensive, happy days!

Everyday Living, an A to Z

9.72 MOT's

The French equivalent of an MOT is the *Contrôle Technique* and it is applicable to all cars over 4 years old. There are differences to the UK system in that the tests are valid for 2 years but you will not be sent a reminder that it is due (and there is a 135€ fine for non-attendance). As of May 2018 the test was made more stringent than previously as regards vehicle safety and pollution control and there are now more than 600 control points as against over 450 previously.

There are 3 outcomes to the test. Success means that your log book *Carte Grise* is updated accordingly and you get a sticker for your windscreen which also states the date the next test is due.

Of the 2 types of failure, cars that don't pass are either classed as *'unfavourable'* which means the owner has 2 months to get the necessary repairs made and to re-submit the car for a retest. Their *Carte Grise* is stamped with a letter *'S'* to indicate this. If the faults are serious then the car is classed as *'critique'* meaning that it cannot legally go back on the road until repaired. An 'R' sticker is placed on your windscreen and you are only able to use it on the road for the remainder of the day, except for being able to drive it to a garage for repair within 24 hours of the test. The control centres themselves don't undertake repairs, and are prevented from doing so by law.

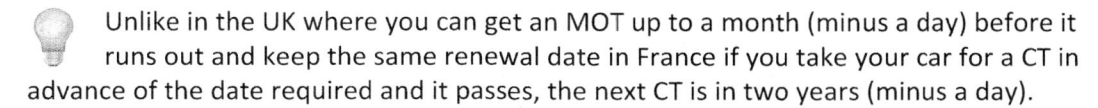

Unlike in the UK where you can get an MOT up to a month (minus a day) before it runs out and keep the same renewal date in France if you take your car for a CT in advance of the date required and it passes, the next CT is in two years (minus a day).

9.73 Municipal Elections

9.73.1 Communal Elections

Note If you are British and living in France but don't have a dual nationality then you can no longer vote in the municipal or European elections. But for information purposes here is what happens:

Unlike the UK with its tradition of Thursday polling elections in France generally take place on a Sunday and locally they allow the residents to elect members of the City Council in each commune. These are called *conseillers municipaux* (city councillors) and their number depends on the size of the local population, i.e.

Number of inhabitants	< 100	< 500	< 1500	< 2500	< 3500	< 5000	< 10,000	< 20,000	< 30,000	< 40,000
Number of councillors	7	11	15	19	23	27	29	33	35	39

Once elected it is the municipal council who elect the mayor, who then chairs the council, as well as deputies to the Mayor. The Mayor, their deputies and the councillors then serve for a term of 6 years although a Mayor can resign or be superceded in the unfortunate event of their death without triggering new municipal elections.

When a new municipal council is elected, their first meeting is held, by law, no earlier than the first Friday and no later than the first Sunday after the election.

Everyday Living, an A to Z

A couple of quirks of the municipal system are that:
- The council is initially chaired by its oldest member before they appoint the mayor and deputies.
- The Mayor is elected by a majority of votes
however, if the number of votes of the councillors is the same for more than one candidates, the older person is appointed!

Where there are less than 1,000 electors in a commune one votes for either individual candidates or candidates (with similar views) from a list. To win a seat in this first round of voting a candidate must obtain more than 50% of the total votes. Because of the list system this may apply to more than one councillor, the other councillors then enter a second round (which generally takes place the following week). At which point seats are given to those who obtain the most votes.

9.73.2 Communal Elections

While municipalities can concern themselves with any subject of local interest, the situation is different for regions and departments, whose competencies are defined by law.

There are 13 regional councils in metropolitan France (including Corsica) and 92 departmental councils. Overseas, Guadeloupe and Réunion each have a regional council and a departmental council, while Martinique, French Guiana and Mayotte are unique communities. Departmental elections (formerly called cantonal elections) and Regional elections are two separate elections normally held every 6 years to renew the composition of regional and departmental councils. However the next set of elections in this 6 year cycle (2027) will clash with the presidential elections that year and so have been deferred to 2028. So representatives have currently been appointed for 7 years.

Regions are concerned with economic development, non-urban transport (e.g the TER train and coach network), regional (land use) planning, Sport & Culture, vocational training and have responsibility for the management of secondary schools.

Departments are in charge of various benefits such as social assistance for children, assistance to the elderly, the disabled. They also manage the college network.

9.74 Mushrooms

Obviously anything bright red or looking like something out of a fairy tale is best to be avoided but what about the others? Well you can by all accounts pick a selection of *the one*s you are unsure of and take them into your local pharmacy and they will advise as to which ones are safe (to eat) and which ones are not.

Everyday Living, an A to Z

There are apparently over 35,000 different kinds of mushroom here so it is very unlikely that a single pharmacist will know them all but they should in theory be familiar with those dangerous ones that grow in their area. As you might expect those rural pharmacists are likely to have more knowledge on the subject than those in big cities simply because they will be asked about it more often.

Keep an eye out for local mushroom societies (*societies mycologiques*) who organise voluntary training sessions on the subject.

9.75 Mutuelle(s)

9.75.1 What Are They?

As I have stated elsewhere the French state only reimburses approximately 70% of one's outlay on healthcare services, consequently many people choose to top-up their health cover to 100% and a *Mutuelle* provides this. *Mutuelle's,* and there are many to choose from, are non-profit organisations that can date back over 150 years. As with any type of insurance there are many providers who will offer you many types of cover with premiums to match and you can obtain policies that will cover dental and optical treatments, prescription drugs etc. if you need them. As with any insurance based product the simple advice has to be, shop around, do not pay for policies with all sorts of bells and whistles you won't use.

Do not confuse a *Mutuelle* with any Private Health Cover that you may be familiar with in the UK. Although you as an individual pay their premiums it does not give you access to private clinics or faster treatment times.

9.75.2 How do they work?

When you go to see the relevant healthcare practitioner you give them your Carte Vitale and then pay for the cost of treatment. Your CPAM are informed automatically and they take steps to reimburse you their percentage amount. At the same time they notify the relevant *Mutuelle* who calculate how much they have to pay you (the part of the cost not covered by the state) and you subsequently get a separate reimbursement.

Just to confuse matters be aware that some Doctors can charge more for consultations (40€) than the base rate set by the state (25€ ex April 2019) and a *Mutuelle* reimbursing at 100% only covers the base rate. To cover the higher rate you will need a policy that provides cover up to 200%!

9.76 Newspapers

I said at the outset that I wasn't going to recommend or endorse products. One exception I will make is ConnexionFrance. As well as an informative website they issue a monthly English language newspaper in 'e' format or in actual print for 46€ for the year.

What they also produce that is very helpful are a series of guides about aspects of moving to and Life in France. I remembered this when my *'French Income Tax – What's new for 2018'* arrived in the post as I started to draft the original version of this book. It goes through each form that you have to complete and explains how to fill it in. I have used it in each year since and find it really helpful. Various French publications produce their own guides too but they are obviously written in French, depends how good your language skills are? (See also section 9.115.1).

Everyday Living, an A to Z

Most regions have their own daily paper(s) that cover local news and events, for example here in the *Corrèze* we have *Le Montagne* (Daily) & *La Vie Corrézienne* (Weekly), in Brittany you will find *Le Télégramme de Brest* on a daily basis, *L'Est-Éclair* in Aube and *Nice-Matin* in Provence-Alpes-Côte d'Azur publish on a daily basis too. You will also find a lot of useful information, papers, magazines and the like at the many regional airports in France. But if you can't do without your fix of physical English newspapers then most of the larger super/hypermarkets sell them, albeit a day out of date.

9.76.1 Sports Newspapers

If you are a sports fan then you are well catered for in France with 2 sports specific newspapers of note.

9.76.1.1 L'Equipe

L'Equipe is a Paris based daily sports newspaper started shortly after the Second World War. It principally features Basketball, Cycling, Football, Formula 1, Rugby and Tennis although notionally will cover all sports.

9.76.1.2 Midi-Olympique

Midi Olympique is one of the oldest French Weekly newspapers, it was started in 1929, based in Toulouse in the rugby heartland of the South West, and is a bi-weekly newspaper on sale throughout the year that specialises in rugby. It is printed on distinctive coloured paper with the red hued edition available on Mondays which summarises and reports on the weekend matches. On the first Monday of each month they issue a colour magazine. The green/weekend edition available on Fridays looks forward to the coming weekend games and provides updates on team selections and injuries. As well as in depth coverage of the higher levels of French Rugby there is a small section on the English game and it covers International fixtures, International Sevens, the Rugby Championship, the Six Nations Tournament, Super Rugby, the Women's game and also the World Cup.

9.77 Nuisance/Cold Calls

In addition to any features on your telephone handset if you start receiving nuisance/cold calls from companies that you do not have a professional relationship with you can register an account on Bloctel, a government run site (See Annex C) and enter the specific numbers to bar them.

Despite the good intentions, after the system was introduced in 2016 consumers found that operators simply bypassed the system by masking their numbers and transferring their operations overseas whilst continuing to use French Landlines. The French telephone regulator has now toughened their stance and as from 1st August 2019 they have made it illegal for companies to mimic a French landline (starting 01 – 05, or 09) if calling from abroad, and any company using such a number must be registered and based in Metropolitan France. Penalties of up to 375,000€ can be levied against offenders. At least now one should be able to be fairly confident as to which part of the country you are receiving a call from (See section 0).

At the same time the French parliament approved further measures to be taken against cold callers in France particularly if the recipients were signed up to Bloctel, with fines of up to 75,000€ for individuals caught cold-calling (as opposed to 3,000€ previously), and

Everyday Living, an A to Z

375,000€ for businesses (previously only 15,000€). The practice of telephone canvassing for energy renovation work, particularly around the scheme to insulate ones home for 1€, is now prohibited unless it refers to an existing contract/request as it was established that some of the work carried out was sub-standard and workers were underpaid.

9.78 Numbers

When writing numbers in French, particularly on cheques and when doing online banking remember that in France one does not use a decimal point '.' between the whole number and the fraction or the euros and the centimes, one has to use a comma ',' instead. Although confusingly some French banking *'Apps'* rely on one using the decimal point when entering values!

9.79 Ophthalmologists, Opticians and Eye Tests

A big difference here in France is that Opticians do not generally perform eye tests and as such are not part of the French healthcare system so always check when you make an appointment as to whether they conduct them? Tests and any treatments are carried out by an Ophthalmologist *Ophtalmologiste* who can give you a prescription for glasses which you can then take to the opticians to choose a suitable pair.

Find your nearest ophthalmologist in any business directory or online and make an appointment directly, it is not necessary to involve your doctor. Their charges will vary, the minimal official rate is 30€ but you will be reimbursed 50% through your Carte Vitale. Any higher charges may be covered by your *Mutuelle* (See section 9.75). Reimbursement for the glasses themselves is minimal unless you are on a low income but there is a better level if they are for children.

When you go to an opticians with your prescription they will give you a written estimate of the costs involved and if you are not happy with it then shop around (including the internet) before agreeing to buy.

9.80 Parapharmacie(s)

As you travel around you will get used to seeing the green cross sign of a pharmacy in cities, towns and villages but unlike the UK there are no national chains of them as most are independently owned. What you may be surprised to see are *Parapharmacie* signs as there is no direct equivalent. These can sell you (usually at a discount price) everything you would expect to find in a fully-fledged Pharmacy except medication. There is likely to be an extensive range of baby products and a variety of health related items ranging from beauty and skincare treatments, cosmetics, hair care, homeopathic remedies, personal hygiene products and vitamins. The *Parapharmacies* though may well belong to chains.

Both *Parapharmacies* and *pharmacies* are likely to have a sign on the doors indicating the details of the nearest All Night Chemist *(Pharmacie de garde)*.

9.81 Parcels from the UK

You will find that it is far cheaper to send yourself parcels from the UK than it is to send parcels back to the UK even after Brexit. So something to consider is that if you plan to travel back to and from the UK at regular intervals and are predisposed to check in additional suitcases on your low-cost flight ask yourself why when

Everyday Living, an A to Z

you can send yourself parcels of up to 29kg for far less than the cost of a suitcase (Though see also 1.3.5.6). The only other proviso being that the parcels can't contain anything with batteries otherwise it will be rejected at customs and returned to you at your expense. This gave me a problem when buying a new laptop (I bought English simply because I didn't want a French keyboard, as I had previous experience) as manufacturers will not ship them to France either, luckily my daughter came to the rescue by acting as courier on her next visit to see us.

9.82 Passport for ID

These days shopping for various items online has become part of our everyday life and many stores operate a *'click and collect'* service. Be warned however, that strange as it seems when going to collect your purchases sometimes having an email print on your phone and showing the credit card you bought it with is not enough. I took these things along to an electrical retailer shortly after we moved when I was trying to collect a new washing machine; we had sold our other one when we downsized, but I was told that was insufficient and they needed a passport. No amount of attempting to use logic, why would I have the printout and credit card it was ordered on if I wasn't me prevailed and I had to return the following day. Not all shops operate this policy but once bitten twice shy, if I haven't used a particular shop before I will take my passport with me as a precaution against a wasted journey.

Some friends recently had an internet problem and spoke to Orange. After some discussion they were given a special security code and told to go to their nearest Orange store to collect a dongle. They duly did but the store would not release it as despite giving them the code the store wanted passport ID, which our friends didn't have with them and which necessitated a trip back home to collect before returning to the store.

9.83 Plan D'Eau

As you drive around you may well see signs for a Plan D'Eau (together with a water graphic) and I used to be quite confused as to what they were. Simply put they are areas of water which can vary in shape, size and depth; so the signage might equally relate to gravel pits or quarries as well as the more obvious lake *étang,* pond or reservoir as they can be man-made or natural. Depending on their size, activities such as fishing can be permissible.

Although they might appear to be stagnant the water is generally renewable, albeit slowly, in that there is some kind of inflow and an outflow, although gravel pits and quarries would be the exception in that they would be filled by groundwater and there wouldn't necessarily be an exit point.

9.84 Policing

When you first arrive here it is sometimes easy to get confused between a Policeman and a *Gendarme*, although if you have been stopped by one or the other the difference is incidental as both Police and *Gendarme* officers are uniformed and armed! That said the essential difference is that a Policeman is a civil servant, has civil status and generally works in urban areas, vis: large towns/cities. S/he are employed by the *Maire* of the municipality although National Police Officers are employed by the Ministry of the Interior.

Everyday Living, an A to Z

9.84.1 CRS

The CRS *Compagnies républicaines de sécurité* are well known but probably for the wrong reasons. They are the general reserve force of the French National Police and specialise in a public order role and are well known for crowd/riot control. One CRS company specialises in VIP escort.

9.84.2 Gendarmes

A *Gendarme* on the other hand is effectively a soldier as the *Gendarmerie* is an Army Corps that belongs to the French Army. As such a *Gendarme* has military status, lives in barracks and can be mobilised if necessary. The *Gendarmerie* is also part of the Ministry of the Interior organised on a *Départemental* basis in a hierarchy of Regions, Groups, Companies & Brigades. Their name is derived from *Gens d'Armes* – armed people. The *Gendarmerie* has 3 branches:

9.84.2.1 Garde Républicaine

In troubled times this branch of the *Gendarmerie* can be temporarily sent overseas to strengthen resident security forces at French Embassies if the local situation dictates, and they also provide the Guard of Honour (on either horseback or motorcycles) to the President and/or visiting heads of state, in particular on the Esplanade des Invalides and on the Champs-Elysée. The Guard supports the presidents of the two parliamentary assemblies (*Sénat* and *Assemblée Nationale*) at the opening of each session.

They are also charged with providing security at key government buildings, for example the *Elysée* Palace as well as the official residence of the Prime Minister, and key ministries, the Foreign Ministry at Quai d'Orsay, the Interior ministry at the Hotel Beauvau and the Armed Forces Ministry at the Hôtel de Brienne.

9.84.2.2 Gendarmerie

This force is deployable in and responsible for policing of smaller towns, rural and suburban areas.

9.84.2.3 GIGN

The *Groupe d'Intervention de la Gendarmerie Nationale* is an elite highly trained military unit of the *Gendarmerie* that carries out extreme police actions as required in the field of counter-terrorism either in France or abroad. It is staffed by volunteers from the other branches of the *Gendarmerie* and recruits undergo a rigorous training programme.

9.85 Pollution Control

Some French cities and towns have introduced a requirement for an air quality sticker to be displayed on vehicle windscreens. The scheme is called '*Crit'Air*' (*certificat qualité de l'air*) and is currently in the process of being introduced in many major cities. It means that some high-polluting vehicles may not be able to enter certain restricted areas during specific times.

There are six categories of sticker (each with unlimited duration) and these are colour-coded according to how much vehicles pollute and range from the cleanest (Crit'Air 1), for electric or hydrogen-powered vehicles, to the most polluting (Crit'Air 6).

Everyday Living, an A to Z

There is no physical test involved, the classification is based on the age, size, and type of your vehicle and is determined by your registration number (See Annex C for more details).

9.86 Poppies/Remembrance Day

In the UK we are used to seeing Poppies start to be sold in Shops, the Street and in Supermarkets in early October as part of the build-up to Remembrance Sunday the following month. However they are not a universal symbol of remembrance for the first World War as instead in France they recognise the '*Bleuet*' or Cornflower. There appear to be two reasons for this, like poppies, cornflowers continued to grow in the mud of the devastated Flanders fields after the conflict had ceased, and secondly the French conscripts who fought there wore blue uniforms in stark contrast to the red trousers that were the standard uniform of a French soldier before the war broke out. Incidentally remembrance day *L'Armistice* which is a Bank Holiday here is not as big a fund-raising day as it is in the UK, and generally the *Bleuets* are only sold on the day so they are not as common amongst French people as the poppy is in the UK.

9.87 Postal Services

9.87.1 Postcodes

Like in the UK, France & *La Poste* uses a system of postcodes to further identify addresses. The structure of these codes is Remembrance Day very simple. They are all numeric and composed of 5 digits. The first two equate to the number of the *département*, and the last three for the number of your commune. The same three digits will often cover several small communes, for example my postcode is shared around 5 adjacent communes.

n.b. These 3 least significant digits usually increment in 10's although in a big city, e.g. Paris they range from 001-020 and indicate the *arrondissement*.

If you want to know the postcode of a particular commune, or the name of a commune from a postcode, you can look it up on the *La Poste* website (See Annex C).

9.87.2 Letters

The French Postal Service *La Poste* has 2 classes of mail here as in UK. *Prioritaire* et *seconde classe* (*Lettre verte*). As of the 1st January 2022 the price of the former will be 1,43€ and the latter 1,16€.

Post Boxes usually have 2 receptacles, one for local and surrounding *Départements* and Other including International mail.

9.87.2.1 *Signed for Delivery*

If you want recorded delivery for your letter/parcel then *Recommandé & Accusé de Réception* is the service to ask for as it provides you with legal proof of despatch as well as receipt by the recipient and is equivalent to the old Registered Delivery. The postal clerk will give you a multi-part document that looks like the picture below:

You fill in where it is going on the Left Hand Side and put your details on the Right. It is then attached to the item and you are given one of the multi-part items from which you get the tracking number (above the barcode) that you can then check online. If the record is for delivery in France you will get a card (the last page of the multi-part set) showing the signature of the receiver and date of receipt a few days later.

Everyday Living, an A to Z

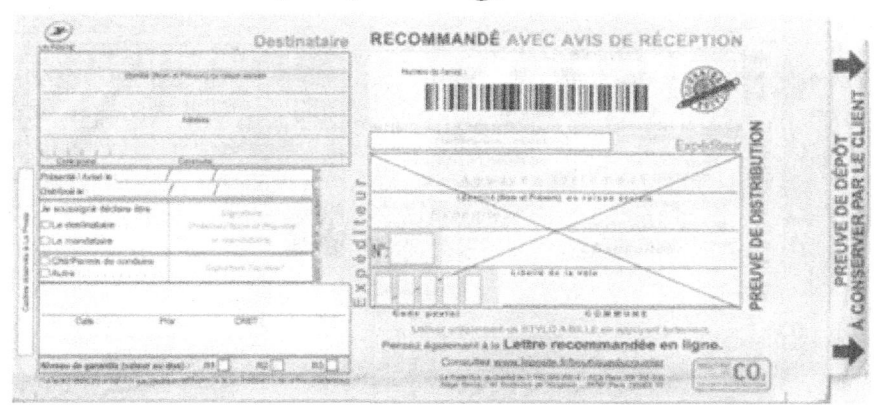

9.87.2.2 Tracked Delivery

If you just want your letter tracked, but not signed for, equivalent to the old Recorded Delivery, then the *Lettre Suivi* service is the one you should ask for. The Post Office will put a tracking sticker on the left hand side of the envelope and give you a copy of the relevant tracking number that you can check online.

n.b. This service is also available for small parcels up to 3kg.

9.87.2.3 Self Printing

For more convenience and to save time it is also possible to print off stamps on your computer at home (at a very small discount to the standard price) and this includes the *Lettre Suivi* and *Recommandé* options.

9.87.2.4 Redirection or Retention

Should you subsequently move house then *La Poste* can redirect your mail for you *réexpédition du courrier* either to another address in France or Internationally. But if you are going away for a period of time and don't want your mail accumulating in your letter box then they can look after it for you until you return *Garde du courrier*.

9.87.3 Parcels

If you want to send parcels through the French Post Office you have a couple of options.
Chronopost: is an express delivery service and in general provides next day delivery for parcels sent to France. It's more expensive but faster. It's the equivalent of Fedex, TNT or UPS; and
Colissimo: is the standard parcel delivery service with delivery times usually between 48 and 72 hours.
Both services provide a tracking ability via the *La Poste* website.

In addition you will find it is possible to send parcels simply by putting them in your own letter box! The *La Poste* website provides the facility to create and print your own label for its *Colissimo* service. You simply provide the parcel dimensions (basically the length, width and height together must not exceed 150 cm, and with no side longer than 100 cm), weight, your address and that of the recipient; then you print it off and stick it on the parcel, pay the appropriate amount and place it in your mailbox before 8am. *La Poste* then inform your local *facteur* that it needs picking up, and he will do so and leave a collection notice. As with all their postage services you can track the delivery of your parcel on the *La Poste* website.

Everyday Living, an A to Z

9.88 Priorité à Droite

💡 A nearby town has 2 very confusing mini roundabouts as far as we are concerned as cars coming onto them have priority over those already on it. Although one is made aware of *Priorité à Droite* when one first drives in France there are no road signs there to indicate same and it seems the key to understanding this situation is to look for road markings. If there is no dotted line across your carriageway on the approach to the roundabout then you can indeed sail right onto it, however beware as at the next access point someone can do the same to you. **Be cautious!**

9.89 Processional Moth/Caterpillar

These are a natural phenomenon which causes problems over large parts of Europe around Oak or Pine trees but one which is not encountered in the UK.

During Winter you can spot their presence by the appearance of numerous *'cotton wool or silky'* type structures on the branches of infected trees where adult moths have laid their eggs. When their larvae pupate they leave their nests at night to feed on the needles/oak leaves. Then in Spring and early Summer the caterpillars leave the nest and climb down the tree to the ground where they travel along in lines to find soft earth within which to make burrows. They have few natural predators and their bodies are covered in tiny barbed hairs and as they climb down the trees or move along in snake like procession along the ground, nose to tail with their neighbour, these hairs fall off, so avoid going anywhere near the nests. Because if you, your children or animals are touched by these hairs you will get a severe skin irritation and if the tiny hairs get on your animal's paws, they will cause irritation and your cat/dog will lick them. Once the hairs are on its' lips/tongue it will induce itching, swelling and possibly vomiting. Noticeable symptoms are white spots in the mouth/tongue, excessive drooling and chomping. If you spot this then rinse the area with water and get your cat/dog to the vet immediately.

Your local pharmacist will be able to provide you with some relief from skin/eye irritation but get to a doctor/hospital if the allergic reaction is severe.

Because of the potential danger you should report the presence of any nests to the *Mairie* and in some *Départements* the *Sapeurs Pompiers* are deployed to remove them, but it is a job best left to the professionals.

9.90 Pruning

You might think it strange to have a section on *'garden maintenance'* in this guide but this pruning *Elagage* concerns maintenance of your boundary if it is adjacent to a main road as it is incumbent on property owners to maintain their hedges/trees particularly if they start to encroach on telephone wires or electricity cables. In this part of the world too there has been concerns raised as the Departmental Council of *Corrèze* believes that pruning (trees and hedges) can increase the lifespan of the road network, especially by preventing falling leaves from rotting on the roadway. Their decision to install optical fibre overground (when it is underground in other *départements*) also contributes to this viewpoint. As a consequence some property owners including one of our neighbours have been served notices ordering them to prune relevant foliage otherwise the Departmental Council will arrange for the work to be done at the owners' expense.

Everyday Living, an A to Z

Where the *département* has got involved directly it has left some areas of woodland and adjoining roads seriously denuded and there has also been claims that owners have been overzealous in their housekeeping as a result. The simple message appears to be prune your boundary on a regular basis.

9.91 Publicity Posters

Do not be surprised if on your travels you see out of date publicity for events. Sometimes the event in question can be weeks or months old, there seems to be no rush to remove them nor to place current posters on top of them to obscure them. In fact last Christmastime our local supermarket still had large posters next to the entrance for events that took place in July and August. Conversely we read in an events guide that there was to be World Championship kayaking on a river in a town some ¾ hour away from us and thought it would be worth a visit. We did not see a single poster/advert for it during the entire journey, even when we got to the town where it was being held there was no publicity in sight. It was only the sound of the Public Address system that gave us a clue as to its location, well that and the river!

Consequently if you are driving in unfamiliar territory, don't get your hopes up when you see a poster/billboard advertising a restaurant as they may not be still trading!

9.92 Radio Stations

As you drive around on your viewing trip or once you live here, you will obviously hear a mix of English and French songs on whatever radio station you tune into, although the English language songs played tend to be a mix of 80's 90's 00's. What you may not realise is that by law DJ's on French Radio stations have to play a minimum of 35% French language songs! This all stems from a 1994 decision by the then government to introduce a 40% quota to protect France from what they deemed was an *'Anglo Saxon'* cultural invasion. *Députés* subsequently voted to reduce this to 35% during the first quarter of 2016.

9.93 Restaurants

It seems that every village hereabouts has a restaurant and obviously some are better than others. It is surprising that many of the smaller restaurants are just operated by a husband and wife team. There are many examples of this locally and it seems that the former is the chef whilst the latter waits on tables, occasionally they may employ someone to run the bar or help out with serving. A point to note however is that they do not always cater for pescatarians, vegans or vegetarians.

I have to say that as a lifelong carnivore albeit with omnivorous tendencies living rurally and walking past fields of cows or sheep with their babies on a daily basis certainly makes one aware of a vegan viewpoint, although I've always managed to dissociate what I see in the field and what is on my plate. However vegetarian options will be an everyday standard in public catering, and this is all part of a *'culture shift'* proposed by Barbara Pompili the French environment minister in her climate and resilience bill, which aims to improve health and wellbeing and help reach net zero greenhouse gas emissions. *'Vegetarians must be able to find menus that cater to their needs in their canteens. This is especially true for young people, among whom the proportion of vegetarians is twice as high as the rest of the population.'*

Everyday Living, an A to Z

That aside it will take you a while when you first arrive to find a restaurant open in the evenings as this is not common outside big cities, irrespective Mondays could be problematic anyway. Also many restaurants are very busy on a Sunday lunchtime as it is a time when many families go out to eat together. Many have a range of fixed price offerings *Formules* as well as *A La Carte*. One difference between a *Menu du Jour* or *Menu Ouvrier* (Workman's Menu) as opposed to a more *A La Carte* offering is that with them you will invariably be expected to keep your knife and fork between courses. With a *Menu Ouvrier* the food can be quite rustic, e.g. *andouillette*, *langue de boeuf*, *tete de veau* etc. and the service will generally be quite speedy, so as to enable the workman to complete their meal before their lunchtime ends. Lots of the supermarkets have a *bistrot du marché* where you can eat cheaply.

9.93.1 Etiquette

Somewhat bizarrely from a British perspective bread is not always given out with a soup course and sometimes doesn't make an appearance until the main course/*plat* is served. In more rustic establishments you might observe that French diners/workers drop a little red wine from their glass into their soup bowl, swill it round and drink from it! Although it is not something that is common in more refined dining places.

Here in France it's perfectly acceptable to drink water with your food if you don't want wine, unlike in the UK where asking for water in a restaurant is liable to lead you to be charged an excessive amount for a bottle of mineral water. So unless you really want mineral water, when you go into a restaurant here just ask for *une carafe d'eau* or *un pichet d'eau* which will guarantee that you get plain tap water (usually chilled), given to you.

In France the law is such that restaurateurs are obliged to provide food/meals for their employees in their workplace.

9.94 Restaurant Guides

However if you are not the type of person who likes taking chances when it comes to eating then you can choose where to eat by looking for a restaurant's membership of/recognition by certain organisations.

9.94.1 Bistrots du Pays

The Bistrot de Pays is a network which aims to contribute to the conservation of the economic and social fabric in rural areas by maintaining - or recreating establishments such as bistros, cafés, and other drinking places in small towns or villages and has a presence in around 25% of *départements*. Membership involves meeting strict criteria such as being open all year round, being sited in a community of less than 2,000 people, supplying local tourist information leaflets, promoting local products etc.

9.94.2 Gault & Millau

The Gault & Millau guide dates from 1969 when it was started by a pair of food critics and journalists and when Nouvelle Cuisine arrived shortly afterwards it became known for actively promoting its' principles and values i.e. lighter, more delicate dishes and an increased emphasis on presentation. Their guide rates establishments on a scale of 1-20 with points being awarded purely based on the quality of the food served, with observations about ambience, price and service kept separate. For many years the

Everyday Living, an A to Z

originators and indeed their successors refused to award a score of 20 using the argument that perfection was beyond the limits of a normal human being.
n.b. Only 2 restaurants have ever been given a 20 score but they are now both closed.

Dependent on the score a restaurant may display between 1 and 4 *toques* (the traditional headwear for a professional chef) equating to a score between 11 and 18½.

For the last 40 years they have announced a Chef of the Year award.

9.94.3 Michelin Guide
9.94.3.1 *Origins*

This is one of the oldest and most famous food related guides in the world. The roots of which are maybe not so well known. At the turn of the 20th Century there were only a few thousand or so cars on French roads. To increase the demand for cars and, thereby car tires, the tire manufacturers and brothers André and Édouard Michelin published a guide for French motorists. The first edition of which was free and contained useful information such as listings of car mechanics, hotels, maps, petrol stations and repair and replacement instructions for tires throughout France.

From these humble origins it has grown into the prestigious guide we know today and Michelin now employs numerous full-time reviewers (called 'inspectors') who visit establishments around the world every day of the week sampling the food on offer. They are barred from talking to journalists and conduct their work anonymously thereby having a dining experience like any other customer.

9.94.3.2 *Reporting*

Having visited a restaurant they produce a comprehensive report focusing on the dining experience using just five separate criteria:
- Consistency of culinary standards and presentation of the dishes;
- Flair and skill in preparing ingredients and combining flavours;
- Quality of ingredients;
- The chef's personality as revealed through their cuisine; and
- Value for money.

All the time the emphasis is on the food. Inspectors do not care about the décor or quality of service or the way the table is laid out. The inspectors then meet and discuss the reviews and the restaurants and decide which of them should receive stars. Those restaurants being considered for stars are obviously subjected to several visits each year. The highest accolade that a restaurant can receive is a coveted Michelin Star, as recipients gain prestige and honour as well as usually an increase in business as a result, and the customers view them as a hallmark of a quality establishment. Michelin state that
- One star signifies *'a very good restaurant'*;
- Two stars are *'excellent cooking that is worth a detour'*; and
- Three stars mean *'exceptional cuisine that is worth a special journey'*.

Michelin Star awards are not announced but are subject to *'revelations'*.

The listing of starred restaurants is updated once a year, as of 2020 there were 29 three Star Michelin Restaurants in France and Monaco, 86 with two stars and 513 with one star.

Everyday Living, an A to Z

However January 2021 saw a Vegan restaurant near Bordeaux awarded a Michelin Star, the first plant based restaurant in the country to receive such an award.

> Something to note, particularly if you like *'fine dining'* experiences is that restaurants keep their stars even after a change of management and bizarrely even after a change of Chef!

9.94.3.3 Bib Gourmand

For the last 60 years or so the Michelin Guide has also highlighted those establishments that in its view offer exceptionally good food at moderate prices (with menu items below a maximum governed by prevailing local economic standards). This feature is called '*Bib Gourmand*'.

n.b. Bib is an abbreviation for Bibendum which is the companies nickname for the Michelin Man, its well known logo.

9.94.3.4 Michelin Recommended

For the last twenty years a third category, that of Michelin Recommended has been in use. Assessed using the same criteria as for the starred or Bib Gourmand restaurants the status is given to restaurants that propose good above average food, using quality ingredients that has been well cooked, and offered at moderate prices.

9.94.4 Petit Futé

The term *Petit Futé* means *'little wily one'* implying in this case the wily and cost-conscious traveller, and the brand's logo is a (wily) fox. *Petit Futé* (founded in 1976) is a series of French travel guides, a bit like the Lonely Planet series covering Accommodation, Currency Purchase, Food, Insurance, Things to do, Travel etc. They produce listings of their recommended restaurants per region.

9.95 RIB

Basically the *RIB* (*Relevé d'Identité Bancaire*) is your statement of identity that you get from your bank that contains your account details:

- The *nom* and *prénom* (s) or business name of the account holder;
- The bank code (5 digits);
- The counter code (5 digits);
- Account number (11 digits or letters);
- RIB key (2 digits);
- The title of the institution and the counter holding the account;
- For international account identification: the IBAN code (International Bank Account Number) a series of numbers and letters (27), including the bank code and the account number, and
- The Business Identifier Code (BIC) (11 or 8 digits or letters).

When you use it i.e. give it to a vendor, it then becomes relatively straightforward to setup Direct Debits etc.

> Some organisations will accept photocopies of these when setting up accounts with them but you will find *'formal'* spares in the front of your chequebook if you need them.

Everyday Living, an A to Z

n.b. The *RIB* may also contain optional information (this depends on the practices of the institution concerned) such as the account holder's address and the address and telephone number of the bank counter.

9.96 Road Tax

There is no road tax here it was abolished for private vehicles in 2001!

9.97 Roads

In a rural environment get used to driving on roads that don't have *'cats eyes'* down the middle and many don't have any form of white lines either.

9.97.1 Classifications

Roads in France are categorised as follows:

A = Autoroute

Some of these or stretches on some of these are free but the majority are toll roads. As in the UK the signage for these is white numbering/lettering on a blue background.

M = Metropole Roads

These are denoted by white numbering on a light blue/cyan background are found in *métropoles* – local government groupings based around larger cities and there are less than two dozen at present. The roads are mostly former Departmental roads and the number has stayed the same.

N = National Roads

(Or *Route Nationale* as they were called when I first came to France in my 20's) are mainly trunk roads and are frequently dual carriageways'. These are indicated by white numbering on a red background.

D = Departmental Roads

These have been delegated to the *départements* over time by the government. It is therefore not unusual to find numerous of them with the same number in different parts of the country. They are designated by black numbers/letters on a yellow background.

C = Commune/*Routes Communales*

Smaller roads, sometimes equivalent to lanes in the UK that are the responsibility of the various *communes*. Although they are all numbered, not all will be signed! Where they are it will be by black numbers on a white background.

9.97.2 Designations

Road designations will be in the format of Annn
where A = Type of road, i.e. A, M, N, D or C; and
nnn = Number (between 1 & 999).

It is not uncommon to see the same road with different numbers. For example on the occasions when I have driven home from Calais I use the A71/E9 where the former is the Autoroute designation and the latter is the European road number (which transcends national borders) and is the product of the United Nations Economic Committee for Europe (UNECE), created in 1947. European road numbering is indicated by white numbers on a green background.

Everyday Living, an A to Z

9.97.3 Tourist Routes

Sometimes you may see direction signs starting with the word *Bis*, in italics or after a road number. This is the equivalent of a less crowded holiday route in the UK. So a sign saying '*Bis Toulouse*' is an alternative route with less lorry traffic that avoids the main roads. The French have an expression *Bison futé* (meaning the cunning bison) for motorists who do not follow the crowd and use less busy roads, thus making their journey easier. The name is also given to a well-known travel website that provides real-time traffic information (See Annex C for more information).

9.98 Rural Families

Famillies Rurales is a national association founded in 1943 with the aim of improving the living environment of rural inhabitants. It gives a voice to the needs and interests of families in regard to the implementation of government policies. There are over 2,000 local associations and they typically organise a range of activities such as Advice Sessions, Cinema Visits, Relaxation Classes, Social Gatherings and Sporting events. It also helps defend the rights of consumers.

9.99 Sans Contact

Over recent years contactless payments have become a boon as one can temporarily forget one's PIN number but still buy things. This is certainly true in France also with a transaction limit of 50€. However it seems that a lot of the EPOS systems here only allow such payments if you say so in advance as it seems the cashier needs to enter same on their till. Just dropping your card on the card reader can result in a payment refused message appearing on screen to your potential embarrassment, but is usually easily overcome if you then say you want to pay *Sans Contact*.

9.100 Schools

We no longer have school age children to concern ourselves with so the days of having to juggle differing school holiday timetables and teacher training days amongst 5 children at 3 schools in the same town have gone, but I appreciate that schooling will be a concern to a large number of you thinking of moving here.

Firstly I have to say things here seem more straightforward, which certainly simplifies things from a parental perspective. The country is divided into 3 coloured zones A, B and C (organised geographically) and all schools within that zone have the same holiday periods. Within these zones the holiday dates are fixed nationally by the Ministry of Education for a period of three years and are spread out for the winter and spring holidays so that children are not all on holiday at the same time, while others such as Toussaint, Christmas and the summer holidays, are taken in parallel. (See Annex F).
n.b. Diaries usually display the colour codes on their year planners.

Everyday Living, an A to Z

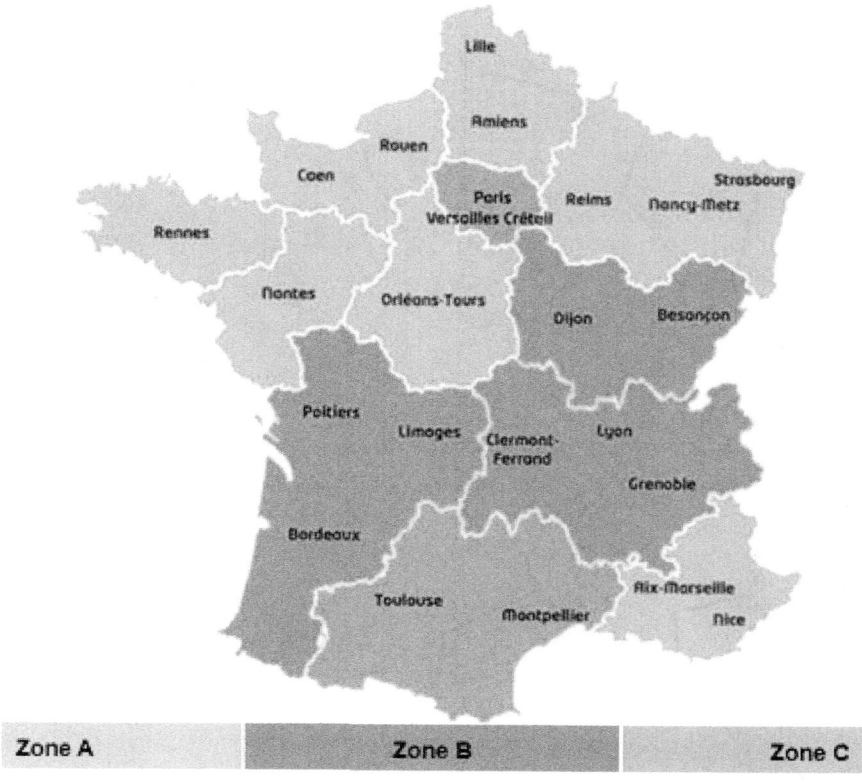

9.100.1   Types of School

The nomenclature of the French school system (and their age ranges) is as follows:
- Nursery *Ecole Maternelle*   3-6
- Primary *Ecole Primaire*   6-11
- Lower Secondary *Collège*   11-15
- Upper Secondary *Lycée*   15-18

Since 2019 it has become mandatory for children to attend Nursery school from the age of 3 and they can start from their birthday. Nursery and Primary Schools have usually have lessons 4½ days a week (with Wednesday afternoons off) though in some areas the half day lessons are on Saturday mornings and all of Wednesday is free. However a couple of years ago schools were given the discretion to implement a 4-day school week, with no lessons on a Wednesday. Secondary School students are taught 5 days a week. During term times school buses operate for children between the ages of 6 & 15. School attendance is obligatory between the ages of 3 to 16 beyond which 16-18 year olds who are not still at school must be in training or work.

Chiming with wider moves to introduce plant based diets School canteens must now offer children at least one vegetarian meal a week.

As to some specifics about the different types of school:

9.100.1.1 *Primary Schools*

Maternelle starts from age 3, 2 if there is room; *Élémentaire* from age 6

Everyday Living, an A to Z

9.100.1.2 <u>Collège</u>
Children have automatic rights to attend their local college, if they/you prefer to attend another will need a *dérogation* from the educational head of the *Département – directeur académique*.

9.100.1.3 <u>Lycée</u>
There are two types, a general academic or a professional *lycée* and the student attends the nearest suitable establishment. Again if they/you want them to attend somewhere else you need a *dérogation* as above.

In contrast to the UK, from the age of 6 (in *Élémentaire*) children will need to take their own writing materials including exercise books & paper, pens etc. Text books are provided in Collège but in Lycée students need to supply both stationery and text books.

9.100.2   Enrolment
To enrol your child(ren) you must sign up at your *Mairie* usually any time between March and June. If you want your child(ren) to attend a school in a different commune you will need to obtain permission from both your *Maire* and the *Maire* of the other commune.

9.100.3   Home Schooling
In October 2020 M Macron implied that this would become more difficult although nothing official has yet happened. If you want to home school your child then you have to inform your *Mairie* and the Departmental *directeur académique*. If accepted you would be subject to at least annual checks.

9.101 Sensory Heritage

In January 2021 the French Government passed a new '*Sensory Heritage*' law to protect the countryside from new arrivals unable or unwilling to understand the realities of rural life and looking to change those aspects of it that interfered with their peace and quiet. One celebrated case – Maurice the Rooster – had resulted in a woman and her rooster being taken to court by her new neighbours who had bought a nearby holiday home and had objected to being woken up. A '*Save Maurice*' petition raised thousands of signatures and the case was eventually thrown out.

The Government Minster for rural life said '*Living in the countryside implies accepting some nuisances*'. So noises from Church Bells, Cow Bells, Ducks and Geese, Grasshoppers, Tractors etc. will henceforth be considered part of France's natural heritage and will be included in its environmental legislation.

9.102 'Shed' Tax

Be careful if you plan to improve your outdoor space by installing e.g. a parking area, shed, solar panels (on the ground) or swimming pool as anything with a ground surface area more than 5m^2 will be subject to a *taxe d'aménagement*. This one-off tax is also levied on any construction or extension that needs a building permit.

It was introduced in 2012 and is aimed at assisting the funding of local work. A base rate is set each year and that is multiplied by the project's ground area and by the commune's total rate (usually between 1 and 5% but can reach 20% if large scale local work is being funded). There are some set rates, e.g. a pool is 200€/ m^2 whereas ground solar panels are

Everyday Living, an A to Z

10€/ m² and some works are exempt. If the total amount is less than 1,500€ it is paid in full otherwise it is made in two payments in the 14th and 26th months after approval is granted.

9.103 Shutters

Want to install shutters on your house to give it a more authentic French look or want to change the colour of the existing ones? It's best to have a word at the *Mairie* to make sure that you are not contravening anything in the local planning guidelines with regard to colour restrictions etc.

9.104 SIREN

The SIREN (*Système d'Identification du Répertoire des Entreprises*) number is a unique 9 digit French business identification number allocated to one's business by INSEE (*L'Institut national de la statistique et des études économiques*) – the national institute of statistics, when one registers one's business. The 9 digits contain an 8-digit business reference number and a single check digit which proves the legality of a business or non-profit organisation. The SIREN number will remain constant throughout the life of the business, in the event of a one man business it ceases on their death or on dissolution/liquidation of the business, whichever comes first.
n.b. French public organisations have 1 or 2 as the first digit of their SIREN number.

9.105 SIRENE

SIRENE *Système informatique pour le Répertoire des entreprises et des établissements* is a business directory managed by INSEE displaying the date of creation, address, no. of employees SIREN and SIRET codes.

9.106 SIRET

The SIRET (*Système d'Identification du Répertoire des Établissements*) number is really a registration number associated with a single place of business and is used to index French companies and proves the existence (and legality) of an establishment. It corresponds to a series of 14 digits, the first 9 digits of which are the SIREN number and the remaining 5 are an NIC (*Numéro Interne de Classement*) number. Consequently a company with 5 physical locations would have 5 different SIRET numbers, all of which contain the same SIREN number as the first part of the SIRET; only the NIC code will vary.

9.107 Skips

So you plan out a whole sequence of work on '*the one*' and look around for Skip Hire so you can book someone to cart away your deconstruction waste. Sadly you may be looking a long time as Skip Hire like you are familiar with in the UK is not that common here, yes you can find a *benne* if you are lucky but it will not necessarily be the kind you are used to and you are likely to find that it comes with a whole lot of restrictions. First up it will likely have metal rollers and be delivered on a low truck with the *benne* itself being a cutdown version of the containers' you see at council tips, and being much larger means it needs to be sited on a road not your property. To do this you need to get special permission (from the *Mairie*) to site it there. Once it arrives you normally can only put one type of rubbish in a *benne*, and you could get charged for sorting once it has been collected. My advice, depending on

Everyday Living, an A to Z

how much of it you have, would be to either hire a tipper trailer or invest in a good trailer for your car and take it to the *déchetterie* yourself.

9.108 Slower Pace of Life

It is highly likely that a more relaxed and slower pace of life featured quite high on your list of reasons to move to France, so if you are impacted by it don't over-react. It is not uncommon to be standing behind someone in the Supermarket queue who then gets into an animated conversation with the cashier at the checkout. Both of them will seemingly be totally oblivious to the queue of waiting people and their, and your, growing impatience.

It is not just the Supermarket where you will encounter this, you may be in a queue of cars at the *Déchetterie* and the person who has just unloaded their car and/or trailer decides to engage the employee in a discussion; equally you could be driving somewhere and encounter a delivery driver, other motorist or even postman blocking the road whilst talking to someone at the side of the road or in another vehicle. It will be obvious they have seen your vehicle draw up but will possibly be in no hurry to finish their discussion. The same applies if seeking assistance in a large store, the assistant may well see you standing there but will continue their sometimes lengthy conversation first or when finished they will even stop to answer the phone before dealing with you. Don't take it personally, it isn't because you are British, it is just what they do. If this occurs just breathe in slowly and smile inwardly that you are no longer on the clock and have all the time in the world yourself. But there are limits, I have had to bite my tongue on a few occasions and I have to keep reminding myself of that as unfortunately I was born impatient.

9.109 Smoking

I don't smoke and I can't say I'm a fan of smoking. After all what is attractive about anyone who wants their breath, clothes and hair to smell of stale cigarettes let alone putting the foul thing in one's mouth. Yes ok I am biased and too much time spent crammed into small airless and windowless meeting rooms in Paris with a team who fancied themselves as ambassadors for *Disque Bleu, Gauloise* and *Gitanes* didn't help. So I have been pleasantly surprised since being here but as with many things France proves to be contradictory. Yes France has to a degree followed the anti-smoking trend around the world and I have yet to go to a restaurant where smoking is allowed. However if one goes to a bar, music venue or a sporting arena it is a totally different matter and people don't think twice about lighting up, it is just unfortunate if one of them happens to be next to me.

9.110 Snakes

I am definitely not a fan of these reptiles, they are not my happy place, although I understand they have a place in the countryside I just don't like the thought of that place being anywhere near me. In all my years in the UK I only ever saw 2 and they were both dead. Since we have moved here I have seen a few dead ones of different sizes on the roads around here but the problem I have is that I have not found anything like a definitive guide as to how to determine whether they are poisonous i.e. dangerous or not, and then you have also got harmless grass snakes *couleuvres* to throw into the mix. It is not even as simple as saying if they have round eyes and straight heads they are OK but slit eyes and or triangular heads are dangerous; not that I want to get that close to work it out anyway. When it comes to things scaly, I have been told that longer is apparently better/safer, but I

Everyday Living, an A to Z

am not so sure, clearly that school of thought never had a King Cobra or Gaboon Viper in their class!! Anyway I have a couple of inquisitive dogs who I can't watch 24/7 and who can't tell me if they have been bitten or not, consequently I have to err on the side of caution.

9.110.1 A tale of two snakes

Having said all that, snakes are not normally aggressive, except in the breeding season (early spring) and they are not overly common. I have seen a total of 9 in our grounds (including the *Etang*) during our time here, that's in over 5 years (but because it is so unusual compared with around our house in the UK, each occasion for me has been indelibly etched in my memory, they are my kryptonite if you like) and Joanne has seen 2. On reflection I think only 1 was an adder and thus potentially dangerous, 7 of them disappeared quite quickly although Keno got very close to trying to catch one of them a few years ago before I managed to grab him but two have appeared in our polytunnel. Alfie, who likes to follow his mistress everywhere alerted Joanne to the first of them when he saw a bag start moving so she beat a hasty retreat, called me and I subsequently had to take more drastic action than I would have necessarily liked, although I realise by so doing that I may offend any herpetologists amongst you. But then again I would have to question why you are attracted to reptiles in the first place? They don't exactly respond to one's commands or have any endearing qualities about them and thus can't be considered pets to my mind.

The story around the second is quite amusing. On this occasion Joanne came back to the house and said she had seen a snake in her polytunnel. On closer investigation it appeared to have slithered in through the rear window, over a table, and as it tried to move down onto the floor got itself caught up in some plant netting. Acceding to Joanne's plea for clemency I ejected it (and the netting) with the aid of a long handled shovel back through the window which I promptly shut. Over the next three days it did move away from the rear of the Polytunnel, but not very far, maybe only a couple of feet but it was still entangled in the netting. Joanne immediately felt sorry for it and casually mentioned it to a friend who had come over. He went to look and pronounced it was a harmless *couleuvre* and immediately said he would free it. I offered him some leather work gloves to wear and the subsequent advice to slide his hand up nearer to its head as it had greeted his presence by turning round and trying to bite him. I then went off to the *déchetterie* and left him to it.

By the time of my return the reptile had been set free. Our friend had requested some scissors to help cut away the netting and Joanne had responded and had also brought her phone out with her for good measure. She then promptly videoed the entire episode and then posted it on a 'WhatsApp' group that a number of us share along with a '*Snake Whisperer*' title. It seems that once our friend started cutting the netting the snake calmed down and let it happen. He then carried it some 50m or so down the garden before releasing it close to the woods. It was only when Joanne then started worrying about going for a walk '*because they can climb trees*' that I secretly hoped a hungry Honey Buzzard might have spotted it and fancied it for lunch!

9.110.2 Safety Measures

Relax, **don't worry though**, if you are a '*normal healthy*' adult there is nothing here that will kill you, there are no Cobra's, Mamba's or Puff Adders here in France, but some of the

Everyday Living, an A to Z

snakes that are can cause your pets some distress that is often acute. So if your pet gets bitten it is best to seek urgent medical/veterinary attention and either take along a description/picture of the offender (or its body) to aid correct treatment!

That said, Snakes are protected in France, but there is the law and ……..!

As it is not possible to eliminate snakes from your property completely some simple basic common sense safety steps should minimise any interaction you have with them.

- They tend to be attracted to ponds and ditches as well as buildings infested with mice, and don't think it is just sunny spots they like; cool, dark, quiet places are appealing too;
- Snakes tend to move away from any area where there is noise or vibration so feel free to be Mr/Mrs Flatfoot and stomp round your Polytunnel or Vegetable patch;
- Don't walk around with bare feet and legs where you can't see properly. Wear Wellington Boots if you haven't mowed the grass for a while and it is longer than you would like as these will protect your ankles and lower legs;
- Be cautious when moving objects which are possible hiding places, e.g. don't plunge your hand into the water meter or electricity meter box or other inspection point without first checking that it is empty;
- Don't leave empty/split bags of compost/peat nor bin bags lying on the floor (as we did) as these too make great hiding places;
- Don't leave piles of grass/cuttings around overnight. If you do so and intend to move them the following day then poke around with a garden fork or rake first;
- Don't delve into the darkest recesses of your barn/garage/workshop to retrieve something without first having a good look around or switching a light on if practicable;
- Be wary of leaving your doors open especially If you have grass paths leading to/from your various doorways. It is not uncommon to find them in a laundry type room, one with an outside door as it is unlikely to be in continual use and it is generally nice and dark under the washing machine and the rooms generally have a cool tiled floor;
- Be careful around log piles as these can be frequent hiding places, even in winter;
- If you are going to pick something (reasonably solid) up off the floor then tilt it towards you first, thereby giving anything that is asleep/hiding underneath it an escape route away from you in the first instance;
- If you buy a compost bin then siting it on a concrete base if practicable will help restrict unwanted ingress; and
- Finally, if you do see one and immediately think you are going to get bitten, understand that snakes generally only bite/strike over a distance between approximately one third and a half of their body length. Clearly this is obviously difficult to gauge if it is laying somewhere curled up but if it is moving, err on the side of caution, and try and stay at least its own length away from it until you see what it is going to do. But be careful as they can move far quicker than you might expect.

If you do have the misfortune to get bitten DO NOT under any circumstances:

- Attempt to suck out the poison;
- Apply a tourniquet;
- Drink a cup of coffee or tea to combat the shock.

Everyday Living, an A to Z

Instead:
- Get assistance as quickly as you can
  (You can call any of the emergency numbers for help, 15-SAMU, 17-Police, 18-Pompiers);
- Try and stay as calm and still as you possibly can as this will slow the movement of any poison around the body;
- Try and remove any tight clothing/watches/bracelets around the bite area; and
- If practicable apply some ice to the bite area
  (as this too slows the movement of venom around the body).

n.b. If you want a quick response, key SOS Serpents dd (Dept No.) into a search engine to find the location of local services who will help deal with it.

9.111 Steak

Despite the burgeoning rise of the Vegan movement a lot of people get great enjoyment from eating Steak and it features a lot on menus here. So that you are equipped to eat out and order one in a restaurant, familiarise yourself with the terms:

Bleu	Extremely rare
Saignant	Very Rare
A point	Medium Rare
Moyen	Medium
Bien Cuit	Medium well
Tres Bien Cuit	Very well done

However don't make the mistake that I did over seeing '*Steack à Cheval*' and telling Joanne that yes the French do eat horsemeat (and you can find horse in some *boucheries* in France). Ok so '*cheval*' in French does mean horse in English but the phrase does not mean '*steak of horse*' but in this instance '*Steack à Cheval*' translates as '*steak on horseback*' and it's just a way of cooking/presentation; a steak with a fried egg(s) on it and on that occasion the egg was truly on my face and not on the plate!

9.112 Supermarkets

9.112.1 Opening Hours

Supermarkets that open 24 hours a day do not exist in France, even in the big cities, and you are even pushed to find late-night opening. As a rule they will open generally around 8.30-9.00am and close between 7.00-7.30pm and slightly earlier in winter. Some, depending on location may even close for lunch. Again some will open for a time on Sundays, usually 09.00 and shut their doors between midday and 12.30pm although associated Petrol stations will stay open for credit/debit card payments only.

> Even DIY stores which you may be used to popping along to on a Sunday will shut their doors on a Saturday night until Monday morning.

9.112.2 Petrol

> (tip) Keep an eye out as those Super/Hypermarkets that have an associated Petrol Station usually (at least around the *Corrèze*) reduce their prices across all grades of fuel at weekends. Assumption week in the middle of August (the major holiday week in France) sees low prices for the whole week in our local supermarket. Irrespective,

Everyday Living, an A to Z

supermarket forecourt Petrol prices respond to market forces far quicker than those in the UK, and have been known to change 4/5 times a week both up and down.

9.112.3 Publicity
You will be surprised in the amount of publicity the supermarkets issue on a weekly basis. All the magazines containing current offers are usually delivered along with your post on Monday or Tuesday's, assuming you haven't blocked delivery of Junk Mail that is. (See section 9.59 above).

9.112.4 Offers
So you have spotted an offer in their weekly magazine, gone along to the supermarket, found it in stock and taken it to the till along with the rest of your shopping only to find that when you get back home your receipt shows a totally different price. I have to say that this not uncommon as there seems to be frequent disconnects between the magazines, the shelf-edge labels and the EPOS systems at the till. So if you are buying something that you expect to be on offer either watch the price as it is scanned or check your receipt before you leave the store. Again it really is really a case of Caveat Emptor. But when Joanne tells me that the price was more than she thought I know she didn't have her glasses on!

That said, if I only spot something when I get home I query it next time I am in store and have not once been refused a refund.

9.112.5 Other
Once you have unloaded your shopping onto the conveyor belt for checking out you will be expected to open your shopping bags for inspection as you pass in front of the till. No, not because you are English because everyone has to do it.

9.113 Swimming Pools and Alarms
You may be surprised to find that there are apparently more pools per head of population in France than in Spain. So having lived in '*the one*' for a period and experienced the climate here you may think that installing an inground or ground level swimming pool will be a good idea?

If you are looking to build/buy a pool don't forget to factor in the running expenses (the pump will need to be on 12 hours a day or more) and daily maintenance. Consider if you will use it everyday/is it just a fanciful idea?

9.113.1 Building a Pool
If you then decide to build a pool the costs are generally given as being somewhere between 15,000€ and 50,000€ for the pool itself and that includes the pre-formed fibreglass ones, but you then have to add on the cost of any surround, be it decking or paved/patio area. You will need to apply for full planning permission if your intended pool has a water area greater than 100m² or if you plan a pool between 10m² and 100m² and want to cover it to a height greater than 1.8m with either a fixed or mobile cover.

If you decide to surround your '*Out of Ground*' pool with decking so it appears '*In ground*' then make sure you have some inspection hatches or means of getting down to the base level of the pool to clear away excess water from the outside as such pools

Everyday Living, an A to Z

generally have metal frame supports and over time these will rust if pool or rain water settles against them and the pool will eventually give way!

9.113.2 Running Costs

Once built, the cost of maintaining a swimming pool varies widely as local factors – such as the price of water, electricity and taxes which all vary depending on where you live. If you have never had one before don't underestimate either the upkeep or the costs involved, vis:

- Chemicals
- Depreciation
- Electricity
- Tax
- Water

9.113.2.1 *Chemicals*

The cost of these will depend on the kind of pool you have/install and salt pools generally have lower chemical bills than chlorine pools. If you have a salt electrolysis pool you will likely have to replace part of the unit every two years or so.

9.113.2.2 *Depreciation*

The pool's pump, valves and other parts wear out and parts might need replacing. Most French pools are built now using plastic liners, which have a life of around 10-15 years, and which cost around a third of the price of the pool to replace, plus the cost of then filling the pool from scratch.

9.113.2.3 *Electricity*

Your pump and salt electrolysis system if you have one are connected to the electrical supply and pumps will typically run for 12-16 hours each day during the summer. So investigate the practicalities of solar energy.

9.113.2.4 *Taxes*

As soon as you build a pool you immediately start paying extra taxes. Initially *taxe d'aménagement*, which for pools is calculated on the basis of 200€/m², multiplied by the index of tax imposed by your commune and your department. (See also section 9.102).

Thereafter once it has been installed for two years your pool will be included in a revised calculation for *taxe foncière*, based on the theoretical rental value of your property, which will increase with a pool.

n.b. If you have a pool with a water surface area of less than 10m² it doesn't have to be declared but if you are living/plan to live in an old village, or your house is close to a historic monument site, you will have to follow the local urban planning code.

Values tend to increase the further south you are located due to the likely increased frequency of use. You cannot claim a reduction for not using your pool, you can only do this by filling it in or removing it!

9.113.2.5 *Water*

Don't forget that filling your pool is a large one-off expense, and this will be followed by regular top-ups to combat evaporation, over-jealous splashing, or dare I say some leaks! It may be you need to drain/partially drain your pool for maintenance activities in which case

Everyday Living, an A to Z

if the property is connected to mains the pool water should be emptied there, otherwise you will need to consider the most suitable place to discharge it to.

9.113.3 Safety and Security

Historically, due to the high rate of infant mortality by drowning in pools, France introduced some of the most stringent rules regarding the building of new swimming pools and consequently they need to be equipped with one of the following standard safety devices. These can be either:

a. A (usually transparent) shelter that one retracts before using the pool although high ones allow one to still swim in poor weather, but sometimes these shelters cost more to install than the actual pool itself;
b. An alarm that activates when it detects entry of a certain weight or more to the water;
c. A pool cover for when the pool is not in use; or
d. A barrier or gated fence surround.

Use of these last two measures in combination is quite common. The rules apply for both paying guests, at your *Gite* or B&B for instance, and your family.

Somewhat bizarrely if you are considering going swimming in a public pool please be aware that you can't use board shorts as they are deemed unhygienic, only '*speedo*' types are permitted!

9.113.4 Pool Alternatives

As a possible alternative there are of course many lakes with artificial beaches for you to enjoy here. Be aware that not all of them feature lifeguards and the rules about wearing trunks not shorts don't seem to apply.

You will also find that during the Spring and Summer the many *Bricolages* offer inflatable (usually circular) pools of varying depths and diameters and you may consider one of these a practical alternative to the expense of creating a permanent pool. Equally you may be taken with the idea of an outdoor Hot Tub. You will need to install a reinforced concrete base to stand it on and overall the cost will be somewhere between that of an inflatable pool and a full sized pool.

9.114 Tabacs

A *tabac* is a shop licensed to sell tobacco products, but with smoking becoming less fashionable and in the face of declining sales they have diversified their activities. Depending on their location they will also likely sell some or all of lottery tickets, multi-journey bus tickets, newspapers, postage stamps, and telephone cards. Some are also used as drop-off or reception points for parcel companies.

Additionally some now provide one with the opportunity to pay fines, taxes or certain Public Service bills or open a *Compte Nickel* (See section 9.10.6.1). 2021 saw the initial rollout of touch screen computer terminals in some to further assist people without regular access to the internet. Users will be able to notify the authorities of a change in their address or car ownership, or email and scan documents. Ultimately every *tabac* will have one. There is also a pilot for installing ATM's currently taking place and once evaluated, if successful, all *tabacs* can opt to install them

Everyday Living, an A to Z

9.115 Tax

As a resident and the owner of a French property you will become familiar with 4 principal taxes.

9.115.1 Income Tax

Over the years we have all become familiar with the HMRC Self-Assessment process with tax returns having to be completed by September or the following January for the tax year ending the previous April 5th. The French system is a little different; it is based on a Tax Household *Foyer Fiscal* and the number of people within it, and the French tax year equates to the calendar year. Returns have to be completed in the following May, the actual date within May varies depending on your *Département* number, the lower the earlier. If you move here you can setup an account on the tax website without first making a tax declaration by applying for a *numéro fiscal* (tax id no.) To do so visit your local tax office or go online to the tax website www.impots.gouv.fr and click on '*Espace particulier.*'

Until 2019 income tax was payable annually in arrears but that year saw the introduction of *prélèvement à la source* (PAS), basically a PAYE system for those in employment, and retirees were also included with monthly payments due based on $1/_{12}$ the previous year's tax payable. Despite this everyone still has to make an annual declaration and everyone has to complete a French Tax return, including if one gets income from letting a property in France irrespective of where one lives. **Remember, the country that one pays tax in is defined in law and isn't a matter of personal choice!**
N.b. As an individual you are responsible for making the declaration,
   non receipt of relevant forms is not acceptable as an excuse.

As a first timer you will need to fill in and send off paper forms that one can download from the Government Tax website (See Annex C). As a minimum you will likely need the following forms *formulaires* and accompanying notes:
   2042   - Formulaire principal
   2042C - Revenu complémentaire
   2047   - Revenus de l'étranger
   3916   - Comptes de déclaration tenus à l'étranger?

Thereafter you can setup an online tax account if you haven't already and make subsequent submissions electronically. Your tax bill is then calculated by the Tax Office and you are sent it and notified of any amount owing during the summer. If you are due a refund it will be paid in September, if you need to pay more any amount under 300€ is payable then, else the difference is split over the 4 remaining months of the year.

There are numerous guides available for one to purchase that can help you with your submission but these are generally published before the Tax Authorities finalise their forms (as like HMRC they constantly tweak them year on year) and so they refer to the previous year's forms. If you are unsure you can always engage the services of an accountant *comptable*.

9.115.2 Taxe D'habitation

Taxe D'habitation is like Council Tax in the UK. It is either payable by the person who is residing in the property on the 1st January each year or the property owner by default. The

Everyday Living, an A to Z

tax is generally payable in October/November of that year though your *Notaire* may make the necessary payment on your behalf as part of the purchase process. The monies raised by this tax go to your commune who set the rate to be paid but it is based on the Cadastral Rental value of the house and its' outbuildings. There are reductions/exemptions for households with lower incomes but it is in the process of being phased out for principal home owners by 2023, although it will continue for second/holiday home owners.

> **The Tax office have started using aerial photos from Google to target home owners who fail to notify them of the installation of swimming pools, tennis courts and conservatories or extensions as this impacts the amount of *taxe foncière* and habitation paid.**

9.115.3 Taxe Foncière

Taxe Foncière can be viewed as a land and building ownership tax and is paid by whoever owns the property on 1st January each year and is based on a notional rental value as adjusted by the age, size and condition of the property. This money too goes to the commune, who set the rate, and amongst other things covers the cost of rubbish collection. This tax is generally paid in October/November although again when you purchase a property the tax for the year is generally paid pro-rata by the Vendor and Purchaser and sorted out by the *Notaire(s)*.

9.115.4 VAT

This is known in France as TVA (*Taxe sur la Valeur Ajoutée*), and as in the UK the main rate is 20% but there are reduced rates of 10% for things like Catering, Hotel Accommodation and Passenger Transport, and 5.5% for the majority of food items, soft drinks, feminine hygiene products etc. For completeness there is also a rate of 2.1% for the TV licence and certain publications whereas in the overseas departments of Guadeloupe, Martinique and Réunion the standard rate is 8.5%.

9.116 Tax Return

When you become resident in France you will have to declare any overseas accounts on your tax return (or get fined 1,500€ per account). Make sure that when you submit the return you send it by recorded delivery – *recommandée avec accusé de réception* – I submitted our very first return in the May as required. I had no acknowledgement or anything until the October when I got an official letter reminding me of my obligations to complete a return and stating the penalties for failing so to do. As I still had the confirmation slip and print of the tracking page I politely wrote back and said that I had submitted it and it had been received into their office on such and such a date and gave the name of the signee, after which I heard no more until I got my statement.

One doesn't usually get a French Tax reference number until after the (tax) assessment is issued – around August in the year following arrival assuming you have submitted a tax return.

9.117 Telecommunications

9.117.1 Networks

As in the UK telephone networks in France have expanded allied to the growth in mobile phones and advances in technology and continues to improve. To recap, the different network capabilities are as follows:

Everyday Living, an A to Z

2G (c1990)   Provides for calls and SMS;
3G (c2003)   Additionally provides limited web access and sending of photos;
4G (c2010)   In addition allows for web access, 'apps' and downloading/sending videos
5G (2020 on) Introduces connectivity to vehicles, augmented reality etc. and delivers a massive leap forward in both speed and quality. Data moves faster, it's more responsive, and you'll be able to connect a lot more devices at the same time.

The independent telecommunications regulator in France is called ARCEP (See Annex C) and in 2020 they announced that 96% of the country is covered by 4G supplied by at least one operating company.

9.117.2 VOIP

As in the UK the Public Switched Telephone Network (PTSN) here was based on traditional copper-wire landlines carrying analogue signals, but network modernisation is slowly replacing these with fibre-optic cable meaning that voice communication is progressively becoming internet based and users landline phones are being switched over to Voice Over Internet Protocol (VOIP) connections. Existing (landline) phones will still work, they are just connect to a different system behind the scenes.

In the UK it used to be that in the rare case of a power cut your landline phone would still likely work due to the different circuitry involved. One drawback of VOIP is that where the old landline phones received power via the line itself, which was separate to the household mains electricity supply. Internet based phones rely on home routers or similar devices so if there ius a power cut then you will have no internet and no phone and you will need a mobile to maintain 24/7/365 availability particularly if 'the one' is in a rural or semi-rural location.

9.118 Telephone Numbers

French telephone numbers have 10 digits and the convention is that people give out their telephone number in 2-digit groupings. Thus a number such as 0517894631 would be read out/stated as:

Zero *Cinq* – 05
Dix-Sept – 17
Quatre Vingt Neuf – 89
Quarante-Six – 46
Trente et Un - 31

Over the years in the UK we have become familiar with the STD codes of the major cities despite the tinkering of Oftel, as telecommunications expanded exponentially with the introduction of first fax machines and then mobiles etc. as well as slowly transferring from Analogue to Digital services. Thus over time London numbers went from 01 to 071/081 to 0171/0181 and then to 0207/0208 and mobiles occupied the 07 series numbers. In France things are a little more straightforward and the prefixes are geographic. Thus a prefix of:

   01 – Signifies the caller is based in the Isle de France area;
   02 – North West region;
   03 – North East region;
   04 – South East region;
   05 – South West region in addition to which;

Everyday Living, an A to Z

06 & 07 – Are allocated to Mobile telephones;
08 – Freephone numbers*; and
09 – Non-geographic number, Internet Service Providers.

* **Freephone prefixes are 0800-0805**; while 0806-0809 signify standard landline rates and 081, 082 and 089 are premium rate prefixes.

If you plan to get a French mobile/SIM, unlike in the UK there are no credit checks here to get contract mobiles or monthly SIM plans.

9.119 Telethon

In the same way as the UK has *'Children in Need'* or *'Red Nose Day'* in France they have the Telethon. It started in 1987 and raises money for various neuromuscular diseases, it officially takes place over the first weekend in December and over 30 hours of live TV are aired on France 2 and France 3 television channels. However many communes setup fund-raising events in their local *Salles de Fetes* in aid of the Telethon during mid to late November and some companies organise fund-raising days for their employees. In 2018 the Telethon raised almost 86 million euro's even though that figure was impacted by certain major events being cancelled due to *Gilets Jaune* activity. In 2020 all the nationwide events were cancelled due to Covid and the telethon was wholly digital.

9.120 TV Licence Fee

There is a TV licence fee payable in France but as with other things there is an exemption for those on a low income. It is called simply the fee *la redevance* and is a *contribution à l'audiovisuel public* which funds the five public television channels in mainland France - France 2, France 3, France 4, France 5, and Arte. The fee is revised annually and collected each November/December with the annual tax demand for the *taxe d'habitation*, (See section 9.115.2) where it will be listed separately.

9.121 Ticks

Part of the spider family, these parasitic insects satisfy all their nutritional needs by feeding on a diet of blood. They are perhaps best known for transmission of Lyme disease to humans although not all their bites are harmful. You can't escape these insidious parasites in France and if you or your dog(s) walk through any grassy areas and/or woodland then you are at a higher risk of tick bites, especially between April through September when they are most active. If you have a large amount of grass with *'the one'* then you need to carefully inspect/examine your dogs on a regular basis or each time after you have walked them. That said we cannot always see them on Keno and he is all white!

If you find that they do have ticks attached you can simply remove them by pressing down on them with your finger and then turning it anti-clockwise up to a dozen times or by twisting them out with Tick Hooks which you can obtain online or from your local vets. Not all dogs are happy with you doing this so alternatively you can take the precautionary route and use Tick collars or obtain Tick tablets for your pets from the vets. The latter are available for periods of one or three months during which they provide them with some resistance to the effects of tick bites.

Everyday Living, an A to Z

If you find that you are unlucky enough to get bitten by one you'll find that Tick Hooks (for Dogs) work just as well on humans, but more importantly if you see the bite area slowly changing into what appears to resemble a *'bulls-eye'* pattern then it is time to go the Doctor as you may well need the aid of anti-biotics to calm the infection.

9.122 Van Hire

There is always the odd occasion when you think that using a van/lorry for a few hours will solve your particular problem either getting to and from the *Déchetterie* with a large load or collecting something bulky like rolls of insulation or a sofa, but getting one from the established car/van hire companies can be prohibitively costly. An unlikely source for your needs is the local Supermarket or *Brico* as they seem to have numerous liveried vehicles around advertised at from as little as 1€/hour.

However just so you are aware the deposit *caution* on such things can be exceptionally high so if you are worried about getting into a scrape then they may not be for you. I stood in line behind a couple at a *Brico* who were hiring a flatbed truck (not sure for how long) but they wrote out a cheque for 1,500€.

That said when I recently hired a wagon mounted cherry picker *Camion Nacelle* to sort out a chimney leak all I was asked for was my address and driving licence before being handed the keys. No deposit, no signing endless insurance indemnity and waiver forms even though it was the first time I had used the company, happy days. Although maybe it was simply because I was leaving my car there for the day, I can't be sure?

9.123 Voting (Euro-elections)

Voting in the recent Euro Elections here was quite different to participating in elections in the UK. To vote in the European elections, you must:

- Be at least 18 years of age;
- Live in France;
- Be an EU citizen; and
- Have full civil and political rights.

For a start one's letterbox is not bombarded with party political material in the weeks leading up to the election, which in France takes place on a Sunday. Instead one receives a single envelope from the Marie between 1 and 2-weeks before the election that contains single sheet leaflets from every party participating for you to read or discard as you wish. As the system here is one of Proportional Representation it means that parties receive seats in direct proportion to the percentage of votes obtained and so one side of the leaflet lists the party's candidates in the order they will be allocated if successful.

On the day when one enters the polling station one will find a table with piles of the different leaflets on together with a small blue envelope. One is supposedly meant to take one of each leaflet into the polling booth, discard all those you don't intend voting for and place the leaflet of your preferred party into the envelope, seal it and then take it to the clerks sitting at a table. They will check your name and address against their master list. Moving on one then places one's envelope into a transparent Perspex box attended by, in our case, the *Maire*, after shaking hands of course. Finally a clerk at the *Maire's* side moves a register of names and addresses in your direction together with a template held against

Everyday Living, an A to Z

your entry line in the book. You sign within the template and your role in the election is then complete.

I found it strange that the leaflet table is visible to all so if you only grab a single leaflet it is clear who one is voting for. The envelope you use has no serial number on either which is another difference to the UK in that there seems to be a complete lack of audit trail with the actual votes.

9.124 VSP

In France it is possible to drive without a licence and I don't mean by driving a car on private land! That is because there is a type of car that doesn't require a compulsory licence to drive and that is a *Voiture Sans Permis*. These are also known as 'A-Cars'.

These are tiny, basic (no air bags or ABS) two-seater cars less than 3m in length, weighing no more than 425kg, with no more than an 8hp motor and pretty slow (with a top speed limited to just 45 kph) because of which they are not allowed on motorways. They are popular with young people because they can be driven from the age of 14, providing the driver has taken a written exam in the French highway code and driven whilst accompanied for 4 hours. Otherwise the *'AM Licence'* needs just 8 hours of training and a theory part which can be taken at school. Whereas the minimum driving age for most types of vehicles is 18 and learner drivers have to be 18 before they can pass the practical driving test for cars. Many young people find them a convenient means of travel as they are potentially safer than a scooter.

There is a serious downside in owing a VSP and that is because there's virtually no vetting process their owners can expect to pay high insurance premiums and insurance is mandatory. They also have a poor overall reputation, not just from those other drivers who get stuck behind one on a narrow winding country lane, but for being driven by older people who have otherwise lost their licence, particularly as the requirement to pass a written exam is waived for anyone born prior to 1988 and they don't need a licence or training to drive one. Which is why they could also be convenient for anyone moving here who has never learnt to drive.

Manufacturers don't view these cars negatively though as there are some 5/6 specific makers of them and Renault recently entered the market. However such cars are not particularly cheap options as the average cost for a new model is around 10,000€ but they vary from about 7,000€ to just over 20,000€.

9.125 Wasps

The day after we moved in we were lying in bed drinking a cup of tea and ended up watching a constant stream of wasps outside flying towards the corner of the dormer window in the bedroom. It felt like we were a powerless air-traffic control! We thought it would have been nice if our vendors had mentioned it or even dealt with it before we arrived, but these things happen. A trip to the local *Brico* furnished me with an aerosol of hornet, horsefly and wasp *frelon taon & guepe* killer and then it was down to me to apply it.

If you are dealing with these insects then firstly make sure you are well protected. I didn't want to be up a ladder with a throng of enraged wasps swarming around me so made sure I was well covered up and with minimal exposed skin. I donned work gloves, long sleeves, a

Everyday Living, an A to Z

mask, and made sure I was wearing eye protection and a hat as well. Then because their activity slows right down at dusk before picking up again just after dawn, I chose my moment carefully. Half an hour after dark I scaled a ladder and released a third of the can into the access hole. For good measure I set our alarm and repeated the process shortly after dawn the following day. They have not returned since.

We did have another occasion when we had seen a nest building up in the external apex of our Utility Room roof. Not wanting to be more than 20ft up in the air whilst spraying them I adopted an alternate approach. This involved reducing the hosepipe to a jet rather than a spray and then getting Joanne to turn the external tap fully open before I directed the jet up to the nest. I kept up the torrent despite nest pieces falling around me but luckily no wasps. I should however mention that this was nearing midnight after we had returned from a very sociable BBQ so I was feeling somewhat emboldened with my approach.

Some of the aerosol sprays you can buy to eliminate Hornets/Wasps will squirt the contents 4, 5 or 6m, which is ideal for dealing with aggressive hornets or wasps if you don't want to get too close to the nest.

9.125.1 Wasp Nests

We do seem to attract our fair share of Wasps here, more so than in the UK, but then there is a lot of wood in and around the house which may be the attraction for them? It is not just that the house is timber framed but we have wooden doors, floors, skirting boards, beams in a number of the rooms, staircase and weather boarding on a quarter of the outside as well as the large wraparound deck and veranda. Consequently since our early encounters with them we inspect the boarding, beams and look in the corners of rooms quite regularly to see if there is any build-up of a pale, opaque, papery type of structure that indicates they have started a nest, and we then deal with it accordingly. We've had cocoons/nests build up in some very strange places so it is worth keeping an eye out as we have found them:

On beams;
- On a pillow in a little used bedroom;
- On the hinge side of a window;
- In a box with little used kitchen equipment;
- In springtime on our winter coats hanging in the utility room;

With our house they seem to frequent the apex of dormer windows as an entry point for their nests and I have dealt with a further 2 since the initial problem.

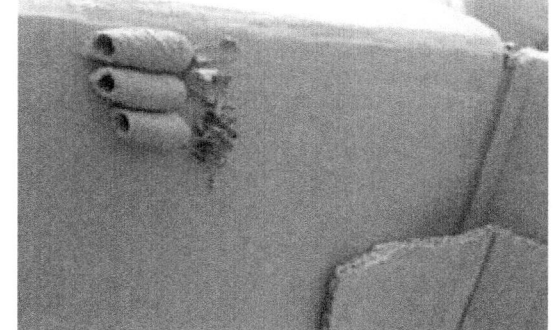

Everyday Living, an A to Z

9.125.2 Wasp Traps

Our wasps are not constrained to the house. Because we have numerous fruit trees they are a nuisance outside too. Taking a leaf out of the local orchards' book we have invested in Wasp Traps. You can buy these in Farmers Co-operatives or Supermarkets. They are basically an enclosed plastic container with a trough in the bottom and a raised entrance hole in the middle. The idea being that you hang these from the branches of the trees you are trying to protect and entice the wasps inside with sweet smelling aromas and they then struggle to get back out. Yes you can buy specially formulated liquid to fill them with but you will over the months spend a pretty penny if you take this route. Beer, stale or otherwise works just as well but my preferred approach is to buy a 1½ litre bottle of cheap sweet cider from the Supermarket and mix it 1:1 with water. It is just as effective and a lot less costly in the long run. Obviously if you have had a day/night with stronger than usual winds it pays to check the levels in the traps as the rocking motion may have lowered the levels or indeed emptied them.

tip When it comes to traps, don't necessarily buy one though, you can take the Blue Peter approach and make your own by cutting up a 1½ litre plastic drinks bottle, putting the top into the bottom, making 2 holes and passing string through to hang from a tree. Use a smooth bottle like Cider is sold in rather than mineral water bottles as they tend to be ribbed. Tape the join and the *'job's a good un'*!

9.126 Water Quality

I have to say that one pleasing aspect about the quality of our local water is that it is extremely soft. Coming from Essex we were used to needing a Water Softener but in almost 6 years in the *Corrèze* I am happy to say that we haven't had to descale our kettle once.

If you are concerned about the quality of the drinking water in the area around *'the one'* then obviously contact your Water Supply Company but you can also try visiting your *Mairie* who should be able to supply you with information on any water quality tests carried out. Failing that then a visit to your *préfecture* who are actually responsible for water quality testing should elicit the information you need. To this end the consumers organisation *UFC Que Choisir* published an interactive map of Water Quality by postcode (in April 2021) using the criteria of bacteria, filtering and pesticides (See Annex C).

Depending on your fluency in French you can also go onto your Water company's website. There is also a government website on which one can find the most recent quality tests for one's commune. (See Annex C).

9.127 Water Restrictions

The recent *Canicules* (Heatwaves) in France have led to water restrictions across many *départements* as water levels in reservoirs ran dangerously low and even some large towns feared for their water supplies. In fact during Summer 2019 even the *Corrèze* which regularly features in the Top 15 wettest *départements* in France saw water tankers deployed to some half dozen or more communes; and in 2020 it experienced its driest July since 1959 with only 10% of its usual 83mm of Rain falling in the month. During such periods householders are restricted in their use of water. For your information France employs 4 levels of alert:

Everyday Living, an A to Z

Type of Alert	Meaning
Level one (grey) *Vigilance*	urges the public to consider their water usage and to cut down where possible.
Level two (yellow) *Alerte*	cuts the amount of water farmers can use by 50% and prohibits activities such as watering gardens, green spaces, golf courses, as well as banning the washing of cars between 10h and 20h each day.
Level three (orange) *'Alerte Renforcé*	imposes more stringent limits on farmers and prohibits watering gardens, green spaces, golf courses or cars
Level four (red) *Crise*	the highest level bans all non-priority uses, including agriculture. Where these decrees have been issued, water can only be used for drinking, sanitation and public health.

During the higher level alerts even householders with wells are told not to use well water to water their gardens as obviously these wells draw water from the same underground aquifers that are ultimately used by the water companies.

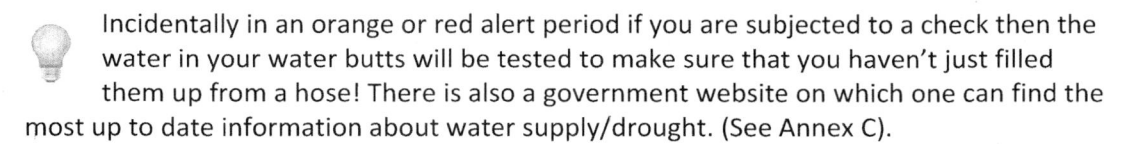

Incidentally in an orange or red alert period if you are subjected to a check then the water in your water butts will be tested to make sure that you haven't just filled them up from a hose! There is also a government website on which one can find the most up to date information about water supply/drought. (See Annex C).

9.128 Water Storage

Finding *'the one'* with lots of land and flowers, plants, shrubs and vegetables is one thing, keeping it looking presentable is another, especially in the summer when temperatures can easily exceed 40°C in the southern parts of the country. For that you need water and lots of it, and that means some form of storage solution. Sure there are always hosepipes, but unless you have access to a Well then you are likely to be on a water meter and I can tell you nothing will set the dial spinning more than turning the hose on each day to water your flowers/plants.

Consequently acquiring containers to store water in is a necessity. If you have any and they are reasonably clean you can use old oil drums else you will need to purchase some purpose built Water Butts from your local *Brico* but you will also then need to buy a connector kit, cover, stand and tap which are all sold separately and the cost then starts to mount up. Instead wait for your local supermarket to run a promotion or *déstockage* event where you can pick up a complete ensemble far cheaper!

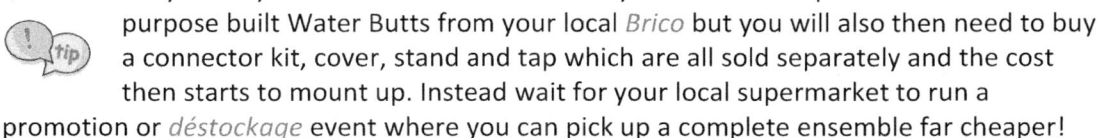

The types of Butts sold generally range in size from 200 to 500 litres or 1,000 litres but as an alternative, and this depends very much on your budget, you could utilise a plastic *Fosse Septique* tank placed above ground which will give you in excess of 3,000 litre capacity (bear in mind that the average UK bath holds c67 litres) however if you go down this route you will likely need a submersible pump with an appropriate hose fitting to be able to extract and utilise the contents. By appropriate I mean a *'semi-*

Everyday Living, an A to Z

rigid' hosepipe rather than one of the *'lay flat'* variety as these are prone to bending over at right angles when they exit the butt and restricting the flow. Using such a pump and hose we have the ability to move the water around from one strategically sited storage container to another if required.

We inherited some such storage and have acquired additional capacity since which we have spread around the property. As such we have some 14,000 litres available for the produce in our polytunnel and vegetable patch as well as our fruit trees which provides some 3-4 weeks supply should we need it during the really hot weather.

If you have/use Water Butts then make sure you place the lid firmly on top so that it locks into place, this keeps out leaves from any adjacent trees, as these can block your taps when the level in the butt approaches the bottom and also ensures your butt doesn't have unwanted visitors such as insects and small animals. I didn't cover the butt at the back of the barn as there are no trees in the vicinity but so far it has accounted for 2 Loir, 6 Mice and innumerable wasps.

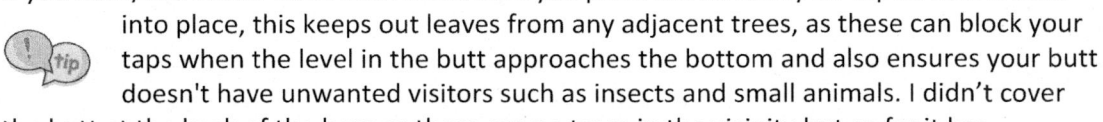

9.129 Websites.

As a society we have become used to buying goods or event tickets or looking up information via a search engine or a company's website. However here in France your digital experience may not be what you are used to. I have already remarked that it is common to see posters (See section 9.91) advertising things that are long since out of date but the same is sometimes also true of company websites as their content management in general is woefully lacking by UK standards.

Even comparatively simple things like the display of opening and closing hours cannot always be believed. If you have not been to a particular store before then do not plan to go just as it opens or just before closing as you may well be disappointed! Give yourself some additional time or call them once your language is up to it.

Many companies that have websites just use them for display purposes with no link to a purchasing function. Equally the in-site search facilities don't always return every product they sell and you will not always find the latest result or match report on sports clubs site's for example.

In connection with this our instant society expects that if we contact a supplier through their website that they respond to our question/complaint within a matter of hours, this does not seem to be the case here and you can easily wait days for a response. I had a problem with a brushcutter that had come apart so I emailed the manufacturers support desk and although I got an automatically generated support ticket number it took them 10 days to reply to my mail. In the meantime I had got fed up with the wait and taken it back to the store.

You will also find that filling in a webform doesn't always guarantee a speedy response, I have completed such forms to try and obtain:
- A dental check-up at my dentist;
- A quote for septic tank emptying;
- A quote for a set of brake pads for my car; and
- A service for my mower.

Everyday Living, an A to Z

None of which elicited any response. Only after I subsequently called/visited them did I manage to arrange the appointment/obtain the quote.

I don't want to single out my rugby club but Brive had a game postponed on the Wednesday evening as some of their opponents players had tested positive for coronavirus yet on Friday morning their phone '*App*' was still counting down the hours to kick-off time.

Finally a word of warning about filling in your details if making an order on a French website. Many of them make it **mandatory** to enter a French mobile telephone number, rather than a landline number. A UK mobile number is also rejected out of hand. Curiously this situation applies when trying to setup ones *DMP Dossier Médical Partage* which enables one to keep all one's health information online and share it with the health professionals of your choice.

Of course the sites' validation doesn't always tell you this and you have to work it out. So if you don't have one enter a friends number if you can or otherwise create a dummy one such as 0600000011 to enable you to move on and complete the purchase.

9.130 Well Water

In certain circumstances having a well can be a positive addition to a property but you need to check that your well is registered at the *Mairie*. Further, if it is used to supply drinking water then you need to get it analysed regularly although you can arrange for this through your local pharmacy who will send samples off for testing.

You need to be careful as in the times the water is not drinkable you will have to rely on bottled mineral water from the supermarket which will start to get expensive but is also an awful lot of single use plastic to dispose of. Be aware too that well water can contain sediment that will discolour it and your clothes through your washing machine. If you suffer a power cut then your pump will stop working and you won't have any water unless you can extract it manually.

Some friends moved into a house that hitherto had been empty for some months, and it had a readily accessible well opposite the front door. On the day they moved in a neighbour's dog seemed to immediately adopt them as she spent all day with them, even seeing off the neighbouring farmer's dog as though it were her house and territory (although to be fair she probably adopted it whilst it was empty). However when she was offered water to drink (from the well) she refused to drink it but later she was happy to drink bottled water. Subsequently the laboratory deemed the well water undrinkable as it bore traces of e-coli, reinforcing to a degree that animals sometimes have more intelligence than we give them credit for and that as humans we can learn a lot from them.

9.131 Wildlife

9.131.1 Wildlife Spotting

If you live anywhere rural then it is likely you will see a large variety of wildlife during your time here. If you acquire a building plot or a house that has recently been built on one in such a location (as ours was) then potentially you will have encounters on a daily basis. Courtesy of my Trail Camera/Camera Trap which I have setup in our garden on many occasions I know that we experience visits from Badgers *Blaireau*, Black Squirrels, Genets, Martens, Red Squirrels, Roe Deer *Chevreuil* and Water Rats as well as a plethora of different

Everyday Living, an A to Z

types of feathered visitor. In particular we have a Heron who frequently visits our *étang*, even more so when our second fallen tree straddled it, as well as numerous Honey Buzzards in addition to the usual suspects – Blackbirds, Crows, Jays, of course the ubiquitous Magpies, Robins, Sparrows, Tits etc. and my particular favourite a Green Woodpecker. We also watched a Great Tit family grow up in a nest box *nichoir* on a table on the veranda and some Redstarts built a nest in the car port in the barn. At different times during the day if you sit on the veranda for any length of time you can listen to the numerous bird species battle for aural supremacy. At night we can be buzzed by bats as well as hear the distinctive call of owls *chouette* (f) / *hibou* (m). In late Autumn we stand enthralled at the sights & sounds of wave after wave of migrating Cranes heading South and South West.

On other occasions we can stand in the kitchen or dining room and watch deer grazing or foxes foraging in the garden, that is until Alfie/Keno spot them and drive them off with the sound of their barking. We are lucky in that Joanne (and Alfie) has seen only one wild boar in the flesh. I say luckily as Farmers hate them because of the crop loss through their scavenging and they can do an awful lot of damage with their digging; although we have an Akbash/Berger Blanc Suisse Croise that can rival them to some degree.

In fact If we had known the extent of the wildlife in our garden we would have thought twice about sending Alfie down the garden with his lighted collar after we moved here. (See section 5.9.3)

Equally don't be surprised to find wildlife on the rural roads day or night. As well as any of the above, depending on the part of the country you ultimately reside in you may even see a Lynx or Wolf *loup*.

9.131.2 Accidents with Wildlife

I hope that you have nothing but positive interactions with your local wildlife but from time to time in rural locations you will likely encounter all manner of dead creatures on the roads, badgers, birds, cats, coypu, deer, dogs, foxes, hedgehogs, honey buzzards, owls, pine martens, rabbits, snakes, squirrels, voles etc. I have seen them all on or at the side of the road and indeed have buried some that were in close proximity to the house but should you have the misfortune to hit and kill either a deer or wild boar then the law states that you can take it home (to eat) providing you inform the local *gendarmerie*/police first. Alternatively you can contact the *Mairie*.

However if you hit any other wild animal whilst driving along then the best advice is to contact the nearest wild animal rescue centre – *centre de sauvegarde de la faune sauvage* https://www.reseau-soins-faune-sauvage.com/
or if it is a wild bird then the *LPO* (See Annex C).

9.132 Winter Truce

La trêve hivernale or the so-called winter truce runs for five months from November 1st until midnight on 31st March and marks a period when French landlords are not legally allowed to forcibly evict their tenants **for any reason**. The truce is meant as a humanitarian gesture, to ensure that people (but not squatters) do not end up homeless in the coldest part of the year. During this period it is also illegal for landlords to cut off gas and electricity supplies in the event of unpaid bills. The exceptions to this are if the house is dangerous to live in or if

Everyday Living, an A to Z

it is in connection with moving the tenants to a better standard of accommodation. However, a landlord can begin proceedings during the winter truce to look to evict any tenants who do not pay their rent, or who refuse to leave after being given the contractual notice period. However, this still requires a court order from a judge at the local *tribunal d'instance*, which the tenants can appeal. Once any final judgment is made then the landlord has to give the eviction order via a bailiff, and the tenant then has, depending on the judgment, at least two months to leave, though it can't take place during *La trêve hivernale*.

Interestingly as part of their response to the coronavirus pandemic the UK Government appeared to copy this measure as they said (10 Sept 20) that there would be a truce on enforcement action for tenants facing eviction in England & Wales at Christmas, neither would it be enforced in areas subject to local lockdown. Bailiffs would also be told they should not enforce possession orders over Christmas apart from in the most exceptional circumstance. Here in France due to the pandemic and the financial impact it caused the grace period has been extended to the 1st June for last year and repeated for this year.

9.133 Wood (for Heating)

If *'the one'* has a woodburning stove(s) you will obviously need to source a supply of wood to use through the winter. This may come from trees on your own land although received wisdom is that anything cut *'this year'* should be allowed to dry out for a year before using it the next. Alternatively you can buy *Bois de Chauffage* from a commercial source. Only experience, or information received from your Vendor, will tell how much wood you need on average each year but what quantities of measure do you buy it in?

- A *stère* (a term which originates from the original metric system) equates to a cubic metre of wood – usually in 1 metre lengths.
- A cord is approximately 3½ *stères* although it depends on the size of the pieces and the airspace between them.

The price you are generally quoted is for 1 metre lengths but do not make the mistake of thinking you can easily cut it to size (say 50cm lengths) just before you need it as even if you use a chainsaw it will take you much longer than you think. Believe me it is far simpler to ask the merchant to cut it to the length you want, before delivery and pay the 20-30€ extra!

9.134 Woodburning Stoves

On a cold winter's day there something satisfying about the glow of a log fire and If *'the One'* is old or rural the chances are that it will have a wood burner *Poêle* which could possibly be the primary heat source although many renovated houses choose to have them as a focal point. On the other hand if you are thinking of installing one make sure you choose one with sufficient heat output for your needs and there are numerous online calculators to assist you with this. They have had a bad press environmentally but at least with the overall supply and the French approach to managing their woodland the wood itself usually comes from sustainable sources.

Everyday Living, an A to Z

9.134.1 Some Tips

Tempting as it may be don't overfill your burner the heat generated could damage it irreparably.

1. Buy a Stove thermometer for either the top of the burner or the flue/stove pipe, these usually have a magnetic base and therefore easily attach. To get the optimum heat output from your stove it should ideally burn at a temperature between 260°C and 460°C. Anything lower and it will be burning too slowly to generate a decent amount of heat and it will likely be producing copious amounts of smoke.
2. To maximise the heat produced use a stove fan, they either attach to your stove pipe or sit on top of the stove and using the heat produced to direct the hot air out into the room rather than it rise to the top of your fireplace.
3. Use properly seasoned dry wood (meaning it should have a moisture content of <20%). Generally any wood you cut this year should be stored for burning next year. Fresh cut (green) wood can hold upwards of 50% moisture. If you try and burn this the extra moisture causes excessive smoke which can blacken your stove glass, make your chimney dirty and lead to a potentially dangerous build-up of creosote in the flue.
4. Wood burners are very effective but do dry out the air in the room very quickly and as a result you may find that you suffer from itchy eyes or even headaches. Simply placing a heat resistant bowl filled with water on top of your burner will add moisture back in to the air as it slowly evaporates.
5. As a bonus, if necessary you can cook some meals on it if you suffer a power cut.

9.134.2 How you can tell if wood is seasoned

As wood loses water it shrinks and small cracks form in the end grain (but different woods behave differently so this is not a totally reliable method);

The colour of seasoned wood changes more to a grey/silvery look rather than the yellowy look of freshly cut wood (shown on the left) and it may start to lose its bark which drops away as moisture reduces; also:

- If it is hard to chop up or split then it is likely to be seasoned enough;
- Try picking up 2 pieces of equal size and bang them together, if the wood is dry there will be some reverberation and they will sound hollow as opposed to the dull thud of wet wood;
- The wood will not give off any odour when burned;

Another way would be to buy a moisture meter but that is taking things to extremes for the average home user.

9.135 Wood Stores

If you either don't have a garage or decide to park the car outside on a regular basis then avoid parking near your woodpile. Friends of ours were in the habit of doing this until their car wouldn't start one day. It was eventually diagnosed that mice had thought the engine

Everyday Living, an A to Z

compartment cosier than the woodpile and as part of making themselves comfortable decided to chew through the electrical wiring necessitating a costly tow to and repair by the local garage! Of course you can get a deterrent spray for the wiring but best not to put you in the position of needing it in the first place. Take care, wood piles can also harbour snakes!

9.136 Your Address

Obviously you know where you live and can describe it to family/friends who visit easily enough but it is not always obvious to delivery drivers, particularly if you are just known by a house name and a commune. Consequently I suggest that if you have accounts on say Amazon, Ebay, or any other supplier that you make regular purchases from or just when making adhoc orders that you change the first line of your address in your customer profile to include your specific GPS Co-ordinates, something in the format of:

<House Name> (GPS nn.nnnnnn, n.nnnnnn)
<Road>
<Commune> etc.

then there should be no excuse for not getting deliveries to your door.

Because a lot of courier companies still give an expected delivery timeslot of between 0800 and 1800 they give one the opportunity to have one's parcels delivered to a nearby collection point, e.g. a *Bibliothèque*, or *Tabac* so if there is something that needs a signature, is valuable, or you are just going to be out for the day then take advantage of this facility.

Boys Toys & Other Useful Playthings

10. Boys Toys & Other Useful Playthings

10.1 Introduction

In this section I am not talking about the tools one might regularly see in a toolbox such as hammers, pliers, saws, screwdrivers etc. Or even the ancillary items that one accumulates over time such as a Circular Saw, Drill, or Sander or depending on your property say a Post Rammer or Winch. No the kind of thing I am talking about is the type of kit that one doesn't necessarily need back in the UK with much smaller gardens to tend.

These may seem like an extravagance, particularly if one's budget is tight but they will more than pay for themselves in a relatively short time period by saving you time and effort and you will soon become proficient in a range of skills you didn't know you had. I am not suggesting that you go out and buy them all at once, it should be needs based, analyse your situation (location, size and nature of plot etc.) first, use that to determine your actual requirements and then fulfil your needs. You can always borrow from friends or hire/rent them in the first instance to inform your decision, better still wait for any clearance *déstockage* events where you can potentially pick up what you need much cheaper. But do buy the tools you need for the job, rather than try and make do.

10.2 Battery, Electric or Petrol

Once you have decided on what tool you need the first question you have to ask yourself is what type of tool do I buy, Battery, Electric or Petrol and when I say Petrol this encompasses Diesel? For the larger than average grounds of a French property I would suggest that you want to strongly consider a Petrol powered device, although that does mean you will likely be spending more on them as they can be 3 times the price of a comparable electric model.

Stating the obvious, basically if you anticipate doing a lot of work in relatively inaccessible places where extension leads are impractical then you need Battery or Petrol tools. If a tool is a bit of a luxury and you don't see a huge use for it then battery powered versions could be cheaper. I took this approach for instance with a circular saw as I don't do a lot of woodworking so don't need an expensive piece of kit sitting around.

10.2.1 Battery Powered

Of course you can consider battery powered devices and believe me where there is a need you can find a device, I was amazed!. Consequently you will not be surprised to find that battery powered All in One's, Chainsaw's, Hedge Cutters, Leaf blower's, Mower's and Strimmer's etc. all exist. There are also Electric Rotavators but I am not sure how they would cope with cloggy soil. I have personally never contemplated such machines on our plot due to its sheer size but if you are thinking battery powered then I guess the type of questions you need to ask yourself are:
- How long does a battery last (from which you can determine how much work you will get done on a single charge)?
- How long does a battery take to charge?
- How much does a (spare) battery cost?
- Are there different rated batteries (power) for each tool?

Boys Toys & Other Useful Playthings

As I am thinking you need at least two per tool, one on while you are working and one charging. In which case a further question then arises:
- Are the batteries interchangeable (between devices)?
  (It is possible that even tools from the same manufacturer will have different fittings in which case that will be more outlay).

What you don't want to happen is to start a job and have to continually stop some way through it to wait for the battery/spare to charge.

10.2.2 Electric Powered

So it may be that you discount battery powered devices for all but the smallest jobs and go with Electrical as that is probably what you have been used to in the UK.

But you have to think practically, how far is it from your front/back door and the nearest socket to the edge of your boundary? It is not just a case of whether you have an extension lead long enough or even multiple leads and a circuit breaker you can use, but can you realistically see yourself outside using your electrical appliances? For one thing wet or even damp weather can greatly restrict your usage, impact your safety and then you need to think of the Electricity consumption if you are spending hours using them. Electricity in France is not cheap.

Using electric powered tools outside is all very well but do ensure that you use an RCD (Residual Current Device) as well as it acts as a circuit breaker and prevents electrocution; for example if you cut through the cable when mowing the lawn or cutting a hedge – which I have done in a previous life. Chances are you will use a portable device that plugs into any standard socket-outlet and you plug your appliance of choice into the RCD which then continuously monitors the current flowing through the circuit it is protecting. if it detects electricity flowing down an inadvertent path, such as through a person who has touched a live wire, then it switches the circuit off very quickly, thereby reducing the risk of death or serious injury.

10.2.3 Petrol Powered

So for these reasons allied to the size of our plot and the distances involved my personal preference is to opt for petrol powered tools. A choice of Petrol gives you more flexibility if you are out and the weather takes a turn for the worse. Conversely should the weather be bad when you open the curtains you can still go out and work with Petrol.

I will now attempt a brief discussion on the type of Petrol toys you might need. The majority of them require a different mix of Petrol and 2 Stroke Oil to run. Consequently I suggest you label up separate bottles with an indelible pen to store the different mixtures in. The tools won't perform well, if at all, with the wrong mixture.

The one thing you will not find in this list is a strimmer. Reason being is that I have had a few but irrespective of the make and the care one takes with them I have found that after a while this concept of a command feed just doesn't work. Whether it is by pressing a button or banging the spool to feed out more line they all jam and to me seem a complete waste of time and money and a triumph of marketing over practicality.

Boys Toys & Other Useful Playthings

10.3   All in 1

You know the kind of thing I mean. Where there is a base power unit and you plug in/on various attachments, extensions and handles. I started off with a 4 in 1 brushcutter, hedge trimmer, pruner, and strimmer. To start with you only tend to use a couple of the attachments far more than the others so you are paying for things you don't really need. I also tended to use the pruner as a substitute chainsaw which it really isn't. But secondly and more importantly I would argue that they cannot necessarily be a master of all trades and that with continual mixed use they will wear out far quicker than a purpose-built tool. Mine did after a year, caught fire in fact!

10.4   Brushcutter

A *Débroussailleuse* is basically a long pole with a triangular/solid metal disc (with or without teeth) on the end that spins around at high speed. It is therefore more robust and can cut through thicker vegetation than a strimmer and is my preference in this department. They come with both motors & blades of differing sizes so you *'pays your money and takes your choice'* depending on the work you have planned for it. They are ideal for cutting a path through brambles or cutting down grass under low hanging tree branches where you might not be able to reach with your mower. A purpose built one will come with a harness that you strap on and helps you bear the weight.

Through experience when using a brushcutter I would always use a helmet with safety visor or safety goggles as a minimum and leather work gloves as if you inadvertently flick up a stone it will travel at high speed, and hurt!

10.5   Chainsaw

The *Tronçonneuse* is an extremely useful adjunct to one's toolbox indeed I would say that having one is fundamental to your new life here.

> **However they are not to be taken lightly as Chainsaws do not take any prisoners. Other tools in your armoury may cut/bruise you if they are mishandled, but any accident with a chainsaw is likely to be serious and involve a rapid trip to the hospital.**

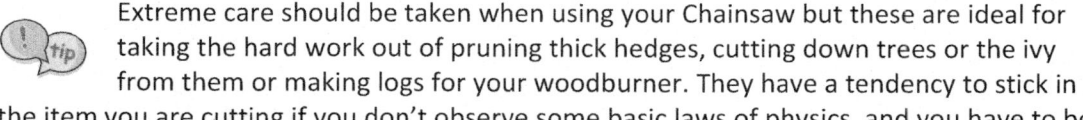

Extreme care should be taken when using your Chainsaw but these are ideal for taking the hard work out of pruning thick hedges, cutting down trees or the ivy from them or making logs for your woodburner. They have a tendency to stick in the item you are cutting if you don't observe some basic laws of physics, and you have to be careful trying to extract them else you can damage the bar and/or the chain and need replacements.

Only buy a longer length saw (more than 12") once you are accomplished using one of the smaller versions.

Depending on how or where you buy it, you may have to assemble the chainsaw yourself. Pay attention as it is possible to put the chain on the bar *'back to front'* in which case although it will spin round it won't actually cut anything. Another rookie

Boys Toys & Other Useful Playthings

mistake is that you fail to tighten the chain sufficiently and that it is too loose which means it will snag more easily and come off the chain bar while you are trying to cut.

It is good practice, some will say a necessity, to at least wear some safety gear when using your chainsaw. Some or all of a helmet with safety visor (I had a chain snap on one occasion) and/or ear defenders, leather work gloves, boots or shoes with '*toe- tectors*' and even Protective trousers which have multiple abrasive resistant layers should be considered, avoid loose clothing too in case it drops into/catches in the chain.

Also through experience when out cutting trees I will take along a bowsaw and a crowbar with me in case the chainsaw gets stuck and you need to free the blade quickly without incurring any damage to either bar or chain.

10.6 Cherrypicker

As toys go I have to say that ever since I hired one of these for just a day (See section 9.122) I have wanted my own one (rather like a Jet-ski but I know unfortunately our *étang* is far too small), but realistically they are way out of budget, not just to buy but the maintenance of the necessary hydraulics adds to the annual expense. However they are ideal for sorting out problems with Chimney Stacks, Hedges or your Roof. Dependent on your needs there are free standing pickers or one's with caterpillar tracks that need to be either towed, trailered or otherwise transported to your site, and don't discount scissor jacks that might work just as well depending on circumstances.

10.7 Compact Tractor

If you are looking for a little more flexibility around your plot then perhaps a compact tractor is more your style, particularly if you intend to develop '*the one*' into more of a smallholding. With more brake horsepower and capable of being easily fitted with a range of useful accessories e.g. auger/post borer, back hoe, bucket, chain harrow, log splitter, rotavator, topper etc as your needs dictate, these versatile *polyvalente* beasts can save you a mountain of time.

Sometimes the weight of attachments, in particular a cutting deck, make these machines '*rear end heavy*' particularly travelling up a slope consequently it's not unusual to see tractors with Gabion Cages or Oil Drums (filled with concrete, rocks, sand or water accordingly) welded to their front to counter-balance/offset the weight of the attachments.

10.8 Crowbar

A Crowbar *pince à levier* is not usually thought of in terms of boys toys but for me it is an ideal piece of kit, providing it is 4ft/120cm long! The type I am talking about has one flat/slightly curved end and one very curved end with a hammer like claw feature. I originally bought mine to assist in dismantling the old decking as the leverage it is capable of exerting using either end will remove even the most stubborn screw.

But since then it has proved to be an extremely versatile tool in the garden and on the drive as our land is extremely rocky once you get say 6" down. You'll know what I mean if you have ever bent a garden fork(s) whilst digging out holes. Trying to remove a large piece of rock or stone just isn't easy with a fork unless you dig a far bigger hole than you need. Using the crowbar makes life far simpler, use the flat end to find the edge of the rock, work your

Boys Toys & Other Useful Playthings

way down the side and then lever it out, works every time. This type of crowbar is also good for prising stuck pieces of wood out of a shredder (that doesn't have a reversal mode) as well as digging post holes, levering off ancient ivy or helping to remove Metposts or small tree stumps providing you use the right fulcrum.

10.9 Generator

Living in the countryside a Generator *Groupe électrogène* really comes into its own as power cuts are a way of life unfortunately, and not just in the winter. Our worst one was on the 4th July (yes really) 2018 when a huge storm crossed the country taking out fences, power lines, roof tiles etc. We lost power at 1800 on the Wednesday and it wasn't restored until around 1330 on the Saturday. I was extremely lucky as I had a pre-booked trip back to the UK from the Thursday to Sunday so Joanne bore the brunt of it with candles in the house and going out in the car to charge her phone and ipad etc. and the compensation we received from EDF a few months later was scant consolation for the annoyance caused.

This was the third such occasion we had lost power for some time (once while we were away on holiday), so I decided that we had lost enough freezer food and that we needed a generator. They come in all shapes, sizes and prices and there are plenty of online calculators available to help determine *the one* that meets your requirements. I was not thinking about something that would power the whole house necessarily just keeping the essentials going like fridges and freezers and being able to make cups of tea or coffee. It doesn't need to automatically start when the power fails as I am happy to go and fire it up as required. A friend has a 3Kw machine but when it is running it trips out if he switches the kettle or TV on which seems somewhat inconvenient so I went for a 5Kw version which gives us a bit more flexibility. We can run the fridges and freezers, have some lights on and make tea without worrying about having to restart it.

Before you start up your generator check over the fuel pipes if they are rubber to make sure they haven't split or perished since the last check/usage. Also when you start it up make sure it is not in your garage as the exhaust fumes can build up in an enclosed space and get sucked in thereby stopping the generator. If you have trouble starting it then you can use '*damp start*' or at worse a normal deodorant and spray it into the air intake as you would with an older car.

Because of the radial circuitry in French houses you need to be careful plugging the generator into your domestic supply. You must ensure your main input circuit breaker/isolation switch is set to OFF, then start your generator and simply plug it into a standard power socket to power your house. But be sure to stop and disconnect your generator first prior to re-setting the breaker when you finish using it.

Different generators have varying sizes of petrol tank and this combined with their hourly petrol consumption gives differing periods of autonomy. In the case of an extended power outage it becomes a matter of personal choice and practicality as to how long you run them for. Consider for example whether you need to run your generator on a 24 hour basis or just during waking hours as freezers will happily go through the night without power with minimal impact on their contents providing the door remains closed? The reason being that some generators use upwards of 25-30 litres for c11 hours electricity production so the costs for running them for a day start to mount up and could easily

Boys Toys & Other Useful Playthings

begin to outweigh the costs of any food you are trying to save but clearly come into their own if enabling heating systems to carry on running.

With luck it will be something you have that you don't need to use, but when you want it to spring into life you want to be sure that it does so it is a good idea to power it up every few months. By power it up I mean switch off the mains supply to the house, connect the generator and start it rather than do it independently. Be comfortable with the process so it isn't a concern when you do it for real.

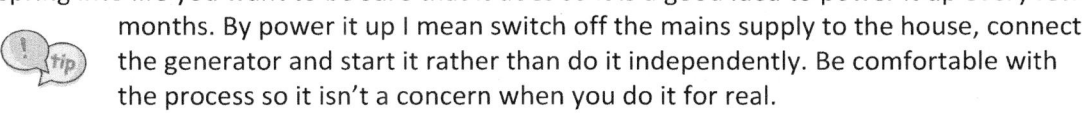

10.10 Hedge Trimmers

A *taille-haie* is essential if like us you have almost 200m or more of hedging boundary that needs upkeep. It would lead to severe cases of RSI (Repetitive Strain Injury) if you had to cut this amount by hand, so having powered assistance is essential. Anything thicker than the hedge trimmer can manage can easily be dealt with by your chainsaw.

10.11 Mower

The typical plot size here renders your average Flymo redundant and you just need some form of powered *Tondeuse*. The standard kind that you walk behind and push is adequate depending on the type of terrain and its size but for most of the larger properties you will need to consider a (*Tondeuse) autoportée* or ride on mower.

Our plot is over 2 hectares and when you discount the Barn, Drive, *Etang*, House, Woods and boundary area I reckon there is still over 3 acres that needs regular mowing. The garden which was pasture in a previous life slopes every which way and the ground is prone to moles *taupes* and their holes and hills *taupinières*. I spoke with a couple of local garden supply shops who were very helpful and offered to come and size up my garden and recommend the right piece of hardware but the cost of the tractors and machinery they were proposing were too rich for my blood. I was also apprehensive as I never previously owned a house that required me to use one before. A chance conversation with a friend at a quiz night helped me enormously. He had 9 acres, with slopes and mole holes and said that his ride-on was more than a match for the job. I then rang a company in England and spoke to a salesman for 40 minutes about the merits of different models and pretty much made my decision based on that. I went to see him when I was next back in the UK, tried out my preferred model with a test drive and then arranged to buy it and have it shipped over as a part load. (See section 6.5). Talking to the salesman had another advantage, he offered to fit a 50mm ball hitch to the back of the mower before I took delivery so I could use it to pull a trailer if I needed/wanted to. Without it I would need a trailer with a universal hitch pin attachment which seem somewhat rarer here.

n.b. I know that earlier in this guide I have advocated shopping locally but in this instance I was far happier having a detailed and technical conversation about something I had no practical experience of in my native language. Whereas when we bought our car I was happy to do that from a French dealership.

Boys Toys & Other Useful Playthings

In the end I went for the next model up in the range than my friend, as well as a slightly bigger engine (656cc/17hp as opposed to 500cc/13hp), better suspension and it had a 120cm cutting deck not 102cm. Not much difference you might think but if your garden is say 100m long isn't it better to make a minimum of 83 passes across to cut it (dependent on contours and the position of flower beds, ponds and trees etc) rather than 98? Then factor in mowing every couple of weeks between say April & September and that is a lot of time saved.

10.11.1 Type of Mower

I said at the outset that I would not get involved in technical challenges so whether you need a lawn tractor, simple ride-on or zero turn model you will have to determine yourself, as I did. I never had the need for such a mower before and found the potential choice a little daunting, until the conversation with my friend. Choose wisely because you will find that a decent ride-on will likely cost as much as any second-hand car you may have bought in an earlier life.

Once you have homed in on your type and make you then need to decide whether you are mowing and collecting the grass or mowing and mulching it? As far as I was concerned it was a *'no-brainer'*. Given the size of our plot compared with the average size collector box on the back of a mower I foresaw endless trips back up the garden to an ever growing compost pile to empty the container and so steered well away from those models as when you're cutting it every week or so in late spring and summer you will have an ever growing mound of the stuff as it just won't decompose quickly enough.

View a mulching mower as like a large scale cross-cut paper shredder as it goes about its business, consequently my mower mulches the grass and spits it out laterally for it to be broken down by sun, wind and rain (and rain seems to work best) rather than gather it up in a collector box.

A word of warning, I would say don't be tempted to buy a mower from your local hypermarket. Yes, some of their prices are extremely attractive but they are not going to service it for you or repair it if it goes wrong. Whereas if you go for a well-known brand it is far simpler to find a service centre.

10.11.2 Advantages of Mulching

Any gardener will tell you that if you mulch your grass it is good for your lawn. The reason being that the quickly decomposing cuttings provide free, essential and natural organic nutrients because as they break down, the cuttings will release nitrogen, phosphate and potash etc. Scientists will also tell you that you will find smaller quantities of calcium, iron, and magnesium that your lawn needs to stay healthy as worms help carry these nutrients back into the earth. What is more this is as good as any commercial fertiliser you might buy and what is even better, it is free. Contrast this to depositing your collector contents into a compost heap which may well attract different types of vermin, or, if you start bagging it up you will have numerous costly trips to the *déchetterie* to make.

Although stating the obvious don't try to do this if it is wet underfoot as the mower will struggle to cut and the grass will clog in the exit chute; by wet I also mean when there is the

Boys Toys & Other Useful Playthings

heavy dew that abounds in early Spring or Autumn. Best to let it burn off and start mowing after lunch if possible.

10.11.3 Basic Mowing Tips

If you drive too quickly you leave clumps of grass behind. When mowing if the grass is long, and before the first cut of the Spring it can reach 8-10" in length, then your mower will struggle if you try and attempt too severe a cut first time out, but irrespective it will likely cut out fairly frequently due to the sheer volume of grass under it and you will also find that you will use more petrol (as I guess the motor has to work harder to get the blades to cut). Whereas in Summer I can just finish the entire garden on a tank the first cut uses at least a tank and a half.

tip: For the first outing of the year cut down to say 4" or the highest setting on your particular mower and a few days later get it down to the 2, 2½ or 3 inches you desire.

You'll soon get the hang of it, if you stop when mowing uphill try shifting your weight first although if you park on a slope don't try and set off and cut uphill as it may not work. Pull forward first to get some momentum before engaging the cutting deck.

Whilst mowing round the edges of the garden the degree I have to limbo or sway in my seat depends on how well I have cropped the overhanging bushes on the perimeter or pruned the trees in the interior.

10.11.4 Basic Precautions/Maintenance

With the cost of even a second-hand ride on likely running to 4 figures I suggest you need to take some basic precautions both before and after using it.

- Follow the manufacturers service schedule, even if you do it yourself;
- Carry out monthly maintenance checks/top up the grease points, the most important generally being the front axle and on each spindle housing on the cutting deck to maintain grease from the top pulleys to the blades. It also ensures the cavity within the housing is dry;
- Prior to going out each time
  - Pick up any large sticks/pieces of wood as they can damage the blades, a particular problem for us Alfie loves chasing sticks when thrown or just taking one off chewing it and leaving the residue wherever he fancies, so we try and encourage him to return them;
  - Pat down all the molehills as any stones/rocks they contain could also damage your cutting blades;
- Whilst mowing I try to ensure that I put the front tyre through any molehills that I might have missed as apart from flattening them you can also easily see if they contain any rocks;
- When out on the mower for any length of time wear ear protection and if prone to hay fever wear a mask too; and
- Brush or vacuum off any residual grass cuttings when you have finished before putting the mower back in the garage.

n.b. You can obviously collect up what the moles have deposited on the surface for use elsewhere, like in flower beds or in our case to fill in the many holes that Keno digs. On

Boys Toys & Other Useful Playthings

occasions this can take a couple of hours as it seems that every mole in the commune has been partying overnight in the garden. Sometimes I think I am going to look out of the window in the morning and see the garden has disappeared into one giant sinkhole!

10.11.5 Flat Tyres

I find mowing quite therapeutic; I use the 2 hours it takes me to plan out any jobs that I have to undertake or think about trips I would like to make. On one occasion I was blissfully away scuba-diving in the Maldives whilst trying to create a path through the long grass between our pond and *étang* but the mower slipped down a small bank and got stuck. I had to walk back up the garden and seek Joanne's help to come and sit on it and engage reverse whilst I lifted the front bumper and applied some serious grunt (it weighs 233kg after all) to shift it back on track. That done I drove it back to the barn only to find that the wheel that had gone down the bank had a puncture. Rather than get into the difficult task of trying to remove it, take it to a garage and look to get it repaired I found that one of those aerosol inflators that pump liquid rubber into deflated bike tyres did the trick in seconds. It worked a treat and that was almost 5 years ago now and I have had no problem with the tyre/wheel since.

10.11.6 Add Ons

10.11.6.1 Chain Harrow

If you have a large amount of land or even a meadow it is unlikely you will get it to lawn standard. My machine has 12 different depths of cut from 1-4" and I never go below 2½". However, providing that you have a reasonably powered mower, say >15Hp you could fit a Chain Harrow. This is best described as an interlinking set of chains that look akin to the springs on an old style bed, the difference being they have a set of spikes pointing downwards that dig into and scour the soil. These are flexible enough to follow the ground contours and can penetrate grass in even the toughest pasture. They help remove dead vegetation from lawns, paddocks and large grassed areas and are also suitable for preparing and levelling seed beds.

10.11.6.2 Trailer

If you have a '*garden*' big enough to warrant acquiring a ride-on mower then chances are you will need a trailer attachment of some description as well. I knew that I would benefit from one, to collect cut up logs from the woods or soil from *taupinières*, to move waste to the bonfire area etc. You need to choose carefully as there will be a weight restriction as to what your mower can safely pull. I was advised not to exceed 500kg in total on level ground and you still have to consider the '*drag*' factor, such as slopes (of which I have plenty), ground conditions and ground cover etc. To be on the safe side I factored in my weight and the weight of the trailer itself in my calculations of likely load capacity.

I figured that my general use car trailer was too big, too heavy and too high to connect up so I needed something smaller and more specific. I eschewed a '*tipping*' type trailer which people usually recommend for gardens as a lot of them are of plastic construction and I couldn't find anything suitable at a reasonable price as I didn't want a type that you have to assemble yourself. In the end I opted for a small, light, single axle car trailer weighing only 63kg with a payload of 337 kg (0.386 m^3). Although these can be problematic, tending to be too heavy and the draw bars too high and the advice is usually for a lawn tractor trailer but

Boys Toys & Other Useful Playthings

my small trailer works a treat on my terrain and I don't have to worry about the electrical connections.

Buying it did present a challenge. Having decided on the model I wanted I drove to the company concerned with my car-trailer and a plan to drive away with the small trailer loaded into it. The salesman was reluctant to let me take it away as he said it would be unsafe and I needed to tow it. Initially I couldn't understand his reasoning then I realised that to do so meant I would have to buy a separate number plate as well as arrange additional temporary insurance, both from them and he was trying it on. The manager took the same tack with me so in my then limited French I told him in no uncertain terms that I was not going to return without my bigger trailer, buy a number plate, get insurance and drive the new trailer away as it was all an un-necessary cost for a one off as I had no intention of ever using it on the road and that besides, the safety of the load on the road was my concern not his. He then accepted my purchase and I drove away with the small trailer in my big trailer as planned.

10.12 Quad Bike

With a *Quad* we really are talking boys toys but if you can justify one to yourself then all well and good. I thought short and hard about acquiring one but once the novelty wore off I wondered what I would use it for? Assuming it was road legal I could use it to go to the local supermarket if I wanted as it is only 1½ miles away but how quickly would I get bored of just riding it around the garden? If you don't have a ride-on mower I can see a case for it if you equip it so that you can attach a small trailer, then it will help you in and around the garden, otherwise it is just pure indulgence, isn't it? Mind you isn't that what a *'Boys Toy'* is meant to be?

Be aware however that Quads fall into two different categories, i.e. those approved for use on public roads and those that aren't. If you anticipate using it to drive out locally it will need headlights, indicators, a licence plate and rear view mirrors. The bad news is that even if you only intend to use it on private land, i.e. in your own garden/field it still needs to be insured. Although you may choose only for this to be of the third party variety, it will cover you if you hit someone on your land or if it is stolen and used on the public roads. Your insurance company may insist on you wearing gloves as well as a helmet when you ride it.

10.13 Towbar

Not exactly a toy more of a necessity if you live in this part of the world. I know it is expensive to have one fitted to your car if you don't already have one, but nevertheless it is essential to be able to pull a caravan, horse box or trailer either using a fixed or detachable towbar. The other consideration for you is your choice of electrical connection it has. If you are going out of your way to have one fitted then a 13 pin plug will give you maximum flexibility when towing and you will usually get a 7 pin-13 pin converter given to you as part of the installation.

10.14 Trailers

Along with a Chainsaw I would say that a *Remorque* is possibly the most essential toy you will need. Believe me you will be surprised. From clearing out old barns and removing the contents to the *Déchetterie*, removal of excess garden waste to collecting assorted

Boys Toys & Other Useful Playthings

materials from the Builders Merchant or *Brico* store your trailer will soon become indispensable. I initially thought about hiring one when I needed it but having used mine on average weekly since I have been here it has soon paid for itself. I was lucky in that shortly before we moved here a Hypermarket opened nearby and they had a very good promotional deal still available which swayed me.

In terms of what to look out for/obtain I would strongly suggest you get a trailer with twin axles rather than a single as it's easier to load a double axle trailer when it is free standing. Not only is it more stable but using a jockey wheel at the front of the tongue near the hitch or coupler is something of a pfaff methinks.

My trailer came with detachable extra height side panels (but I opt not to fit these as it places extra strain on the back when trying to lift things out) and also a cover/tarpaulin *bâche* to keep the contents dry if needed.

Each trailer will have a Safety Chain, which is a length of chain strong enough to restrain the trailer from complete separation if the hitch or coupler should fail. Safety chains must be dropped over the ball hitch before setting the trailer coupler down on it every time a trailer is towed. One can then attach the electrics via a din-plug connection to the socket on the car. Trailers come with their own '*road documentation*' – details of the weight they can legally carry etc. It is therefore best to keep this in your car as you need to be able to produce it if the trailer is attached and you are stopped by the authorities. However, if your intended trailer carries over 500 kg it will need its own number plate and will have to be registered (and insured separately) but you will need to check that your driving licence allows you to tow it (See section 1.3.5.7).

When it comes to using your trailer connect it to your car before loading it as it is far easier to manoeuvre when empty as even grass cuttings/leaves/plant materials weigh a lot more than you think and it is easier to lift the trailer up when it is empty although a trailer with a jockey wheel would help in this respect.

10.15 Waders

You may have bought a property oriented around a fishing business or intend to setup one but there are also lots of rural properties that come with pond or lakes, so you don't need to be a fisherman to use these. They aren't so much a toy more of a practical necessity if you have any form of lake or significant water feature at '*the one*' as they enable you to venture where simple '*wellies*' don't. Our *Etang* is not overly big, perhaps 35*20m with 3 shallow sides but the other is quite deep at the edge, it is also allegedly 14' deep in the middle. In our time here we have had 2 trees fall into it probably caused by a combination of Coypu digging and Wind. Removing one makes for a good boys morning out but to do it you really need chest high fisherman's waders. With the first tree a friend was on water duty but I felt guilty as he did most of the work. Thereafter I bought my own set and was happy to jump in to do the necessary cutting when it came to retrieving the second.

10.16 Wood Chipper

If you have or anticipate a lot of garden waste of the woody variety then a *Déchiqueteuse* or *Broyeur de Végétaux* is a good idea. The principal drawback of this is that petrol ones are very expensive, think 4 figures for a moderate sized one. This leads one to an immediate

Boys Toys & Other Useful Playthings

dilemma. How do you know that the specific model will do the job you want it to and you haven't wasted your money? Particularly as in the past I have found that the stated thickness of wood that it will shred can be a bit of an exaggeration.

I explained the dilemma to my local *Motoculture* – Garden Equipment man and he was very understanding. We worked out prices for hiring for a day and also for a weekend, that way I could see whether the large scale investment would be worth it and whether I would have enough demand too. After all there are only so many paths you can create or weed suppressant you can use. Ideally whatever machine you opt for needs to have a reversible mode, you don't want to try and prise any jammed log out of it and the difficulties that brings if it doesn't have one, a bit like paper jammed in your shredder but on a more industrial scale.

However when you say wood chipper or shredder most people think of the vehicle mounted machines used by councils, like *the one* shown here. If this is indeed what you think you need then it is in fact called a brush chipper and is far more expensive again.

10.17 Accessories/Final Thoughts

So many tools could be seen as an extravagance, but as I found with my overworked 4 in 1, one size doesn't fit all. Having the right tool for the right job is half the battle, thereafter it is down to the inexperience or incompetence of the operator.

If you know that '*the One*' will need a lot of fencing then perhaps a post digger and post rammer would be good additions to have, after all its horses for courses at the end of the day.

If those courses include renovating an old property and re-covering a lot of ceilings a plasterboard hoist may well be worth its weight in gold but I have no personal experience of such a device as when I boarded a garage ceiling back in the UK I fashioned two wooden 'T' props to help me. Equally in this case a concrete mixer might be worthwhile.

I have shaped this section based on the requirements of our property but depending on the characteristics of '*the one*' there might easily be a case for you obtaining say: a Bench/Chop Saw, Compressor, Leaf Blower, Pressure Washer etc.

10.17.1 Ear Defenders

It will get quite noisy when using these tools so do invest in a pair of good quality ear defenders to use when out mowing or using a Brush Cutter or Chainsaw rather than rely on say a pair already attached to a helmet and safety visor as the former will be purpose made

Boys Toys & Other Useful Playthings

for the job. I tend to use foam ear plugs that you can push right into the ear canal and then ear defenders over them for added protection when chain sawing/mowing.

10.17.2 Knee Pads

Although not something one immediately thinks of but if you need/plan to do a lot of ladder work like hedge cutting/painting or need to tend to your guttering/roof tiles or intend laying lots of floor tiles then strongly consider acquiring some knee pads *genouillères* made of polystyrene/rubber as you will find these indispensable. Even spending 15 minutes up and leaning against the rungs or side of a ladder will likely leave your knees bruised/sore the next day. Some of the work trousers you can buy even have inbuilt flaps on the knee area to facilitate the insertion and holding of generic knee pads.

10.17.3 Petrol

As regards Petrol powered tools I have not yet encountered such a tool using diesel, it is always unleaded fuel. But be careful as it does go 'off'/stale if left for any length of time. Here I will quote the RAC Website.

'Once you've put fuel in a container you only have a few months before the quality starts to fall away – even less if the fuel is contaminated in any way. Petrol has a shelf-life of 6 months if stored in a sealed container at 20°C or just three months if kept at 30°C. The more it's exposed to heat, the more quickly it will go off. If the container isn't tightly sealed, you'll be able to keep it for even less time and there's increased fire risk due to flammable vapours escaping'.

So the lesson to be learned here is do not keep fuel for excessive periods of time in your Generator/Mower as you may find you have to drain it out and refill it before using. Which in the case of a Generator in a power shortage is not ideal!

Girls Gadgets

11. Girls Gadgets

I like alliteration in sentences and the phrase Girls Gadgets goes with that of Boys Toys in the preceding chapter, it is not because I am sexist.

That said some of the following may be stereotypical in that the gadgets are food oriented and therefore geared towards the fairer sex. I can't help it, my girlie is the sort that will look in the fridge 5 minutes after I have said *'we need to go shopping'* and concoct a stunning 2 course meal. Consequently the things that float her boat are mainly in the edible department. So the following things may prove useful.

11.1 Apple Peeler

We live surrounded by orchards and indeed have a few apple trees of our own, the difference being that ours have no chemicals used on them. However even our small number of trees produce far more apples than we can eat at any one time, and that is after taking some down to the staff at the *Mairie* or giving them to friends.

The choice therefore is to throw the excess away/let them rot or to try and store them for cooking at a later point. Consequently a simple Apple Peeler *Pèle Pommes* helps prepare them for this. It looks like a spiraliser and is just a giant corkscrew on which you mount the apple and a spring blade which removes the skin as you turn it. Using it makes light work of peeling and you can do dozens in a fraction of the time it would take manually, our grandson loves it. The apples are then in an ideal state to cook and puree before freezing.

11.2 Apple Steamer

Still on the subject of apples, a *Vapeur Pommes* is just a simple three tier steamer. This is a real boon for us as our tress easily produce upwards of 150kg of apples each autumn. Cram the unpeeled apples into the top, put water into the bottom and boil for about an hour. The steam rises and the juice is extracted from the apples and falls into the middle container where it can be siphoned off and once cooled can be consumed immediately or stored for future use.

11.3 Automatic Watering System

The additional land that comes with many French houses compared with the UK means that one doesn't need to consider taking an allotment as there is usually more than enough space to create your own vegetable patch *potager* and the better climate means that you can consider growing a wider variety of produce than you may be used to as well.

Once planted though it needs constant tending if it is not to go to waste and all your hard work will count for nothing. During the long hot summers this means regular watering so what better than to install a *Système d'arrosage automatique* or Automatic Watering System. Utilising timers and with hoses linked to a water source, an external tap or water butt, the system will switch on/off at designated times of the day and run for pre-determined lengths of time to deliver water to your plants or vegetables. If getting an electricity supply to the area is not practicable then investigate solar powered options, there are plenty of them out there. Obviously depending on relative locations you can always extend your *Système d'arrosage automatique* to include your polytunnel.

Girls Gadgets

11.4 Electric Bicycle

I have to state up front that we don't possess a *Vélo à assistance électrique* but when I asked the memsahib what sort of things would improve her life here this is what she chose. Although some of them have prices that would make your eyes water, like most technological items their price will (surely) lower over time. Taking their power from on-board batteries these *'e-bikes'* assist your pedalling efforts and do a lot of your work for you meaning you can be more relaxed whether you have a type that is designed for the road or a mountain type model. The top speed of such bikes are limited to 25kph by law, after which or if its' power unit exceeds 250w you would need a helmet and gloves and a moped licence, without which it can't be ridden on public roads! The powered assistance it provides lets you ride at a constant speed without having to break into a sweat. There are some fairly steep hills near about and I am sure she had visions of going to the local boulangerie on a road bike and pedalling back with her wares in a little basket on the front. Still, if your budget runs to it why not?

11.5 Polytunnel

A polytunnel *serre* is a simple semi-circular tunnel made from hoops of steel and covered in polythene and they are extremely popular here. Like greenhouses they are placed in sunny spots in the garden and work on basic physics in that the inside heats up faster than hot air can escape the structure and thus they help provide a fertile environment for your plants or vegetables. You still have to tend and water them but the extra heat inside stimulates growth and also protects them from any bad weather. Just a cautionary note, in high summer it can get very hot inside your polytunnel, too hot in fact and it is best to leave the door and window(s) open during the day otherwise the contents can easily die off. Note it would be beneficial if you had gauze/mesh fittings inside the doors and windows as this will allow air to circulate but keep animals/reptiles out.

11.6 Rotavator

In keeping with the theme of vegetable patches and Polytunnels, digging them over in Springtime can be backbreaking work so mechanical assistance is desirable. So a Rotavator *Motobineuse thermique* is ideal, and as with the many *'Boys Toys'* (See section 10) the most practical is a petrol powered device, particularly as any such patch/tunnel is likely to be some distance from the house. These machines have a series of rotating blades which enable the soil to be easily broken up and turned over and in so doing they aerate the soil. This improves drainage and makes it more receptive to growing your chosen plants or crops.

11.7 Staple Gun

I don't mean the kind of Staple Gun *Agrafeuse* that you use for building jobs and the like but the smaller electric kind that one would use for craft type projects and that *'fire'* staples or tacks. They are very handy for securing upholstery to furniture like Chairs or Headboards which you may already own or may have picked up from a Flea Market *Brocante* or *Vide Grenier*. If you are renovating a house or getting ready to open a *Chambres d'hôte* then I figure you will have a lot of this type of work to do, so go get one. They also are really indispensable outside the house when for example lining Vegetable or Plant Boxes with sheeting that you need to secure before filling them with earth/compost.

Amusing Incidents/Only in France

12. Amusing Incidents/Only in France

The point of this section is not to ridicule France or the French people, but to highlight how things here are so different in certain aspects to life in the UK. These little incidents/observations/stories gave some amusement at the time and I think are worthy of sharing to illustrate my point. So apologising to the producers and scriptwriters of Friends for the format; here is:

12.1 The One about the Accident

Even though we wouldn't class ourselves as remotely '*horsey*', having a racecourse on our doorstep provides an ideal opportunity to take a picnic along whilst watching some racing. We did exactly that on a glorious summer afternoon a couple of years ago as we had friends from England staying with us and some local friends came along in their car too as we couldn't fit everyone in. We both parked in the road alongside the course, bought our tickets, found a shady spot to setup in and enjoyed some four hours of racing. The problem came when we returned to the cars as to our horror we found that we had been subject to a hit and run and both vehicles were badly damaged on the offside. We started to take pictures of the scene when a passer-by stopped and said that we should go to the racecourse office as they knew what had happened. At the same time a lady from that office appeared and said we should follow her. Luckily neither car boot had been damaged so we were able to open them up and secure the picnic baskets, tables and chairs in there before doing so.

We all trooped inside and the explanation was surprising to say the least. The racecourse had employed the services of a *Calèche* (Horse drawn carriage) and driver for the afternoon to take people around the outside of the course and the local town. It had just returned from a trip and disgorged its passengers when one (or both) horses were startled so they bolted. Bolted out of the course, into and along the adjacent road with the carriage swinging from side to side behind them crashing into whatever was in its path. It must have been quite a site as she told us 10 cars had been damaged (although the next day the local paper reported it was just 7) and that they had called the *Gendarmes* who had taken all the necessary pictures and had all the information if the insurance company wanted it. The *Calèche* driver had admitted responsibility (not that he would have had a choice) and they had made announcements over the public address system for the owners to come forward. Obviously we hadn't been paying attention as although the tannoy was quite clear we hadn't heard, or been expecting to hear, our registration numbers called out. She gave us a glass of champagne and all the information we needed to complete the necessary accident report forms as well as complimentary tickets for another race meeting. It was then that we realised the miserable looking guy in the corner was actually the *Calèche* driver, although I hasten to add that '*no horses were hurt during the creation of this spectacle*'!

12.2 The One about the Charity

One morning after bowls we were told about the opportunity of climbing a 13th Century Tower one coming Saturday morning for charity. Great, we thought it involved abseiling down and so myself and two buddies were quite keen to do this, but it seems we got lost in translation as there was to be no abseil. However all those that made the climb would be recipients of a three course lunch and wouldn't need any sponsorship. That all seemed

Amusing Incidents/Only in France

quite strange and we figured there would be more to it so resolved to find out on the day. On the Saturday in question we did indeed climb the stairs of the 30m tower and released balloons on the summit to publicise the forthcoming *'Telethon'* in December. It transpired that the local fundraising committee had excess funds from the previous year to dispose of and so they decided to put on a lunch! I thought that it might have been better to actually allocate the money to this year's efforts if they couldn't top up last year's contributions, but no they were going to spend it! As it transpired, having waited 90 minutes after our descent during which we listened to 3 different speeches, then walked to the *Salle de Fête* accompanied by a band, and then heard more speeches, I was slowly losing the will to live so gave my apologies and came home instead. I heard later than lunch started at 1300 and didn't finish until almost 1800 and a good time was certainly had by all, but it wasn't charity fundraising as we know it.

12.3 The One about the Chestnuts

One autumnal Sunday afternoon the year after we moved in Joanne was out in the garden picking some walnuts. When she came back to the house she said that she thought there was someone in our woods further down the garden. Off I trotted to investigate and was surprised to see a guy on his knees picking up sweet chestnuts. Bizarrely, back over the fence were what appeared to be his mother, wife and young daughter who were either staying out of harm's way or not agile enough to climb over the fence. I asked him what he was doing and he said that they always came here to pick chestnuts. I pointed out our signs and told him it was a private garden and that he should leave. It certainly wasn't my idea of a weekend family outing but he was clearly annoyed I had interrupted him, particularly when I video 'ed him and his car as they were leaving. He stopped, got out and came over and I assume swore at me (luckily my French wasn't that good as I didn't understand), again I captured it on video which I subsequently reported to the local *Gendarmes*. It was all unnecessary really, because the ridiculous thing is that we have far more chestnuts than we can ever hope to use and if they had rang the doorbell and asked rather than try and steal them we would have given them a bagful to take away.

12.4 The One about the Concert

We went out to a tribute concert one Friday evening. Standing at the back of the steeply raked seating I thought I saw something odd but couldn't be entirely sure. At the end of the performance when the lights came up, sure enough sitting in the front row were an older couple and they had brought their small/handbag dog along too! What makes one think, *'oh I'll take the dog along with us'* let alone assume that it will be let in? Bizarre.

12.5 The One about Customer Service

Earlier I alluded to the fact that getting replies to an email to customer services was nowhere near as speedy as it is in the UK and neither is the performance of that function. To illustrate this point I will offer two personal examples.

A couple of years ago we arranged for a local electrical company to come in and retune our satellite dish that had moved in a storm. They did so and I popped in a couple of days later to pay them. All was well for a couple of weeks until another storm caused us to lose tuning on most channels that we watched. I had been told by a friend that with this company if there was an issue with their work they did not charge for coming out again so I called them

Amusing Incidents/Only in France

about the new problem and after they finished for the second time I thought no more of it. Almost one year later I got an invoice for an outstanding amount through the post with the date highlighted. Obviously they did expect paying, which wasn't a problem but caused me to wonder how many UK companies would sit on an unpaid debt for 12 months without chasing it up?

The second example was for the possible installation of solar panels. During Spring and Summer we get an awful lot of sunshine and as we have uninterrupted views to the South and South East thought that we should consider solar panels. I contacted a local company who came out the next week with an *'expert'* to do a survey. The following week the owner came and delivered the quotation personally, talked us through it and said he would wait for our comments. When I responded I did so with a list of about 10 questions but in the meantime had discounted the whole idea as the return on investment was far too long and I had resolved that unless there were significant changes to the quote I would decline. But I heard nothing. Nothing that is until 6 months later when I got an email from a secretary in the company asking me if the project was still relevant?

12.6 The One about the Dead Vendor

A couple of years ago I had arranged a trip back to the UK in the October to attend a formal dinner, and as these things pass pretty quickly had arranged to meet up with an old school friend for a couple of beers beforehand. He knew that I now lived in France and said that his girl-friend Annette, who was recently divorced, was looking to buy a holiday home here and had put in an offer on a property (which turned out to be just over 90 minutes' drive from me). He then started to explain some of the problems she had encountered in so doing. I said that he might be interested to know that I had recently written a book on the subject and proceeded to explain what to do in her situation. A while later I returned from the bar with a new round whereupon my friend said *'oh I've just been online and ordered a couple of copies of your book'*, one was for him and the other for Annette, as he wanted to add it to the Christmas presents he was giving her. He also asked me to dedicate them too which was quite a compliment and arranged to send them on for me to do so.

Anyway, with the problems brought about by coronavirus and national lockdowns I hadn't heard from him and as I now felt I was invested in their transaction subsequently mailed him to ask about Annette's progress. Here is what he said:

It's a bit of a saga at the moment. As you know last summer Annette made an offer which was accepted and then we heard that the vendor was not well and had gone to live/recuperate on the island of Reunion. We heard nothing for months and then late November we were told that the lady had had passed away. As Annette was in no hurry she said that she was still interested and would wait for probate. In mid-January, after hearing nothing over Christmas, we went to a French property show at Olympia and Annette spoke to a representative of the estate agents who said she knew the property in question and would chase it up for her. Somewhat surprisingly within two days she got back to us saying that the vendor was not dead! However the following day the original estate agent phoned and re-confirmed she was dead, although the day after he rang again, 'she's ALIVE'! This went on for a couple of days and the latest is that she is alive and well and wants to proceed. So we are waiting for it all to happen and so its wait and see at the mo.

Amusing Incidents/Only in France

Footnote - Unfortunately lockdown did not work out well for my friend's relationship as sadly he told me that he and Annette had drifted apart during it because of the travel restrictions. So Annette if you read this edition of my book please let me know how it worked out for you?

12.7   The One about the Delivery

It would seem that not all companies use satellite navigation as on one expected delivery I received an email saying that they couldn't find my address and needed explicit instructions. Incredulous I know and clearly their schedule did not allow time to stop at the *Mairie* to find out where the house was. I did state in my reply that it was impossible to be more explicit than GPS Co-ordinates and also referred to the competence and intelligence of the driver but rather than start a long rant I just sent them directions from the Supermarket in town. The parcel arrived the next day.

12.8   The One about the Doctor

I rarely go to the Doctors but when one does one expects their complete and undivided attention. On one visit the consultation was interrupted on two separate occasions by the receptionist putting through telephone calls, from presumably patients but it could have been anyone whereupon separate discussions took place between the doctor and them for a few minutes each before my diagnosis continued.

12.9   The One about the Fibre Optics

Just before Christmas 2020 we had a letter from the *Préfecture* via our *Maire* saying that Fibre was now available in our Commune and inviting us to select a supplier. As a first step I went online to the map showing our commune and although our house was there, no availability was shown. I called the appropriate number and explained about the letter and the map and that no connection was shown for us. I confirmed our address and was told *'there is no number 36 in this road'*. I explained that earlier in the year the commune had renamed the roads and re-numbered the houses. I then sent them a screenshot of the map annotated with our house and also showed the nearest fibre connection point – on a post just the other side of our hedge. Later that evening I received a copy of an email from the infrastructure company saying the map will be updated.

Early In the New Year I decided to check the map again and was pleased to see that our house was shown with connections available from a range of operators. I selected the first, which was Orange but was horrified to see that the connection they were proposing was 2-8Mbits, not even a good ADSL connection let alone *'Internet at the Speed of Light'* but as none of the other operators displayed a speed I decided to call Orange the following day using their English speaking helpline. I explained my concern that we were being offered a fibre service but at slow ADSL speed. Reassuringly the operator said *'No, fibre will be over 100Mbits'* but I needed to speak to Business Services, her attempt to transfer me failed as she said they were busy and that I should call back later and take Option 2 when connected.

That afternoon I called back, 6 times in fact. 4 times the connection just said that the line was busy and to ring back later! On my 3rd attempt I got through, pressed option 2 and was told the wait time was about 10 minutes. As I was using our portable landline handset I switched on speakerphone and carried on with other things while listening to the music.

Amusing Incidents/Only in France

After some 35 minutes a voice said *'hello'*. I replied only to hear, *'are you there, I can't hear you'* I started to speak and our phone went dead. Annoyingly, I guessed it had run out of charge. This happened again on my 6th call at the end of the afternoon whereupon I thought that we might never get fibre installed. To my surprise later that evening I received 2 separate email from Orange containing both the details of the fibre service package we had been offered and an installation date 2-weeks later. The deal offered was an attractive one so I was happy.

However this was just the start.

The Tuesday for installation arrived, as did the technician, so far so good. But he then asked me where the existing ADSL line came into the house. I was clueless as it wasn't in any information we had received from the vendor. I told him that Orange had installed it so must have some installation drawings/notes? If they did they hadn't been passed on so the next hour was spent walking up the road to various posts & telegraph poles as well as walking round and then crawling around under the house in the crawlspace *Vide sanitaire*, all to no avail. He said he would make a report and they would be in touch. Friday came and we'd heard nothing so I rang and was told that the reports take between 5-7 working days. I called the following week and was told that we had to do some work to enable the installation. As to what, I would be contacted within the next week by email/phone to be told. We weren't and this went on for another three weeks during which there had been mutterings that I had to dig a trench from a pole 100m away or that I had to cut down a tree.

You will have gathered I'm not the most patient person so now almost one month on from the original date I rang and said I wanted to complain and explained why. I also said that there were approximately 200m of conifers around the house so telling me I had to cut a tree was not overly helpful. This at least got me the direct line for the installation team albeit that it would be on a wholly French speaking line, and a further promise of contact within 5 days. Some 3 days later and thoroughly fed up I called the installers and said that I had been told to do some work to enable the installation and it was now done and I wanted to book an appointment. My intention being to do any necessary cutting, but not digging, when the installers arrived. *'Sure sir, next week, Wednesday 18th any time from 0800'*! Trouble was it turned out that the Wednesday was in fact the 17th and on that day EDF had announced a 5 hour electricity shutdown so they could work on their network. I was up early and opened the gates in preparation just in case but no technician arrived. Same on the Thursday but it was apparent after lunch that they weren't coming then either. A further call elicited that they had called me yesterday, 8 minutes after the power (and the phone) was cut, but they didn't come because the address was wrong ☺! They then said they would come back next Friday morning. but they didn't see the funny side of it when I said if the address is wrong how are they going to get here? I confirmed it with them again, and gave my English mobile number. I asked for an email address so I could send in directions from the Supermarket in town or give them the GPS coordinates but she said they didn't have that facility! Neither would it seem that their technicians have the ability to call a UK mobile number, somewhat ironic given they work for/subcontracted to a telecoms company.

Amusing Incidents/Only in France

Endnote. The new date came, along with another technician. He wasn't remotely interested in the route of the existing ADSL line and was happy with my suggestion of routing the Fibre (aerially) to a telegraph post at the end of our drive, then down the post and along the ground to the house in conduit, which I subsequently buried. Unexpectedly he also installed the new router for me and checked the connectivity which he wasn't meant to do, so happy days in the end. Perseverance again.

12.10 The One about the Garage

On two separate occasions now and with two different sets of friends, problems arose after their cars were either involved in an accident or broke down. In each case they called their insurance company to report the problem, try and arrange the delivery of courtesy cars and collection/removal of their vehicles to a repair shop. So far so good you may think. But the problems arose when simply trying to find out where their car was located after it had been transported away. In both instances there was a reticence of the insurance company to explain where the car was located or could be viewed and in one disturbing instance one friend had an ongoing argument with the insurance company for some days as they told him that his car had been taken to an unauthorised garage and he wasn't entitled to a courtesy car. The fact that they had arranged and authorised the collection and subsequently delivery of the car to the supposedly unauthorised garage in question which had caused the problem seemed beyond them.

I won't name names but both of these were English related insurers. Our car is insured with a French company and when we had an accident (*the one* with the *Calèche* – see section 12.1) I was told which garage to take our car to and to collect our courtesy car from and what time it would be available. When we found that the repair would take longer than expected, it had run into August after all, getting the courtesy car extended indefinitely wasn't a problem.

12.11 The One about the Heart Attack

I strongly suspect that this story is an exception rather than the rule but I know of someone who a couple of years ago thought they were having a heart attack so their wife phoned the Pompiers. The Pompiers immediately called for an Ambulance and when it arrived at the person's house unexpectedly it already had the person's GP in the back. As if this wasn't surprising enough, on route to the hospital they stopped at what they subsequently found out was a Cardiac Surgeons house and collected him too, so that on arrival at the Hospital the man in question had already benefited from expert treatment on the journey.

12.12 The One about the Insulation

One afternoon our landline rang and being nearest to it Joanne picked it up. I heard her ask if the person spoke English and then overheard one side of a very strange conversation that took place. It started off about loft insulation, the government here had a scheme where householders could install more energy efficient devices/materials or get their house insulated to improve the energy efficiency of their properties for 1€ subject to certain conditions; but as you might expect there were various scams that sprung up as a result. Anyway having said that no we didn't need any insulation the discussion moved on apace. In a short period of time I heard her decline a date, as she was married, and then say that no she didn't have a daughter or sister living with her who might be interested. It seemed

Amusing Incidents/Only in France

that the guy on the other end liked her voice and decided to chance his arm with more personal questions.

12.13 The One about the Llamas

Driving through a local scenic village one afternoon I had to slow down because the road was coned off to enable some work to take place on an adjacent wall, causing the carriageway to reduce to a single lane. That gave me ample opportunity to look at a group of 5 people walking on the single lane taking 3 llamas for a walk on leads! At the time I wasn't sure if they were Llama's or Alpaca's until I managed a quick image search when I got home, but even so.

12.14 The One about New Year's Eve

Some new found friends of ours had a holiday home here in a nearby village for several years during which they had progressively improved it such that they then decided to move here and into it full-time. They had previously enjoyed lengthy summer holidays and Christmas's here which helped convince them to relocate. One almost unbelievable story they told us was that during one Christmas period they were invited by the builder who was undertaking their house improvements to a New Year's Eve celebration in another local village. To their surprise the multi course meal didn't finish until almost 0430, however shortly before this the local *Maire* interrupted proceedings with an announcement. He said that he had just had a conversation with the local *Gendarmes* and somewhat incredibly he then told the assembly that anyone planning to leave the event by car should turn left out of the village and **not** right!!!

12.15 The One about the Petrol Pumps

Our local supermarket had two sets of pumps enabling 4 cars to fill up simultaneously and a kiosk where one pays but there is a narrow exit from the forecourt by the Kiosk and consequently when things are busy it takes ages for the cars to creep forward, pay and leave. One of these sets of pumps had some fairly antiquated credit card machines enabling them to be used out of hours or at lunchtimes when the kiosk is shut. A while ago all the pumps were replaced over a two-week period by new machines, each with their own LCD selection panel and individual credit card slots and are far more efficient. However one would think that this would be the precursor to dispensing with the kiosk and attendant? Not so, the kiosk is still there but the credit card machines are disabled until lunchtimes or the Supermarket closes and you still have to queue to pay at the kiosk, although this may be to facilitate those people who want to pay for their fuel by cheque but certainly not for efficiency reasons.

12.16 The One about the Petrol Station

As I have just related, the queues for petrol/diesel at our local supermarket can be quite lengthy, particularly at weekends when the prices are reduced. Being born impatient I consequently try and go on a Saturday evening if we are not busy, or failing that on a Sunday morning before the Supermarket opens if I am up in time. One Saturday night before the pump refurbishment took place both of the credit card operable pumps were busy so I queued. The guy in front was having trouble with the credit card machine but eventually took the hose out and walked round the far side of his car to fill up. He struggled

Amusing Incidents/Only in France

for some time and had multiple attempts to fuel up. He then (despite the signs saying do not use them on the forecourt) took out a mobile phone and called someone before returning the hose to the pump. At this point, checking there was no one behind me I rolled back a few car lengths so that the effects of any ensuing explosion wouldn't be so severe! Because of the time he was taking I couldn't even change lanes as there was a bigger queue on the other one so had to sit still and watch him re-enter his bank card which clearly didn't work a second time so he then had to take out an alternate card before this time filling up the car with unleaded rather than the Diesel he first attempted.

12.17 The Other One about the Petrol Station

On a separate occasion I pulled in to the same supermarket late one afternoon and drove straight up to my usual pump so that the filling cap is on the side of the hose. I selected Diesel and waited for the Kiosk attendant to activate the pump. Looking over to the adjacent pump I saw someone who had driven in there with their small micro tractor and was filling it up directly. I thought this strange as most people go down and fill up a jerrycan with the appropriate fuel before transferring it at home but he, like me, was obviously impatient.

12.18 The One about the President

France has had its share of terrorist incidents in recent years but some security matters remain low key and contrary to expectations. The year after we moved here was the 73rd Anniversary of the atrocity at Oradour sur Glane, and, being a Saturday was the same day of the week as the original event. It therefore seemed to me to be a poignant day to visit. On my journey there once I got past Limoges I saw lots of *Gendarmes* in the vicinity and when I arrived in Oradour I had to drive to an overflow car park. I then found the *Centre du Memoire* was shut until early afternoon but assumed it was all to do with the anniversary. With an hour to kill I went into the new town in search of sustenance. Arriving in the square I saw flags outside the *Mairie* and a little crowd in front of it and a few obvious security types dotted around. Figuring that something was going to happen I found a spare doorway to stand in and observe proceedings. A few minutes later a small convoy swept in from a side road and stopped near to the *Mairie* itself. Turning to two security men who had appeared next to me I asked who it was *Qui est la? Qui est la?* they replied, looking me up and down, *C'est le President*! Unbeknown to me it seemed that M Macron had decided to pay a personal tribute to the village that year, his first year in office. I wandered across the square to take some photographs and it struck me as strange that there had been no searches, were no barriers, no security passes necessary and that I, a total stranger to all intents and purposes, could get within 10 feet of the president, all the while taking pictures when I could have had my mind set on other things, but in other respects was quite refreshing.

12.19 The One about the Restaurant

Equally bizarre, we were in an upmarket restaurant one Thursday lunchtime for a Lunch Club outing, much to the amusement of everyone sitting at our table a couple walked through from the dining room at the back of the restaurant holding their cat which was on a lead. Again like the couple taking the dog to the concert, why would you do that?

Amusing Incidents/Only in France

12.20 The Other One about the Restaurant

One of the joys of running Lunch Club is trying out new eating places. On this particular occasion we sampled the food and I talked to the owner-chef about a possible booking almost two months hence. He promised to email me a proposed menu in a few days. Well the weekend came and went and half of the next week. I called him and he said he had been very busy but would send it in a few days. They too sped by and I called again. He apologised and said tomorrow. Sure enough I did get an mail from him but the attachment was in Apple Notes format which doesn't convert well to someone who uses Microsoft software. I couldn't find an easy way to convert it so I mailed back suggesting he just send it as a picture, pdf, or even text format in an email but never got a response. Figuring he wasn't interested I made alternative arrangements. Fast forward some 5 or 6 weeks to the day prior to Lunch Club and I got a phone call after breakfast from the restaurant asking me to confirm our attendance tomorrow! We hadn't agreed a menu, price or the number of people he would cater for, and he still thought we were going to come?

12.21 *The One* about the Tractor

I had never quite appreciated how long and hard farmers work until we moved to France. We have orchards on two sides of us and the guys that own them work incredibly hard and at all hours it seems. Consequently I understand how time is precious for them so I shouldn't be surprised when on two separate occasions I have pulled into local supermarkets only to see very large tractors occupying parking spaces. I wasn't sure if they were my local farmers but I mean why go home to swap into your car when you can just go and pick up your lunch with your tractor!

Questions for Estate Agents

Annex A – Questions for Estate Agents

Here are the questions that worked for us when we asked, modify it according to the features of the property you are enquiring about.

1) When did the property go on the market?
2) What position are the owners in?
3) Can we have a floor plan - hand drawn is ok (and it doesn't have to be to scale) so we can see if the layout works for us?
4) Do you have any aerial view or plan cadastral (with *parcelle* no.s) if possible?
5) What type of heating system is used?
6) Is there underfloor heating?
7) Is there double glazing?
8) Is there ADSL (although now Fibre is more relevant) already at the property?
9) Do you have any other pictures than those posted on the advert?
10) An indication of the location, is it on a main/village road etc?
11) Is there any commerce in the nearest village?
12) Are there any electricity pylons/sub-stations, quarries, or TV masts adjacent to or visible from the property?
13) Is the land around the house fenced, if not how is it delineated
14) Does the septic tank conform to the 2012 regulations?
15) How much is the *Taxe Foncière*?
16) How much is the *Taxe D'habitation*?
17) What size is the swimming pool?
18) Is it fresh/salt water before being chlorinated?
19) Is it covered?
20) Is it heated?
21) Is it alarmed?
22) Is it fenced?
23) Is the *Gite* currently let out and if so during what period?
24) What income is generated from this?
25) Is there a separate website for advertising the *Gite*?
26) If so is it included in the sale?
27) Do the outbuildings have light, power and water installed?

Everyday Abbreviations

Annex B – Everyday Abbreviations

Abbrev	Short For	Equivalent, Meaning, Translation
AdV	*Acte de Vente*	Equivalent to Completion on a UK house sale.
AERL	*Auto Entreprise à Responsabilité Limitée*	Limited Liability Auto-entrepreneur
AFB	*Agence française pour la biodiversité*	
AOC	*Appellation d'Origine Contrôlé*	A protected designation of origin for French agricultural products.
AOP	*Appellation d'Origine Protégée*	French & European protection of geographic products.
ARCEP	*Autorité de Régulation des Communications Électroniques et des Postes*	The independent agency which regulates telecommunications.
ASPAS	*Association pour la protection des animaux sauvages*	Society for the protection of wild animals.
CA	*Le chiffre d'affaires*	Turnover (of sales/services).
CdV	*Compromis de Vente*	Equivalent to Exchange on a UK house sale.
CEDEX	*Courrier d'Entreprise à Distribution EXceptionnel*	An identification system/box number for businesses that receive large volumes of mail.
CNAM	*Caisse Nationale de l'Assurance Maladie*	The main public health insurer in France.
CNE	*Commune*	Abbreviation displayed on location signs.
CNIL	*Commission Nationale de l'Informatique et des Libertés*	Management of internet domain names
CPAM	*Caisse Primaire d'Assurances Maladie*	The local *département* level of CNAM.
CRS	*Compagnies républicaines de sécurité*	Reserve force of national Police who specialise in public order
CT	*Contrôle Technique*	Equivalent to an MOT Test.
CU	*Certificat Urbanisation*	Equivalent to outline planning permission.

Everyday Abbreviations

Abbrev	Short For	Equivalent, Meaning, Translation
DGCCRF	*Direction générale de la concurrence, de la consommation et de la répression des fraudes*	Equivalent to Trading Standards
DGFiP	*Direction Générale des Finances Publiques*	Public Finance Directorate
DMP	*Dossier Médicale Partage*	Personal digital health record that allows sharing information with chosen health professionals.
EARL	*Exploitation Agricole à Responsabilité Limitée*	French: Limited Farm Liability
ENEDIS	formerly *Électricité Réseau Distribution France*	Electricity distribution network managers
EPHAD	*Établissement d'hébergement pour personnes âgées dépendantes*	General term for Care/Nursing Home
Ets	*Établissement*	Establishment.
EURL	*Entreprise unipersonnelle à responsabilité limitée*	Single member limited liability company. (The 1 partner has 100% of the shares).
FAI	*Frais d'agence inclus*	(Estate) Agency fee included
GRDF	*Gaz Réseau Distribution France*	Principal distributor of Gas
GIGN	*Groupe d'Intervention de la Gendarmerie Nationale*	Specialist French counter terrorism unit, part of the Gendarmerie Nationale.
HAI	*Honoraires d'agence inclus*	now replacing *FAI*
HT	*Hors taxes*	Price equivalent to net of VAT
IGP	*Indication Géographique Protégée*	The lowest ranking wine classification in the AOC system. Also relates to the Origin and Quality of Gourmet Food products and/or ingredients.
LPO	*Ligue pour la Protection des Oiseaux*	National bird protection society.
MSF	*Médecins Sans Frontières*	Doctors without borders, equivalent to the Red Cross.
OFB	*Office français de la biodiversité*	Was the result of a 2020 merger between the *AFB* and *ONCFS*

Everyday Abbreviations

Abbrev	Short For	Equivalent, Meaning, Translation
ONCFS	Office National de la Chasse et de la Faune Sauvage	National office for Hunting and Wildlife.
PGE	Prêt garantis par l'état	A state guaranteed loan.
SAMU	Service d'Aide Médicale Urgente	Emergency Medical Services
SARL	Société A Responsabilité Limitée	This is the same as a limited company, it has its own legal entity.
SAV	Service Après Vente	Equivalent to after sales service.
Siren		A 9-digit number that uniquely identifies a business and proves one is fully registered.
Siret	Système d'Identification du Répertoire des Établissements	Formal (14 digit) Company Number of an enterprise at a specific location.
SMIC	Salaire Minimum de Croissance	Minimum wage
SPANC	Service Public d'Assainissement Non Collectif	Public Service for Non-Collective Sanitation
TTC	Toutes Taxes Comprises	If you see an advert or have a receipt with an amount that says TTC it means all taxes are/have been included.
TVA	Taxe sur la Valeur Ajoutée	This is the equivalent to VAT.
VO	Version Originale	A film in its original language.
VF	Version Française	A film in or dubbed in French.
VSP	Voiture Sans Permis	A Car without a licence being necessary to drive it.
ZA	Zone Artisanale	Small industrial estate
ZAC	Zone d'Aménagement Concerté	Integrated development zone
ZAE	Zone d'activités économique	Economic development zone
ZAI/ZI	Zone (d'activité) industrielle	Industrial activity zone/business park

Useful Addresses

Annex C – Useful Addresses

This Annex is shown purely for information purposes and all web addresses are valid at time of publication! If the website of a commercial enterprise is shown here its' inclusion should not be interpreted as an endorsement of their services/products. I have mainly shown the web addresses of sites you may find useful until you source your own favourites, I have deliberately not included any Banks or Insurance Companies as I don't want it alleged that I am giving financial advice, nor Estate Agents as they tend to be regional in focus although I have included a well-known 'E-Agency'.

4G Network Coverage

Check 4G coverage in your/any particular area	https://www.arcep.fr/cartes-et-donnees/nos-cartes/la-couverture-4g-en-france-par-departement.html

Animal Adoption

30 Million Friends	https://www.30millionsdamis.fr/jagis/jadopte-un-animal/
Orfee	http://association-orfee.forumactif.com/f7-les-chiens-d-orfee-a-adopter
Second Chance	https://www.secondechance.org/
SPA	https://www.la-spa.fr/adopter-animaux

Animal and Pet Transport

Pets 2 Go	https://www.pets2go2.co.uk/
Pets Abroad	https://www.petsabroaduk.co.uk/

Animal Protection Societies

ASPAS	https://www.aspas-nature.org/
LPO	http://www.lpo.fr

Animal Training

Julie & Gary Stansbridge	57 route de Beaulieu 16460 Ventouse Tel: 05 45 68 91 25
That mutt (dog blog)	https://www.thatmutt.com/

Autoroute & Toll Management

APRR	https://voyage.aprr.fr/
SANEF	https://www.sanef.com/fr/home
VINCI	https://www.vinci-autoroutes.com

Business Advice

	https://www.frenchbusinessadvice.com/

Cadastral Plan

	http://www.cadastre.gouv.fr

Useful Addresses

Car Buying

Car registration & plate creation	https://www.eplaque.fr/
Carte Grise Cost Calculator	https://www.cartegrise.com/france/prix-carte-grise

Car Clean Air Sticker

	https://www.certificat-air.gouv.fr/en/demande

Car Pooling

	https://www.blablacar.fr
	https://www.ecologique-solidaire.gouv.fr/covoiturage-en-france
	https://www.mobicoop.fr/
	https://www.roulezmalin.com/

Checking as a Consumer

Bank Charges	http://www.tarifs-bancaires.gouv.fr
Car Buying History	https://histovec.interieur.gouv.fr/histovec/home
CT History	https://www.utac-otc.com/infos-pratiques/demande-dhistorique
Driving Penalties (Points per Offence)	https://www.service-public.fr/particuliers/vosdroits/F31551
DVLA	https://www.gov.uk/taking-vehicles-out-of-uk
Find a Care Home (4 different Types)	https://www.pour-les-personnes-agees.gouv.fr/annuaire-ehpad-et-comparateur-de-prix-et-restes-a-charge
Find a garage to register your car	https://immatriculation.ants.gouv.fr/Services-associes/Ou-immatriculer-mon-vehicule
Power Outages	https://coupures.enedis.fr/particulier
Trading Standards	https://www.economie.gouv.fr/dgccrf/contacter-dgccrf https://www.economie.gouv.fr/mediation-conso/mediateurs-references
Understand risks around *the One*	https://www.georisques.gouv.fr/

Consumers Association

Union Fédérale des Consommateurs	https://www.quechoisir.org/
Institut National de la Consommation	https://www.inc-conso.fr/

Useful Addresses

Customs

	http://www.douane.gouv.fr
Brexit Guide for Travellers	https://www.douane.gouv.fr/sites/default/files/2021-01/19/Brexit-guide-voyageurs-travellers.pdf
Sending Parcels	https://www.douane.gouv.fr/sites/default/files/2021-02/26/preparing-for-brexit-customs-guidelines.pdf

Cyber Security

Fraudulent/phishing /scam emails	https://www.signal-spam.fr/
Report cybercrime/ terrorism	https://www.gouvernement.fr/la-plateforme-pharos

Dechetteries

	https://www.annuaire-mairie.fr/decheterie.html

DIY Stores, Building Supplies

Brico Depot	https://www.bricodepot.fr
Castorama	https://www.castorama.fr
Chausson	https://www.chausson-materiaux.fr/
Leroy Merlin	https://www.leroymerlin.fr
M Bricolage	https://www.mr-bricolage.fr

Drought Monitoring

Find current water restrictions in your *département*	http://propluvia.developpement-durable.gouv.fr/propluvia/faces/index.jsp

E-(Estate) Agency

PAP	https://www.pap.fr/

European Road network

	http://highwaymaps.eu/

Expat News

Connexion	https://www.connexionfrance.com/
The Local	https://www.thelocal.fr/

Fibre Optics & Broadband

Check connectivity at an address	https://maconnexioninternet.arcep.fr/
Fibre optic deployment	http://www.cartefibre.arcep.fr/

Useful Addresses

Foreign Exchange

FCA register of approved FX dealers	https://register.fca.org.uk

Fuel Price Check

	https://www.prix-carburants.gouv.fr/

General Guidance

UK Govt Site	https://www.gov.uk/guidance/living-in-france

Healthcare

Find local doctor(s)	http://www.Doctolib.fr
French health insurance program	https://www.ameli.fr
Guide to French Healthcare	https://www.santepubliquefrance.fr/docs/livret-de-sante-bilingue-francais-anglais

Hunting Society

Fédération Nationale des *Chasseurs*	https://www.chasseurdefrance.com/pratiquer/dates-de-chasse/

Internet Domain Names

CNIL	https://www.cnil.fr/

Maison France Services

	https://www.cohesion-territoires.gouv.fr/france-services

MOTs

Explanation of tests conducted	https://www.ecologie.gouv.fr/controle-technique-des-vehicules

Mountain Departments

	https://www.securite-routiere.gouv.fr/chacun-son-mode-de-deplacement/dangers-de-la-route-en-voiture/equipement-de-la-voiture/nouveaux

Notaires

Find by location	https://www.notaires.fr/en

Nuisance/Cold Calls

Bloctel	www.bloctel.gouv.fr/

Useful Addresses

Online Learning

Duolingo	https://www.duolingo.com/
Kwiziq	https://www.kwiziq.com/
Rosetta Stone	https://www.rosettastone.com/

Online Market Places

Leboncoin	https://www.leboncoin.fr/
Manomano	https://www.manomano.fr/

Parcel Shippers

Ecoparcel	https://www.ecoparcel.eu/
Eurosender	https://www.eurosender.com/

Postcode Finder

By Area	https://www.laposte.fr/particulier/outils/trouver-un-code-postal

Property Valuations

By Area	https://app.dvf.etalab.gouv.fr/

Radio

France Info	https://www.francetvinfo.fr/en-direct/radio.html
Independent Radio Group	https://www.lesindesradios.fr/
Understand the world in French, (with Transcriptions)	https://savoirs.rfi.fr/fr/apprendre-enseigner/langue-française/journal-en-français-facile

Restaurant Guides

Bistrots du Pays	https://www.bistrotdepays.com/
Michelin	https://guide.michelin.com/fr/fr/restaurants/
Petit Futé	https://www.petitfute.com/destination/france/

Road Travel

Bison Futé	https://www.bison-fute.gouv.fr/

Rugby

Top 14	https://www.lnr.fr/rugby-top-14
Pro D2	https://www.lnr.fr/rugby-pro-d2

Rugby Papers

L'Equipe	https://www.lequipe.fr
Midi-Olympique	https://www.midi-olympique.fr

Useful Addresses

Service-Public

ANTS	https://www.immatriculation.ants.gouv.fr
CERFA	https://www.demarches.interieur.gouv.fr/formulaires
Official administrative site for France	https://www.service-public.fr/

Sewage & Septic Tanks

SPANC	http://www.assainissement-non-collectif.developpement-durable.gouv.fr/le-service-public-d-assainissement-non-collectif-r11.html

Speed Cameras

Locate fixed cameras	https://radars.securite-routiere.gouv.fr/#/

Sport

National Fishing Federation	https://www.federationpeche.fr/
Flashscore	https://www.flashscore.com/
Refereeing	https://www.tousarbitres.fr/

Supermarkets

Carrefour	https://www.carrefour.fr/
Casino	https://www.supercasino.fr/
Intermarche	https://www.intermarche.com/home.html
Leclerc	http://www.e-leclerc.com/
Lidl	https://www.lidl.fr/fr/index.htm
Monoprix	https://www.monoprix.fr
Super U	https://www.magasins-u.com/

Tax Office

	http:www.impots.gouv.fr
Obtain a *numero fiscal*	https://www.impots.gouv.fr/portail/contacts?778
Setup personal space (with *numero fiscal*	https://www.impots.gouv.fr/portail/particulier/acceder-mon-espace
Make one off payments (with *numero fiscal*)	https://www.telepaiement.dgfip.finances.gouv.fr/stl/satelit.web?templatename=accueilcharpente&contexteinitial=2

Telecomm's Regulator

ARCEP	https://www.arcep.fr/

Useful Addresses

Telephone Companies

Bouygues Telecom	https://www.bouyguestelecom.fr
Orange	https://www.orange.fr
SFR	https://www.sfr.fr

Television

Canal+	https://boutique.canal.fr/
Eurosport	http://www.eurosportplayer.fr
France 2	https://www.france.tv/france-2/

Tyres

	http:www.1001pneus.fr
	http://www.centralepneus.fr
	https://www.pneus-online.com/

Utilities

Guide to setting up your utilities	https://en.selectra.info/guide-moving-to-france/utilities

Veterinary and Phytosanitary Border Inspection Office

SIVEP	https://agriculture.gouv.fr/importation-animal-products-live-animals-animal-feed-and-plants

Visa's

France Visa Applications	https://france-visas.gouv.fr/fr_FR/web/france-visas
General Info	https://www.schengenvisainfo.com/france-visa/

Visit Calculator

90 in 180 days Calculator	https://ec.europa.eu/home-affairs/content/visa-calculator_en

Volunteer Help

	http://www.freevolunteerworkabroad.co.uk/free-volunteer-work-in-france.shtml
	https://www.gooverseas.com/volunteer-abroad/france
	https://www.workaway.info

Water Quality

	https://solidarites-sante.gouv.fr/sante-et-environnement/eaux/eau
	https://www.quechoisir.org/carte-interactive-qualite-eau-n21241/

Weather

Forecasts	http://www.meteofrance.com/accueil

Public Holidays

Annex D – Public Holidays

2022

Date	French Name	Day of Week	Holiday
1 Jan	*Jour de l'an*	Sat	New Year's Day
15 Apr	*Vendredi Saint*	Fri	Good Friday *
18 Apr	*Lundi de paques*	Mon	Easter Monday
1 May	*Fête du travail*	Sun	Labour Day
8 May	*Victoire 1945*	Sun	Victory Day
26 May	*L'Ascension*	Thu	Ascension Day +
6 Jun	*Lundi de Pentecôte*	Mon	Whit Monday $
14 Jul	*Fête nationale*	Thu	Bastille Day
15 Aug	*L'Assomption*	Mon	Assumption Day
1 Nov	*La Toussaint*	Tue	All Saints' Day
11 Nov	*L'Armistice*	Fri	Armistice Day
25 Dec	*Noel*	Sun	Christmas Day
26 Dec	*Deuxième jour de Noel*	Mon	St Stephen's Day *

+ Ascension (40 days after Easter)

$ Pentecost is celebrated on the 50th day (seventh Sunday) from Easter Sunday

* *Vendredi Saint* and *Deuxième jour de Noel* are observed in the Alsace and Moselle *départements* only

Public Holidays

2023

Date	French Name	Day of Week	Holiday
1 Jan	*Jour de l'an*	Sun	New Year's Day
7 Apr	*Vendredi Saint*	Fri	Good Friday *
10 Apr	*Lundi de paques*	Mon	Easter Monday
1 May	*Fête du travail*	Mon	Labour Day
8 May	*Victoire 1945*	Mon	Victory Day
18 May	*L'Ascension*	Thu	Ascension Day +
29 Jun	*Lundi de Pentecôte*	Mon	Whit Monday $
14 Jul	*Fête nationale*	Fri	Bastille Day
15 Aug	*L'Assomption*	Tue	Assumption Day
1 Nov	*La Toussaint*	Wed	All Saints' Day
11 Nov	*L'Armistice*	Sat	Armistice Day
25 Dec	*Noel*	Mon	Christmas Day
26 Dec	*Deuxième jour de Noel*	Tue	St Stephen's Day *

\+ Ascension (40 days after Easter)

$ Pentecost is celebrated on the 50th day (seventh Sunday) from Easter Sunday

* *Vendredi Saint* and *Deuxième jour de Noel* are observed in the Alsace and Moselle *départements* only

2024

Date	French Name	Day of Week	Holiday
1 Jan	*Jour de l'an*	Mon	New Year's Day
29 Mar	*Vendredi Saint*	Fri	Good Friday *
1 Apr	*Lundi de paques*	Mon	Easter Monday
1 May	*Fête du travail*	Wed	Labour Day
8 May	*Victoire 1945*	Wed	Victory Day
9 May	*L'Ascension*	Thu	Ascension Day +
20 May	*Lundi de Pentecôte*	Mon	Whit Monday $
14 Jul	*Fête nationale*	Sun	Bastille Day
15 Aug	*L'Assomption*	Thu	Assumption Day
1 Nov	*La Toussaint*	Fri	All Saints' Day
11 Nov	*L'Armistice*	Mon	Armistice Day
25 Dec	*Noel*	Wed	Christmas Day
26 Dec	*Deuxième jour de Noel*	Thu	St Stephen's Day *

\+ Ascension (40 days after Easter)

$ Pentecost is celebrated on the 50th day (seventh Sunday) from Easter Sunday

* *Vendredi Saint* and *Deuxième jour de Noel* are observed in the Alsace and Moselle *départements* only

Holiday Absences

Annex E – Holiday Absences

OPÉRATION TRANQUILLITÉ VACANCES

Formulaire de demande individuelle (hors Paris et petite couronne)

Pour bénéficier de la surveillance de votre résidence en votre absence, merci de remplir ce formulaire en ligne, de l'imprimer et de vous rendre, muni de celui-ci, à votre commissariat ou brigade de gendarmerie.

ATTENTION :
- Si vous habitez Paris, les Hauts-de-Seine (92), la Seine-Saint-Denis (93) et le Val-de-Marne (94), ne remplissez pas ce formulaire. Rendez-vous sur le site de la préfecture de police pour faire votre démarche : www.prefecturedepolice.paris, rubrique Vous aider > Actions de prévention > S'inscrire à une opération > OTV.
- L'opération tranquillité vacances doit être demandée en avance (48 h avant votre départ au minimum).
- En cas de vacances interrompues, prévenez le commissariat ou la brigade de gendarmerie de votre retour.

VOUS
Nom* :   Numéro de téléphone mobile :
Prénom* :
Né(e) le* :   à :
e-mail :

VOTRE PÉRIODE D'ABSENCE*
Du : (JJ/MM/AAAA) au (JJ/MM/AAAA)

VOTRE ADRESSE (RÉSIDENCE A SURVEILLER)
Numéro et type de voie (allée, rue, avenue, etc.)* :
Code postal* :   Ville* :

INFORMATIONS SUR VOTRE RÉSIDENCE
Type de résidence* :
☐ Maison   ☐ Appartement. Dans ce cas, merci de remplir les deux lignes suivantes :
Digicode d'accès à l'immeuble :   Bâtiment :
Étage :   Numéro de porte ou autre précision utile :
Existence d'un dispositif d'alarme* :
☐ Non   ☐ Oui. Dans ce cas, précisez lequel :

PERSONNE À PRÉVENIR EN CAS D'ANOMALIE
Nom* :   Prénom* :
Code postal* :   Ville* :
Numéro de téléphone portable* :   Téléphone fixe* :
(un numéro à préciser au minimum)
Cette personne possède-t-elle les clés du domicile ?*   ☐ Oui   ☐ Non

RENSEIGNEMENTS UTILES
Votre lieu de vacances : code postal :   Ville :
Êtes-vous joignable pendant votre absence :
☐ Non   ☐ Oui, à ce(s) numéro(s) de téléphone
Ou à cette adresse électronique :
Autre renseignement :
(à préciser si besoin)

Je déclare ces renseignements exacts et m'engage à signaler tout retour anticipé.
☐ J'autorise la conservation de ces données pendant deux ans aux fins d'une éventuelle réinscription à l'opération tranquillité vacances. En l'absence de réinscription, ces données seront effacées. Conformément à la loi informatique et libertés du 6 janvier 1978, je bénéficie d'un droit d'accès et de rectification à ces données, auprès du service de police ou de gendarmerie qui a traité ma demande.

Date :   Signature :

Mise à jour : mai 2016

School Term Dates

Annex F – School Terms

2021/22

Holidays 21/22	Zone A	Zone B	Zone C
La Rentrée	Thursday 2nd September 2021		
Toussaint	Saturday 23rd October 2021 to Sunday 7th November 2021		
oel	Saturday 18th December 2021 to Sunday 2nd January 2022		
Hiver	Saturday 12th February 2022 to Sunday 22nd February 2022	Saturday 5th February 2022 to Sunday 20th March 2022	Saturday 19th February 2022 to Sunday 6th March 2022
Printemps	Saturday 16th April 2022 to Sunday 1st May 2022	Saturday 9th April 2022 to Sunday 24th April 2022	Saturday 17th April 2022 to Sunday 2nd May 2022
Ascension	Thursday 26th May 2022 to Sunday 29th May 2022		
Vacances d'été commencent	Thursday 7th July 2022		

2022/23

Holidays 21/22	Zone A	Zone B	Zone C
La Rentrée	Thursday 2nd September 2021		
Toussaint	Saturday 23rd October 2021 to Sunday 7th November 2021		
oel	Saturday 18th December 2021 to Sunday 2nd January 2022		
Hiver	Saturday 12th February 2022 to Sunday 22nd February 2022	Saturday 5th February 2022 to Sunday 20th March 2022	Saturday 19th February 2022 to Sunday 6th March 2022
Printemps	Saturday 16th April 2022 to Sunday 1st May 2022	Saturday 9th April 2022 to Sunday 24th April 2022	Saturday 17th April 2022 to Sunday 2nd May 2022
Ascension	Thursday 26th May 2022 to Sunday 29th May 2022		
Vacances d'été commencent	Thursday 7th July 2022		

Decisions about school life and holiday dates are the responsibility of the *Ministère de L' Éducation Nationale de la Jeunesse at des Sports* found at https://www.education.gouv.fr/

My Meeting with the Local Chasse

Annex G – My Meeting with the Local Chasse

Background

On safety grounds and having previously encountered *Chasseurs* in our garden I was concerned about the impending start of the hunting season for 2020. I had looked on our Commune website to find out about the local *Chasse* but was somewhat disappointed to see that the last entry on there referred to their annual dinner 5½ years previously. On that basis I wrote to the mayor suggesting that he could perhaps ask the *Chasse* to update the site each week with the location of where they were going to be hunting so as to help people avoid them if they wanted to walk their dogs or just enjoy a quiet weekend walk.

The *Chasse* secretary wrote back saying how unfortunately they could not predict where they will be hunting from week to week or even day to day as they rely on hunters or farmers to call them to tell them about places where wild boar in particular are frequenting. Understandable but not overly helpful I know. Consequently when he invited me to meet him and discuss my concerns I was happy to do so, as I saw it as an ideal opportunity to engage with a group of people whose passion I did not share, though I declined his invitation to join in the actual hunt.

Logistics

Our meeting broadened my understanding but did not allay all my fears. I didn't know what to expect and my pre-arranged 8am arrival found 8 *Chasseurs* (of advancing age) already in attendance in their clubhouse and I sensed a group indifference rather than hostility to me. Despite the hour they were seated around a table eating bread and soup, although most worryingly there was alcohol and wine on the table too! Their meeting place was fairly nondescript, a simple single-storey two room unplastered building with a mishmash of furniture. At the very least I was expecting to see a large map of the commune on the wall highlighted with 'no-go' areas as I had been told in my initial meeting back in 2018 (See section 7.4) but this was not the case, the walls were bare. While the secretary was explaining the what and how (and I was extremely grateful he did that in English) and answering my questions about hunting another half dozen or so members trickled in over the next 40 minutes.

I was told that they hunt up until 1pm at weekends and yes in terms of formal organisation there was a log book/register with pages for each hunting session containing the date, hunt leader, area being hunted, signatures of all in attendance, details of the type of game being hunted etc. although I sensed that much of this would be filled in after the event. There were quota's for some types of animal determined by different levels of government. The hunting of Red Deer *Cerf* for example is subject to a national plan whereas the numbers of hares, pheasants and partridge are subject to local level plans determined by the *préfecture*. During the 20-21 hunting season in the *Corrèze* the quota for Roe Deer *chevreuil,* who are prone to damaging the apple trees which are plentiful in our locality allowed for upto 27 to be killed whereas there was no quota for Fallow Deer *daim,* or Red Deer *Cerf.* The departmental federation gives the hunt special bracelets/identity tags to put on the deer's legs once they have been shot so as to keep a tally.

My Meeting with the Local Chasse

As for the wild boar there is no quota for them due to the amount of physical and financial damage they cause to the farming community through the harm they cause to crops and fields by digging them up. In other areas it seems people are in the habit of dumping rubbish in bushes/woods and the boar thrive on eating this so score high on nuisance value too. He went on to explain that if the weather is poor, through either heavy rain or fog, or for example there are herds of cows adjacent to the proposed hunt site then it is abandoned. In a cupboard they had A3 colour photocopy maps of the different areas they hunt but it seemed that most of the attendees knew where they were going and their roles when they got there as these sheets stayed in the cupboard apart from *the one*'s extracted to illustrate points being made to me.

Use of Dogs

As there were various dogs in vehicles outside when I arrived I moved the conversation onto them. There are restrictions on the type of dogs that are used in that Whippets and Greyhounds are not permitted, nor Border Collies nor anything with a large mouth like a Great Dane or Rottweiller. The *Chasse* themselves have hunting dogs and across the country what they use depends on what is being hunted, in particular beagles when after wild boar; dachsunds *teckels* who excel at hunting '*below ground*' or in flushing out and retrieving game; fox terriers or jack russell's for hunting foxes; pointing dogs (*chiens d'arrêts*) such as pointers, spaniels, or setters for hunting pheasants, pigeons or rabbits; labrador-retrievers if shooting ducks; and running dogs *cheins courants* like bassets, griffons or weimaraner's who will scent and then chase game. The training tended to be by putting younger dogs with older more experienced ones.

Prelude to the Hunt

Once the bread and soup was finished and as the local hunt President had arrived the assembly moved outside. To a man they were either in Orange '*Hi-Vis*' Jackets or Hats or Orange Camouflage clothing as it was believed the prey animals do not distinguish this colour very well. Before setting off they focused on putting radio collars on some of their dogs, a necessary precursor it seems as the previous week one of them was apparently found some 6km away from the scene of the actual hunt! From my point of view I was expecting some kind of general briefing or indeed a weapons check to start the morning's activities but there didn't seem to be any kind of formal safety instructions given out at this point, nor when they got to the scene of that morning's hunt (I had followed them up to that point as I was still asking questions).

On arrival at the scene they simply dispersed to what I assumed were well-known or established positions; there certainly wasn't any allocation of sites and who went where or discussion about fields of fire or what was going to be done. I suspect that they all knew each other, the area they were in, the roles they would be undertaking and the procedure that would be followed as they had all done it countless times before. Worryingly for me, there was nothing in the way of warning signs being put out and it had been previously explained to me that a way of knowing that a hunt was taking place was if you encountered a number of cars, pickups or 4*4's parked together along a lane or road in '*the middle of nowhere*' it was a good indication that a hunting party was in the vicinity. Though to my mind the interconnection of alcohol, dogs, firearms, the general public and hunters means they should at the very least go through the motions just to

My Meeting with the Local Chasse

remind everyone of their responsibilities, and what about checking that everyone still has a valid licence with them?

Prior to our meeting I was of the belief that *chasseurs* were not allowed within 150m of a property with loaded weapons let alone fire them but was disabused of that when I was told that providing they were facing away from the property when they fired they could get as close as 50m. Sadly there wasn't enough time to get into too much detail about the type of weapons used, their ammunition nor their effective range other than for him to tell me that there were restrictions on using weapons with a silencer and that if hunting wild boar then bullets not balls had to be used, which ruled out the use of shotguns, and that they didn't use lead bullets because of concerns about pollution. None of what I had heard was particularly reassuring and certainly nothing had made me change my view or habits about walking out at weekends in the hunting season.

Closing

Before he disappeared off for the morning we briefly covered what for me was another disturbing aspect. It matters not how efficient, organised or publicised a particular hunt is, as the scariest part of the discussion for me, and why I restrict what we do and where we go during hunting season, is that there are also numerous individual licensed hunters in the surrounding areas who can roam the local woods in search of small game – partridge, pheasant, rabbits or small mammals etc. and they don't need to tell a soul where they are going. Unfortunately I was also not overly encouraged when I was told that mostly these hunters are either shooting up in the air (for birds) or down at the ground (for rabbits), especially given the effective range of rifles or shotguns and the fact that rabbits run!

n.b. After my return home I realised I'd forgotten a couple of other, probably obvious, questions which I emailed to him. He replied that:
- The deer/wild boar that have been slaughtered are then valued and then given to the owners of the land on which they are hunting. Once the distribution is complete, the meat is shared among the hunters; and
- In the event of an accident arising, the Secretary himself is a lifeguard and there are also firefighters on the team. There is also insurance that allows them to take care of any people injured.

INDEX

'

'the One', 6, 39, 46, 55, 197, 211

A

Alfie, 4, 11, 42, 77, 78, 79, 80, 81, 82, 83, 87, 92, 105, 179, 196, 207
ANTS, 13, 118, 119, 134, 145
Autoroute, 116, 173

B

Brexit, 2, 3, 6, 8, 12, 13, 14, 15, 16, 18, 19, 21, 22, 117, 138, 163
Brico, 142, 189, 190, 193, 210
budget, 3, 21, 29, 30, 39, 53, 56, 57, 64, 72, 85, 101, 108, 133, 140, 142, 193, 200, 203, 214

C

CERFA, 17, 23, 26, 63, 105, 118, 122, 128
Chasse, i, 88, 127, 148, 152
Chasseur, 151
chateau, 29, 100, 103, 126
Commune, 41, 55, 115, 132, 146, 150, 157, 173, 199, 218
Corrèze, 4, 36, 38, 43, 46, 89, 93, 106, 148, 150, 162, 168, 181, 192
Coypu, 2, 92, 126, 127, 210

D

Déchetterie, 140, 178, 189, 209
département, 2, 34, 37, 106, 115, 119, 120, 129, 131, 137, 138, 166, 169

G

Gendarme, 164, 165
Gendarmerie, 9, 88, 89, 90, 135, 138, 147, 150, 157, 165
gendarmes, 105

K

Keno, 4, 77, 78, 79, 80, 81, 82, 83, 85, 105, 109, 110, 127, 143, 179, 188, 196, 207

L

La Poste, 71, 103, 113, 122, 145, 147, 166, 167
La Rentrée, 154, 155

M

Macron, 8, 76, 148, 176, 222
Maire, 36, 65, 72, 73, 75, 87, 88, 99, 102, 105, 110, 126, 130, 131, 157, 164, 176, 189, 218, 221
Mairie, 22, 23, 44, 63, 66, 74, 87, 88, 102, 105, 108, 110, 115, 126, 128, 129, 130, 131, 134, 140, 143, 150, 156, 157, 158, 168, 176, 177, 192, 195, 196, 213, 218, 222
minimum wage, 24, 27, 71

N

Notaire, 42, 45, 48, 49, 50, 51, 54, 67, 69, 75, 130, 132, 144, 186

INDEX

P

préfecture, 7, 25, 36, 120, 121, 140, 143, 150, 192
Préfet, 36, 115, 131, 132, 151

R

Restaurant, 32, 52, 56, 63, 74, 75, 91, 170, 222, 223

S

Schengen, 7, 16, 20

Sénat, 34, 151, 165
SIRET, 71, 177

T

Tabac, 23, 113, 199
Taxe D'habitation, 185
Taxe Foncière, 30, 54, 75, 140, 186
Tourist Board, 72
Transition, 3, 6, 7, 8, 10, 16, 76, 134

W

WA, 7, 11, 15, 16, 22
Withdrawal Agreement, 3, 7, 8

Printed in Great Britain
by Amazon